NUCLEAR SHOWDOWN
IN IRAN

REVEALING
THE ANCIENT PROPHECY OF

ELAM

FROM THE AUTHOR OF
Psalm 83 : The Missing Prophecy Revealed

BILL SALUS

First printing July 2014

Printed in the United States

For information contact:
Prophecy Depot Ministries
P.O. Box 5612
La Quinta, CA 92248

Design Director: Matthew Curtis Salhus
Image Designer: Lani Harmony Salhus

ISBN – 978-0-9887260-4-8

(All Bible verses are taken from the New King James Version, unless otherwise notated).

Please visit our website for other Prophecy Depot Ministries products:
http://www.prophecydepot.com

Acknowledgements

The LORD will be awesome to them, For He will reduce to nothing all the gods of the earth, People shall worship Him, Each one from his place, Indeed all the shores of the nations.
(Zephaniah 2:11)

I will set My throne in Elam, And will destroy from there the king and the princes,' says the LORD. 'But it shall come to pass in the latter days: I will bring back the captives of Elam,' says the LORD."
(Jeremiah 49:38-39)

Heartfelt thanks to my wife, children, and grandchildren who inspired me to write this book. A further debt of gratitude is extended to all those below whom in one way or another, through prayer, encouragement, support, research, or otherwise, genuinely blessed this book.

The Holmes's, Holton's, Gaskin's, Peterson's, Wheeler's, Hart's, Fulmer's, Mercer's, Stearman's and Ulrich's, Sean Osborne, Brad Myers, Hormoz Shariat, Allyn Huntzinger, Mark Conn and the elite members of the reading focus group.

Lastly, to the multitude of Iranian believers that are fighting the good fight, running the race and keeping the faith. You are an inspiration to many.

Best reading regards,
Bill Salus

Table of Contents

Introduction

As world leaders script the final pages of human history, events foretold long ago continue to unfold. Amidst the backdrop of global uncertainties, one thing remains unchanged.

"The end has been declared since the beginning." (Isaiah 46:9-10)

Ancient prophecies cleverly disguised in sovereign circumstances present wisdom to the wise. To Know or not to know, this is the question.

Nuclear Showdown in Iran, The Ancient Prophecy of Elam provides the reader with invaluable insights into the imminent future. This book reveals the potential relevance of an ancient prophecy that may pertain to Iran's nuclear program, which has been vastly overlooked. Additionally, it explores and sequences other age old biblical predictions that are also about to happen.

There is a tug of war going on in the world's next nuclear hotspot, and it's partially political, but mostly spiritual. While Iran's Islamic leaders experiment with the atom, scores of their countrymen embrace its maker. There is a crisis taking place in Iran, and it's far more reaching than the mainstream news media is reporting. Seventh Century Islam and state censored media have finally met their match in Christian satellite TV.

Have you heard that miracles, visions and dreams are occurring with regularity, causing throngs of Iranians to convert to Christianity? From approximately 500 believers in 1979, to several million today, Iran is the fastest growing evangelical population in the world. Christianity is burgeoning so rapidly that the rogue Islamic regime has instituted harsh policies intended to curb its growth.

Over the past couple of years, home churches in Iran have been closed, pastors imprisoned, and believers severely persecuted. Meanwhile, the modern marvel of satellite TV is being directed by the Holy Spirit to transform Iran into a Christian nation.

Why should you care? Perhaps because,

- Ancient predictions are unfolding in modern times,
- Present paranormal events are shaping mankind for a supernatural future,
- Advanced human technologies are being manipulated by invisible forces,
- The Middle East Theater is being staged for the final showdown between good and evil.

Not enough? Then what about,

- An uncontrollable nuclear arms race unleashed in the Middle East?
- Thousands of missiles launched into Israel?
- OPEC oil supplies cut off from world markets?
- Increased terrorism throughout the world?

Need more? Then imagine this,

- Gas prices hovering over $12.00 per gallon,
- Favorite public places targeted by terrorists,
- Sizeable metropolitan areas infected with incurable viruses,
- Wide scale ATM shutdowns for lack of electricity,
- NO GAS, NO MONEY, NO FOOD, NO WATER!

As you can tell by now, this is not a bestselling woman's devotional book. However, it is a biblically based manuscript that explains the prophetic relevance of certain key current events, and deposits hope for the reader throughout.

As you traverse through these pages, you will come face to face with a generally unrevealed prophecy. Evidence will be provided that enables you to decipher whether or not this prediction is meaningful to you. Painstaking lengths have been undertaken to provide the reader with ample research to make a final determination.

In the end analysis you might conclude along with me, that the ancient prophecy of Elam predicts nothing short of a *Nuclear Showdown in Iran.*

Chapter 1

Introducing the Ancient Prophecy of Elam

(Jeremiah 49:34-39)

"Open Doors: Growth of Christianity in Iran 'Explosive'"

Christian Post 3/23/12

"Church in Iran undergoing revival and facing persecution"

Christian Telegraph 5/7/09

"Greatest Christian Revival in the World" in Iran

World Net Daily 7/25/12

Roll…Camera…Action; It was Friday night August 30, 2013, when I found myself sitting on the Trinity Broadcasting Network's (TBN) TV set staring at Jeremiah's prophecy of Elam on another guest's IPAD. It was just minutes before we were going live in front of an international audience of millions on a "Praise the Lord" (PTL) TV show.

The program that night featured Jonathan Cahn as a guest to talk about his bestselling book, *The Harbinger*, along with yours truly to discuss my latest book, *Psalm 83, the Missing Prophecy Revealed*. Cahn and I had been together on a (PTL)

TV program a few months prior, but this show was slightly different for us because it also included a panel with additional guests.

Sitting to my immediate left was Reza Safa of TBN's Nejat TV. Nejat TV was the brainchild of TBN founder Dr. Paul Crouch and Reza Safa. It originated in the fall season of 2005. It reaches out to millions of Muslim's worldwide, with a special emphasis on those living in the Middle East. Due to its communications in the language of Farsi it has been influential in the massive Christian revival currently taking place within Iran.

Reza Safa and I had never met before that night, and our introduction to each other was through Jeremiah's prophecy about Iran. It was just moments before the show, and we had scarcely separated our welcoming handshake before Reza held up his IPAD in front of me and privately inquired if I was familiar with Jeremiah's prophecy concerning Elam.

Safa had his IPAD Bible program opened in place to Jeremiah 49:34-39 and enthusiastically informed me, "*This prophecy has many Iranian Christians excited.*" My best recollection of how our personal conversation went from there is detailed below.

SALUS: Yes Reza, I am very familiar with Jeremiah's prophecy concerning Elam. I authored an article on the subject in the summer of 2010, and subsequently devoted two chapters of commentary to the prophecy in each of my last two books.[1]

SAFA: Did you know that Iran is experiencing one of the biggest Christian revivals in the world, and that many of the Iranian Christians are hoping Jeremiah's prophecy about Elam will happen soon so that they can leave Iran and spread the gospel throughout the world?

SALUS: I have heard about the Christian revival in Iran, but did not realize that many of the Christians within Iran were focused in on Jeremiah's prophecy about Elam." *Then I asked*, "What is the size and scope of the revival and are you frequently traveling back and forth to Iran?

SAFA: The revival is exponential. When Nejat TV started there were several thousand believers, but now there are several million. And, no I don't travel to Iran, the present Iranian regime is very repressive, and it is extremely difficult for Christians to get in or out of the country. Jeremiah's prophecy encourages the Christians trapped in Iran because it predicts a massive dispersion of Iranians into all the nations of the world. They see this as an opportunity to accomplish two things. First, leave Iran so that they can worship Christ freely in another country. Second, preach the gospel of Christ throughout the world.[2]

SALUS: That's an interesting way for them to interpret the prophecy considering it predicts a disastrous judgment for Iran that appears to necessitate the expulsion of a multitude of Iranians out of the affected territory. In the Lord's infinite wisdom and mercy the end result of the judgment could make it more conducive for these Christians to depart from Iran and spread the gospel elsewhere, but the bottom line is that this appears to be a calamitous episode coming in Iran's nearby future. This is not a scenario that softens the hearts of the ruthless Iranian regime to the extent that they pass out free exit visas to all the Christians.

At that point the TBN producer said "Roll… Camera… Action," and Reza and I had to end our private conversation and focus on the live broadcast at hand.

Prophecy Experts Focus on Persia, not Elam!

When it comes to the future of Iran according to Bible prophecy, most expositors focus primarily on Persia rather than Elam. Persia is listed as a participant in a major Bible prophecy found in Ezekiel 38. However, the ancient land of Elam, also located within modern-day Iran, existed long before the name of Persia was ever introduced on the world scene.

The land of Elam predates the time of the Hebrew patriarch Abraham who lived approximately 4000 years ago. The date of origin of the name Persia is harder to pin down. One of the most notable Persians was King Cyrus the Great and his life spanned approximately from 600-529 BC, which offers a possible start date for the name of Persia around 600 BC or shortly before.

No biblical reference that is specific to Persia predates the general inception period of Cyrus the Great. The oldest biblical references to Persia in the Bible are found in the books of Daniel and Ezekiel. Daniel was probably born sometime between 628-623 BC. His prophetic calling began shortly after being deported to Babylon about 605 BC. Ezekiel's was born around 622 and his calling as a prophet came around 593. In stark contrast, Elam is referenced as far back as the book of Genesis 10:22, 14:1, 9.

A Google word search of (Elam Prophecy) on January 15, 2014 netted 137,000 results. On the same day a similar Google search for (Persia Prophecy) achieved 2,580,000 results.

Why are the prophecy pundits so focused on Persia rather than Elam for Bible prophecies concerning Iran's future? There appear to be a few reasons for this.

1.   Persia, listed in Ezekiel 38, is located within extremely important and well defined passages in scripture. Ezekiel 38 and 39 connect together and contain fifty two passages of some of the most easily understood prophecy within the entire Bible. You don't have to be a biblical scholar to make some general sense out Ezekiel's prophecy. Most prophecy buffs are very familiar with Ezekiel 38, which is commonly referred to as the "Gog of Magog" invasion.

   I believe the Lord purposely made Ezekiel's prophecy well detailed and generally easy to understand because it is the marquis event in the end times that He will use to uphold His holy name in the midst of His chosen people Israel.

"So I will make My holy name known in the midst of My people Israel, and I will not *let them* profane My holy name anymore. Then the nations shall know that *I am* the LORD, the Holy One in Israel. Surely it is coming, and it shall be done," says the Lord GOD. "This *is* the day of which I have spoken." (Ezekiel 39:7-8)

2.   Jeremiah's prophecy concerning Elam in his 49th chapter has been generally overlooked by some of today's top Bible prophecy teachers. Although it appears many Iranian Christians are paying close attention to the prophetic details of Jeremiah 49:34-39, that enthusiasm hasn't trickled across the shores of the Persian Gulf into the embrace of many western eschatologists.

3.   In the minds of some top biblical scholars the prophecy has already found fulfillment. This is a clumsy assessment because Jeremiah 49:39 clearly states that it is a prophecy that will come to pass in the "latter days."

"'But it shall come to pass in the latter days: I will bring back the captives of Elam,' says the LORD." (Jeremiah 49:39)

Summary

Scores of Iranian Christians are anxiously awaiting a prophecy concerning their future that was written in Jeremiah 49:34-39 around 596 BC. Millions of other Christians outside of Iran don't even have a clue about the existence of this prophecy. Either the Iranian Christians are gravely misinterpreting Jeremiah's prophecy concerned with Elam, or millions of other Christians living outside of Iran need to get with the prophetic program.

Perhaps Jeremiah's prophecy has already been fulfilled and many Iranian Christians are merely holding onto wishful thinking. If so, they need to formulate an alternative exit strategy to escape the repression occurring within their homeland. A different departure plan might be advisable anyway, because the prophecy predicts a coming disaster.

Maybe your local pastor or favorite Bible prophecy expert is correct to classify the prophecy as past history rather than a future prophecy.

On the other hand, *Nuclear Showdown in Iran, The Ancient Prophecy of Elam* may convince you that Jeremiah's prophecy about Elam is an extremely serious impending matter; definitely for the Iranians, and also for you!

Chapter 2

Introducing Ezekiel's Prophecy Concerning Persia

(Ezekiel 38, the Gog of Magog Invasion)

Future Headline:
"Global Tensions Soar as Russia Targets Israel."

This fictional headline is the title of chapter ten in Joel Rosenberg's bestselling book from 2006 called *Epicenter: Why the Current Rumblings in the Middle East Will Change Your Future.*[3]

The central theme in Rosenberg's bestselling book is the ancient Bible prophecy described in Ezekiel 38. This biblical prediction ranks as one of the most important and well defined prophecies of the apocalyptic end times. As such, there are many prophecy experts that currently teach about this timely topic.

The general consensus among many pastors and prophecy pundits familiar with this prophecy is that Russia spearheads a nine-member coalition, inclusive of Turkey, Iran and Libya along with other predominately Islamic countries, to invade Israel. Ezekiel points out that Persia, rather than Elam, is among the invaders. Persia was renamed Iran in 1935, which is why Iran is one of the easier nations to identify within this coalition.

> "Persia, Ethiopia, and Libya are with them, all of them *with* shield and helmet." (Ezekiel 38:5)

The primary reason for this invasion is to capture the "plunder and booty" in Israel's possession.

> 'Thus says the Lord GOD: "On that day it shall come to pass *that* thoughts will arise in your (*Russian leader's*) mind, and you will make an evil plan: You will say, 'I will go up against a land of unwalled villages; I will go to a peaceful people, (*Israelis*) who dwell safely, all of them dwelling without walls, and having neither bars nor gates'—*to take plunder and to take booty*, to stretch out your hand against the waste places *that are again* inhabited, and against a people gathered from the nations, who have acquired livestock and goods, who dwell in the midst of the land." (Ezekiel 38:10-12; *emphasis added*)

Fortunately for the Israelis, Ezekiel 38:18-39:6 clearly declares that these aggressors won't succeed! Additionally, the location and last days timing of the event is well defined:

> "After many days you will be visited. In the *latter years* you will *come into the land of* those brought back from the sword *and* gathered from many people on *the mountains of Israel*, which had long been desolate; they were brought out of the nations, and now all of them dwell safely." (Ezekiel 38:8; *emphasis added*)

> "You will *come up against My people Israel like a cloud, to cover the land*. It will be in *the latter days* that I will bring you against My land, so that the nations may know Me, when I am hallowed in you, O Gog, before their eyes." (Ezek. 38:16; *emphasis added*)

Although Iran participates in the invasion, the battle is fought outside of Iran on the foreign soil of Israel. This fact is emphasized further in Ezekiel 39:4, which says the corpses of the invading troops will all fall upon the mountains of Israel.

Ezekiel's prophecy will undoubtedly rank among the most massive Mideast invasions of all times and will be explored in greater detail in subsequent chapters.

Overview of Jeremiah 49:34-39
"The Prophecy of Elam"

Jeremiah's prophecy concerning Elam is going to be unpacked, explained and contrasted to Ezekiel's prophecy in several portions of this book, but encapsulated in a nutshell below is what Jeremiah informs about an important part of Iran's future.

Iran fiercely angers the Lord. As a result of the Lord's burning anger, a disaster occurs in Iran, not Israel. It is important to make this geographical distinction because Ezekiel 38 puts the primary location of that impending invasion inside of Israel.

The disaster is of a nature that it necessitates a wide-scale expulsion of Iranians out of the affected area. This worldwide dispersion may have the makings of the magnitude of a humanitarian crisis.

Although Iran lies within about 90% seismically active land, the catastrophic tragedy appears to be the result of a military attack rather than a great earthquake. It is important to note that the Bushehr nuclear plant is filled with Russian nuclear fuel rods, and sits squarely in the heart of Elam. It is a strategic target of any strike upon Iran's nuclear program. Some have speculated that an attack on Bushehr could result in a nuclear disaster.

There appears to be a shift in sovereignty over the subject territory that coincides with the destruction of the presiding king and princes at the time the prophecy finds fulfillment. Additionally, the Iranian Revolutionary Guard Corps (IRGC) suffers a devastating blow as they are struck at the chief place of their might. At the time of the catastrophe Iran has enemies that witness the calamity. It is uncertain who they are, or what part they may play within the disaster.

The good news is that there will be surviving Iranian refugees that will be restored to their homeland in the latter days.

Ezekiel 38 Omits Elam

The brief overview of Ezekiel 38 presented at the onset of this chapter points out that neither the land nor the people of Elam are part of Ezekiel's prophecy. The invaders include Persians and the battle is fought in Israel.

Ezekiel 38:2-6 identifies a very specific group of populations that come together in a confederacy to invade Israel. These specific verses can be read in the addendum called "The Text of Psalm 83 and Ezekiel 38:1-39:20." (*The image locates these populations by their ancient names on a map alongside their probable modern-day equivalents*).[4] Some scholars disagree with the modern identities of these historical peoples, but all can agree that Elam is not specifically mentioned by Ezekiel.

Why did Ezekiel omit Elam from the Gog of Magog invasion? Was it an oversight, or is Elam not a participant of the battle?

Jeremiah and Ezekiel were contemporaries of each other. They both wrote around 2,600 years ago at a time when Elam and Persia occupied two adjoining territories and maintained separate civilizations with distinct ethnic populations. (*The image identifies the general locations. Note the location on the image of the Bushehr nuclear facility in Elam*).

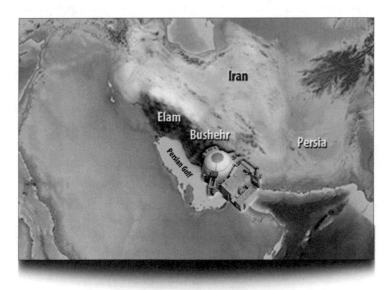

Pictures provided by Lani Harmony at *http://www.laniharmony.com*

Why did Ezekiel prophesy about Persia, and Jeremiah about Elam? Ezekiel was extremely familiar with Elam. Like Jeremiah, he also issued a prophecy concerning Elam.

> "There *is* Elam and all her multitude, All around her grave, All of them slain, fallen by the sword, Who have gone down uncircumcised to the lower parts of the earth, Who caused their terror in the land of the living; Now they bear their shame with those who go down to the Pit. They have set her bed in the midst of the slain, With all her multitude, With her graves all around it, All of them uncircumcised, slain by the sword; Though their terror was caused In the land of the living, Yet they bear their shame With those who go down to the Pit; It was put in the midst of the slain." (Ezekiel 32:24-25)

This prophecy appears to correlate with Jeremiah's prophecy about Elam. Ezekiel says that a multitude has been slain by the sword. He attributes Elam's demise to their sponsorship of terror within the world. This may not refer to terrorism as it is interpreted today. However, it is coincidental that the US State Department website designates Iran, Syria, Sudan, and Cuba as countries that sponsor terrorism.[5]

US Foils "Iranian Terror Plot To Assassinate Saudi Ambassador"
Huffington Post 12/10/11

Iran Is "Most Active State Sponsor of Terrorism" In World: US
Huffington Post 5/25/11

Jeremiah also declares that Elam's destruction has a connection with the sword, which is often used in the Bible as a typology for a war or military conflict.

> "For I will cause Elam to be dismayed before their enemies And before those who seek their life. I will bring disaster upon them, My fierce anger,' says the LORD; 'And I will send the sword after them Until I have consumed them." (Jer. 49:37)

Moreover, immediately after predicting Elam's destruction, Ezekiel issues a similar scathing prophecy about Meshech and Tubal (Turkey). Both Meshech and Tubal are listed alongside Persia in the Ezekiel 38 confederacy.

> "There *are* Meshech and Tubal and all their multitudes, With all their graves around it, All of them uncircumcised, slain by the sword, Though they caused their terror in the land of the living. They do not lie with the mighty *Who are* fallen of the uncircumcised, Who have gone down to hell with their weapons of war; They have laid their swords under their heads, But their iniquities will be on

their bones, Because of the terror of the mighty in the land of the living. Yes, you shall be broken in the midst of the uncircumcised, And lie with *those* slain by the sword." (Ezek. 32:26-28)

This demise of Meshech and Tubal seems to be the result of their participation in the Ezekiel 38 invasion. Why would Ezekiel write about Elam, Meshech and Tubal in chapter thirty two, and Persia, Meshech and Tubal in chapter thirty eight?

One plausible answer is that Ezekiel intentionally omitted Elam from the Gog of Magog coalition. The omission of Elam from Ezekiel 38 invaders is probably because Elam is not part of the epic battle. Elam may not be a participant because the disaster predicted in Jeremiah 49:34-39 may occur prior to the formation of the Ezekiel 38 confederacy.

Ezekiel was very specific about the peoples he listed in the Magog coalition and he appears to be very specific about the populations he intentionally omits from this coalition. He omitted Elam and all of the Psalm 83 Arab states (Syria, Jordan, Egypt, Iraq, Saudi Arabia, and Lebanon) that share common borders with Israel.

Why did Ezekiel eliminate these Arab countries? The answer is probably because these Arab states are not participants in the Ezekiel invasion. The reason for their absence is because they have been defeated prior as a result of the Psalm 83 prophecy.

Summary

Ezekiel 38 and 39 will be one of the most epic battles of the end times. The land of Israel will become a massive battle zone of biblical proportions. The world will be shocked when the God of Israel stops the Ezekiel invaders dead in their tracks. However, the world will probably not be surprised to see that the Arab states of Psalm 83 are not part of the Ezekiel invaders. Mankind will have probably witnessed the fulfillment of Psalm 83 prior to the commencement of Ezekiel 38.

Iran will probably not be a battle ground during the Ezekiel 38 invasion, but will be the sight of a major disaster when Jeremiah's prophecy concerning Elam takes place. The calamity in Elam could precede the Gog of Magog invasion and that may be why Elam is not listed in Ezekiel's coalition.

Unlike the prophecy of Elam, which many Iranian Christians are anxiously anticipating the arrival of, the Ezekiel 38 prophecy is probably not something for them to look forward to. For those Iranians that fail to flee after the disaster in Elam, they may be forced by their repressive government to fight in Ezekiel's war.

This is what the "WORLD FACTBOOK" says about mandatory military service in Iran on the Central Intelligence Agency website.

"18 years of age for compulsory military service; 16 years of age for volunteers; 17 years of age for Law Enforcement Forces; 15 years of age for Basij Forces (Popular Mobilization Army); conscript military service obligation is 18 months; women exempt from military service (2012)."

Chapter 3

The Ancient Prophecy of Elam
Part 1 (Jeremiah 49:34-36)

"The word of the LORD that came to Jeremiah the prophet against Elam, in the beginning of the reign of Zedekiah king of Judah, saying, "Thus says the LORD of hosts: 'Behold, I will break the bow of Elam, The foremost of their might. Against Elam I will bring the four winds From the four quarters of heaven, And scatter them toward all those winds; There shall be no nations where the outcasts of Elam will not go." (Jeremiah 49:34-36)

"Israel Has Days to Strike Bushehr" (Iran)

Jerusalem Post 8/17/10

"Iran Opens First Nuclear Power Plant"

UPI 8/21/10

By now the reader might be asking "who, what, when, where, why, and how the scenario hypothesized on the back of the book cover could occur. Is this disastrous situation coming soon or is it a textbook case of newspaper exegesis? Is this the author's speculative attempt to manipulate current Mideast events into biblical prophecies? Perhaps some liberties were taken in predicting future events, but unpacking the prophecy of Elam provokes grave concerns about the potential for an upcoming apocalyptic world crisis.

This and the next three chapters will approach Jeremiah 49:34-39 as a pending event in its entirety. These four connecting chapters of verse-by-verse commentary will primarily address the details given within the prophecy, allowing the reader to imagine the events in the aftermath. Future chapters will explain why Elam's judgment seems to have no historical fulfillment and why the back cover scenario may not be too far-fetched!

The prophet Jeremiah issued an interesting prophecy that could involve Iran's highly controversial nuclear program. The subject of Jeremiah's prophetic utterances is Elam. During the prophet's time, Elam comprised what consists of the central western portions of Iran today. Elam basically hugged much of the northeastern coastline of the Persian Gulf, while Persia encompassed much of today's southern and eastern parts of Iran. It was bounded by Elam to the west and Media to the north.

These chapters of commentary concerning Elam suggest that Iran is involved in dual end time prophecies, a double jeopardy of sorts. This would include the prophecies of Elam by Jeremiah and those regarding Persia in Ezekiel 38-39.

Jeremiah 49:34-39

The complete text of Jeremiah's prophecy is presented below. These verses will then be separated chronologically into numerically ordered sections to assist with the biblical commentary that corresponds.

"The word of the LORD that came to Jeremiah the prophet against Elam, in the beginning of the reign of Zedekiah king of Judah, saying, "Thus says the LORD of hosts: 'Behold, I will break the bow of Elam, The foremost of their might. Against Elam I will bring the four winds From the four quarters of heaven, And scatter them toward all those winds; There shall be no nations where the outcasts of Elam will not go. For I will cause Elam to be dismayed before their enemies And before those who seek their life. I will bring disaster upon them, My fierce anger,' says the LORD; 'And I will send the sword after them Until I have consumed them. I will set My throne in Elam, And will destroy from there the king and the princes,' says the LORD. 'But it shall come to pass in the latter days: I will bring back the captives of Elam,' says the LORD." (Jer. 49:34-39)

Jeremiah 49:34-39 Numerically Ordered

You will probably want to insert a separate book marker here as you read through these combined four chapters of Jeremiah's commentary. As I authored them, I found it helpful to have these numerically ordered breakdowns readily available to refer back to. This helped me to maintain a broad overview of the prophecy. It will help the reader differentiate between the *forest*, which embodies the entire prophecy, and the *trees*, which represent the individual verses.

1. The word of the LORD that came to Jeremiah the prophet against Elam, in the beginning of the reign of Zedekiah king of Judah, saying, "Thus says the LORD of hosts:

2. Behold, *I will* break the bow of Elam.

3. The foremost of their might.

4. Against Elam *I will* bring the four winds From the four quarters of heaven, And scatter them toward all those winds;

5. There shall be no nations where the outcasts of Elam will not go.

   The following sections are listed in order, but will be interpreted in the next three chapters.

6. For *I will* cause Elam to be dismayed before their enemies.

7. And before those who seek their life.

8. *I will* bring disaster upon them.

9. My fierce anger,' says the LORD.

10. And *I will* send the sword after them Until I have consumed them.

> **11.** *I will* set My throne in Elam, And will destroy from there the king and the princes,' says the LORD.
>
> 12. But it shall come to pass in the latter days:
>
> **13.** *I will* bring back the captives of Elam,' says the LORD.

Jeremiah 49:34-36 Commentary

The biblical commentary has been divided into four chapters due to its length. This prophecy is brought about by the Lord, and it is totally directed at the territory and the people of Elam. Although other nations are mentioned as either the enemies of Elam or places of refuge for the Elamites, they are not subjects of this judgment.

Seven times in these six verses, the prophet says "*I will*," alluding to what the Lord intends to accomplish concerning Elam. After each *I will* declaration, follows an important *detail added* assertion that helps to clarify the extent of the predicted events. Observing how the *I wills'* and *detail added assertions* complement each other assists with understanding the specifics of the prophecy.

> 1.   The word of the LORD that came to Jeremiah the prophet against Elam, in the beginning of the reign of Zedekiah king of Judah, saying, "Thus says the LORD of hosts:

Zedekiah was the last king of Judah. He reigned approximately between 596-586 BC. The word of the Lord came to Jeremiah in the beginning of Zedekiah's reign, which means the prophecy was issued sometime around 596 BC. This means that the predictions are for a future time from that date.

> 2.   Behold, *I will* break the bow of Elam.

The Hebrew word used for bow is "qesheth," and it appears to correlate with a similar use in Isaiah 22:3-6 to convey that the Elamites were expert archers. The fact that they were proficient in this method of warfare may also be implied from Jeremiah 50:9.[6] Genesis 14:1, 9 evidences that during the time of Abraham the Elamites were warriors. This means that the Elamites had centuries to refine their archery skills. By addressing the bow of Elam, Jeremiah appears to be directing our attention to the historical heart of Elam's military might.

The first *I will* suggests that Elam's missile launching capabilities might be destroyed. Oddly, Jeremiah only addresses the bow of Elam and doesn't allude to any arrows. This differs from the prophecy concerning Persia and its allies in Ezekiel 38 and 39. Ezekiel's prophecy addresses both, the bow and the arrows.

> "Then I will knock the bow (qesheth) out of your left hand, and cause the arrows to fall out of your right hand." (Ezekiel 39:3)

Jeremiah's omission of any arrows may mean that the focus of the judgment is on Iran's missile launching capabilities, more so than its specific missiles. Without a bow an archer is unable to shoot the arrows in his quiver. Today, this may suggest that Iran will be unable to effectively launch its rockets at its enemies. They may have a multitude of high-tech missiles in their silos but their delivery systems could be incapacitated. It also implies that Iran could be limited in its capability to defend itself from its enemies. According to Jeremiah 49:37 Iran will have enemies that will seek to destroy them when this prophecy occurs.

Israel, one of Iran's enemies, is presently concerned about Iran obtaining a nuclear bomb, and being capable of launching it across the Levant at the Jewish state. Israeli Prime Minister Benjamin Netanyahu has stated, "*We need to dismantle Iran's ability to manufacture and launch nuclear weapons.*"[7] Observe that Netanyahu's statement addresses both the bow (*launch*) and the arrows (*nuclear weapons*).

The Jerusalem Post (JP) quoted Netanyahu on February 25, 2014, as saying to German Chancellor Angela Merkel during her visit to Jerusalem, "*The goal is to prevent Iran from having the capability to manufacture and deliver nuclear weapons. I believe that means zero enrichment, zero centrifuges, zero plutonium, and of course an end to ICBM development. Because none of these elements – none of them – is necessary for developing civilian nuclear energy, which is what Iran has claimed that it wants.*"[8]

This quote expresses Israel's dual concerns. Netanyahu repeated himself, "*none of these elements – none of them.*" In so doing he was apparently clarifying that not only nuclear weapons, but Intercontinental Ballistic Missiles (ICBM's) are problematic. The two elements are inseparable. Is it possible that Israel and / or other enemies of Iran may attempt to destroy, or otherwise hinder Iran's *"ICBM's development"* program?

Iran appears to be on a fast track to develop atomic arrows and long range missiles that can be hurled into Israel. If Iran obtains nuclear weapons but is unable to propel them, then the danger posed to Israel is minimized.

It is noteworthy to mention that presently Iran's enemies primarily exist to its west rather than to the east. Military prudence would dictate that Iran's military installations should be located in the closest proximity to their enemies as possible. As such, many of the bases are located in the north, central and western parts of the country. Almost half of Iran's main military sites are located within the broader vicinity of ancient Elam.[9]

Perhaps an electro-magnetic pulse weapon might be detonated strategically over Elam hampering Iran's electronic capabilities to wage war effectively.[10]

Below is a quote taken from a commentary written by intelligence expert Sean Osborne about Jeremiah 49:35.[11]

> *"This verse informs that Elam's (Iran's) foremost military might, its offensive military might, is suddenly and inexplicably broken. This event is singular unto itself. The plain text metaphor qesheth (battle bow or archer) given here informs us that the choice part or best of the military might of Iran that God will break is an offensive weapon system that launches projectiles at the enemy.*
>
> *Even without nuclear warheads, Iran possesses an incredible number of rocket and missile platforms that as with all modern military forces provide coverage from short to long ranges and in multiple types for engaging land, sea and airborne targets. These rocket and missile systems are the qesheth that Jeremiah speaks of. There is no reason given for the breaking of these weapons systems, it's just that the Lord of hosts has declared it will happen.*

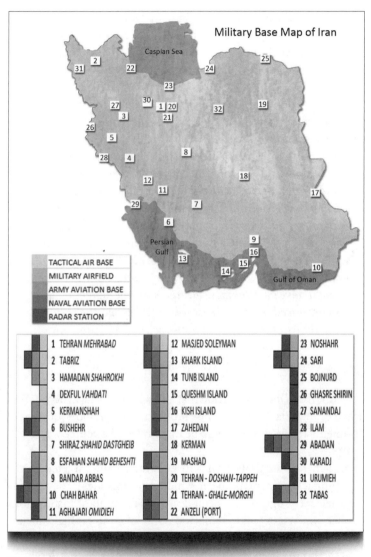

Picture made by Lani Harmony at www.laniharmony.com. Image of Iran's military sites was taken from the Internet on 1/28/14 at this website. http://commons.wikimedia.org/wiki/File:Military_installations_of_Iran_-_2002.jpg

As in ancient times when Elamite and Persian/Median armies launched massive barrages of arrows at their enemies, so too the Iranian military of today relies very heavily on their modern day equivalent. Iranian warfighting *doctrine dictates mass barrage-style launches. Iran can be seen exercising this capability every couple of months or so, and in some instances photo shopping the images to convey ridiculous numbers of rockets being launched.*

Nevertheless, the question is, how will God break such a qesheth (bow) as this? I would speculate, aside from a supernatural act by God, this will occur by the same electronic warfare means as Israel has thus far kept all enemy missile systems from firing at their F15-I Ra'am and F-16I Sufa strike aircraft for the past seven years over Lebanon, Syria and the Sudan. Israel not only can put an enemy into an electronic black hole, but the evidence is that the IDF can actually take control of an enemy's weapons systems. Israel's airborne Suter electronic warfare system, or whatever the more mature version might have as its nomenclature today, the system really is so advanced, that I suspect it is even beyond the very real capability of the rumored non-nuclear EMP capability."

3.	The foremost of their might.

This *detail added* assertion that follows the first *I will* declaration clarifies that Elam's bow will be broken at the foremost location of its might. This assertion might be interpreted in a couple ways.

a. *First*, this suggests Iran will be strategically targeted at the pinnacle point of its power, which today includes its developing nuclear program. This could include its military installations, headquarters, and armories. One of Iran's chief nuclear site is in the area of Bushehr, which is today located inside the boundaries of ancient Elam. It is possible that Jeremiah predicted an attack upon Iran's nuclear site(s) approximately 2,600 hundred years ago.

"Attack against Bushehr nuclear reactor could kill hundreds of thousands"

Examiner 9/6/12

Some Bible translations say the bow of Elam will be broken at "the finest of their might" (NASB), "the chief of their might" (KJV, ASV), "the mainstay of their might" (NIV, RSV, NRSV), and "the best of their marksmen" (NLT).

b. *Second,* The Hebrew word for foremost is "reshith" and can also be translated as *the beginning or first, in place, time, order or rank (specifically like a firstfruit).*[12] Perhaps this suggests that the first nuclear facility that Iran established as a mainstay of its military might could be attacked.

Bushehr is the location of Iran's first nuclear site. It was first to be started, first to be finished, and first to become operational. It was loaded with Russian fuel rods in August of 2010 and became operational shortly thereafter.

"Construction of the plant was started in 1975 by German companies, but the work was stopped in 1979 after the Islamic revolution of Iran. The site was repeatedly bombed during the Iran-Iraq war. Later, a contract for finishing the plant was signed between Iran and the Russian Ministry for Atomic Energy in 1995. There have been safety concerns about the Bushehr plant, associated with construction of the plant itself, aging equipment at the plant, and understaffing."[13]

The safety concerns are wide reaching because the facility was constructed with unmonitored German, Russian, and Iranian parts over a prolonged period of time. Also, the plant was built near tectonic plates, and some studies suggest that a radioactive disaster at Bushehr is possible and could threaten the water supplies of the Arab Gulf States.[14]

It is possible that Jeremiah is attempting to describe an attack on Iran's nuclear program, at least in Elam where the Bushehr reactor exists. When he prophesied there was no Iran or nuclear technology in existence. He would have to warn of a powerful destruction with the words of the vernacular of his time. It could be that he was predicting that Iran's nuclear program will be struck and their ability to launch nuclear tipped missiles will be prevented. This possibility takes on an added dimension in the next *I will* declaration and *detail added* assertion.

4. Against Elam *I will* bring the four winds From the four
    quarters of heaven, And scatter them toward all those winds.

The second *I will* affects both the territory and the people of
Elam. After Iran's bow is broken at the foremost of its might, the *four
winds* are ushered in. Jeremiah is the first and only prophet to use
the term *the four winds from the four quarters of heaven*, and this is
his only usage. This means we have no other biblical references to
glean from. The only other Old Testament applications of a variation
of this phrase are subsequent uses by Ezekiel, Daniel, and Zechariah.

Zechariah's use of the idiom is the one that most parallels
Jeremiah's usage.

"Ho, ho, flee from the land of the north, saith Jehovah; for
I have spread you (Jews) abroad as the four winds of the
heavens, saith Jehovah." (Zechariah 2:6)

Zechariah points out that the Jews were scattered abroad outside
of the land of Israel in correlation to *the four winds of the heavens*. We
might presume that Zechariah is alluding to the same *four winds from
the four quarters of heaven* that Jeremiah had previously identified.
In similar fashion as Zechariah addresses a spreading abroad of the
Jews, Jeremiah predicts a vast scattering of the Elamites. Jeremiah
and Zechariah both use the *four winds* expression as a typology for a
worldwide dispersion of an indigenous people from their homeland.

None of the Old Testament references to the *four winds* refer
to literal occurrences of natural disasters resulting from a massive
tornado, hurricane, or tsunami. In every instance, the prophets
utilize the *four winds* as an idiom to describe some significant
sovereign act. The four winds coming from every direction creates
the biblical picture that something on an international scale,
ordained by God, is forthcoming, and will be unpreventable.

A summary of the six Old Testament uses of the *four winds* is
provided in this paragraph. Jeremiah 49:36 and Zechariah 2:6 refer
to a worldwide dispersion. Ezekiel 37:9-13 alludes to a worldwide
regathering of the Jews back into Israel. Daniel 7:2 references the
stirring up of the "Great Sea," from which come the four powerful
Gentile empires, Babylonian, Medo-Persian, Greece, and Roman.

Daniel 8:8 and 11:4 seems to describe the breakup of Alexander's kingdom (Greece).

5. There shall be no nations where the outcasts of Elam will not go.

This *detail added* assertion clarifies that the expanse of the expulsion of the Elamites will be worldwide. This implies that a massive evacuation occurs in the aftermath of Iran being strategically struck at the foremost location of its might. It may hint of a humanitarian crisis in the making.

Now would be a good time to reflect back upon the conversation between Reza Safa and me described in chapter one. Safa pointed out that many Iranian Christians are anxiously awaiting the fulfilment of this verse. They apparently long to be among the "outcasts of Elam," that escape the oppression within Iran.

Moreover, these Christians don't plan on playing the role of victims but are seeking to seize the opportunity to preach the gospel worldwide. This verse clearly announces that "there shall be no nation" where the scattered Iranians won't go. They probably realize that the price of their passports comes at the cost of Elam's harsh judgment.

Turning what has the trappings to be an extremely negative event into a positive episode in Christian history would be reminiscent of the historic story of Joseph. After being bitterly betrayed by his brothers, he made the following comment;

> Joseph said to them, "Do not be afraid, for *am* I in the place of God? But as for you, you meant evil against me; *but* God meant it for good, in order to bring it about as *it is* this day, to save many people alive. Now therefore, do not be afraid; I will provide for you and your little ones." And he comforted them and spoke kindly to them. (Genesis 50:19-21)

If Jeremiah's prophecy concerning Elam remains unfulfilled and is as imminent as it appears, then the humble mindset of these Iranian Christians is sobering. Unless the Rapture of the church precedes the fulfilment of Jeremiah 49:34-39, many of them could achieve the high-calling of their Christianity, which is to proclaim the "Good News Gospel" of Jesus Christ throughout the world!

> "And Jesus came and spoke to them, saying, "All authority has been given to Me in heaven and on earth. Go therefore and make disciples of all the nations, baptizing them in the name of the Father and of the Son and of the Holy Spirit, teaching them to observe all things that I have commanded you; and lo, I am with you always, *even* to the end of the age." Amen. (Matthew 28:18-20)

> "And He said to them, "Go into all the world and preach the gospel to every creature. He who believes and is baptized will be saved; but he who does not believe will be condemned." (Mark 16:15-16)

Paralleling the aspirations of these Iranian Christians is the grim reality that Jeremiah's prophecy results in a disaster to the territory and its local populous. The dispersion of the Iranians will undoubtedly include people from all walks of life alongside the Christians, including the Muslim majority and religious minorities of Bahá'ís, Mandeans, Hindus, Yarsanis, Zoroastrians, and Jews.[15]

The catastrophic calamity appears to carry with it a lion's share of casualties as per Jeremiah 49:37, which says: "For I will cause Elam to be dismayed before their enemies And before those who seek their life. I will bring disaster upon them, My fierce anger,' says the LORD; 'And I will send the sword after them Until I have consumed them."

Summary

Jeremiah 49:34-36 predicts a coming disaster to the western central portion of Iran where the ancient territory of Elam existed. The magnitude of this tragedy will create a massive worldwide dispersion of the affected population. It may turn out to be a humanitarian crisis of epic proportion. Among those being scattered will be Christians looking for the opportunity to depart from Iran in order to preach the gospel worldwide.

The IRGC will be struck hard at the heart of its military might. This attack appears to minimize the IRGC's ability to respond effectively. The strategic targets might include Iran's nuclear program, which could result in an unprecedented nuclear catastrophe.

Chapter 4

The Ancient Prophecy of Elam
Part 2 (Jeremiah 49:37)

"For I will cause Elam to be dismayed before their enemies And before those who seek their life. I will bring disaster upon them, My fierce anger,' says the LORD; 'And I will send the sword after them Until I have consumed them." (Jeremiah 49:37)

"Iran: Pre-emptive strike against enemies possible."

CBS News 2/21/12

"A senior Iranian military commander signaled the Islamic Republic might launch a pre-emptive strike against its "enemies" if the nation's leaders felt an attack on Iran was imminent, providing another example of ever-escalating tensions between Tehran and the West over its nuclear program."[16]

"A Grand Coalition Against Iran."

The Diplomat 5/7/13

"Whatever the intent of Iran's nuclear program, it appears regional tensions and fears surrounding Tehran's possible motivations could be pushing together some interesting partners. Various outlets are reporting that Israel and nations such as Turkey, Jordan, Saudi Arabia and the United Arab Emirates (UAE) could be forming a defensive pact with Iran in mind."[17]

The first two *I wills'* and #1-5 passage breakdowns of Jeremiah's prophecy concerning Elam were commented upon in the previous chapter. This chapter will explore the next three *I wills'* along with the #6-10 passage breakdowns that carryover. The following two chapters will complete the biblical commentary of Jeremiah 49:34-39.

6.   For *I will* cause Elam to be dismayed before their enemies.

In the fourth *I will*, we discover that Elam has enemies! Not just a single enemy, but a plurality of enemies. One of them is the Lord, and according to Jer. 49:37, He is absolutely infuriated with something Iran has done or plans to do.

Like many biblical prophecies we don't always find out in the beginning verses what has upset the Lord. Nor do we often learn until later on in the prophecy why a judgment is rendered upon a country, or what nation or nations are empowered to execute the divine decree. A perfect example of this is in Isaiah 19. In Isaiah's prophecy the nation of Egypt unravels at the seams in the first 15 verses until the reason is given in verses 16-18. These key Isaiah versus tell us that Egypt confronts Israel and gets defeated by the powerful IDF.

> "In that day Egypt will be like women, and will be afraid and fear because of the waving of the hand of the LORD of hosts, which He waves over it. And the land of Judah (Israel) will be a terror to Egypt; everyone (Egyptian) who makes mention of it (the Jewish state) will be afraid in himself, because of the counsel of the LORD of hosts which He has determined against it. In that day five cities in the land of Egypt will speak the language of Canaan (Hebrew the official language of Israel) and swear by the LORD of hosts; one will be called the City of Destruction." (Isaiah 19:16-18, emphasis added)

A detailed verse by verse commentary for Isaiah 19 is available inside my book entitled, *Psalm 83, The Missing Prophecy Revealed.*

Similarly, Jeremiah 49:34-36 issues a destructive report about Elam, but we still don't know why as of yet. In Sean Osborne's quote in the prior chapter, he suggested that Israel might be responsible for breaking the bow of Elam. This may be the case, but it is difficult to ascertain the specific cause and perpetrator of Elam's judgment in Jeremiah 49:34-39. The judgment is clearly called for by the Lord, but by whom it is executed is unspecified. It is highly possible that the Israeli Defense Forces (IDF) plays a critical role, but they may not go it alone.

In addition to the Lord, Iran has no shortage of enemies today, and for a variety of differing reasons. Below is a basic list of three notable adversaries of Iran:

1. Israelis are concerned that Iran wants to wipe Israel off the face of the map and transform the country into another Iranian proxy state called Palestine. This is why Israel keeps the threat of military action against Iran on the table.

2. The GCC (Gulf Cooperation Council of Arab states), which includes Saudi Arabia, Kuwait, Bahrain, Qatar, United Arab Emirates (UAE) and Oman, are deeply concerned about Iran's rogue regime, unchecked nuclear program, and attempts to spread its hegemony throughout the entire Middle East. This is one of the primary reasons the GCC is forming its own combat coalition and formed a committee to study the potential dangers of the Bushehr nuclear plant.

"Iranian radiation a threat to GCC water security?"

Al Arabiya 7/24/13

"The risk of radiation from Iran's Bushehr nuclear power plant, if there is an accident, is extremely high to the GCC states. Studies and analyses suggest that any leak from the plant will affect the GCC's water supplies especially desalinization plant operation. In the event of a radiation leak, clouds of radioactive material will drift to the GCC states in just 15 hours. While the radiation would affect only about 10 percent of the Iranian population, in the GCC states, 40 to 100 percent of the population would be affected."[18]

Potable and drinkable water is a rare commodity in in the Arab Gulf States. Approximately two-thirds of the world's desalinization plants are supposedly located within these Arab countries. Considering the fact that Iran is one of the most seismically active countries in the world, the Arab Gulf States are justifiably concerned about the potential dangers of a disaster emanating from the Bushehr nuclear facility that sits on the east side of the Persian Gulf.

Iran experienced its largest earthquake in forty years on April 16, 2013, around the border of Pakistan that lasted about twenty-five seconds. It measured 7.7 and was followed by an apparent aftershock of 6.3 near Bushehr. At least thirty-five people were killed and eighty others were injured in this quake.

As a result of this quake and the radiation fallout disaster caused by the 9.0 Tohoku quake to the Fukushima nuclear plant in Japan in 2011, the GCC national emergency members met in mid-April of 2013 to discuss the potential crisis emerging from a disaster at Bushehr. This committee assessed that the greatest potential threat from Bushehr to the Arab Gulf States was to their water supply. Below is a quote from an article that was written about this matter.

> "In mid-July, the GCC Secretariat General announced plans for the construction of a joint water supply system, which will reduce the overwhelming reliance of member states on the Arabian Gulf as their primary water source. Few details have yet been released, but the GCC Assistant Economic Secretary, Abdullah al-Shibli, has said that 'the water link is to build a line from the Gulf of Oman to Kuwait, passing through the GCC countries.' The pipeline will utilise water from outside the Arabian Gulf and will include storage facilities to stock potable water and distribute drinkable supplies across member states. The logistics of the plan are not yet available and it is unclear whether the water will be desalinated in Oman then pumped to its GCC neighbours, or whether salt water will be pumped for utilisation in domestic desalination plants...Planning and construction of the pipeline are now in the works and it is expected that the project could be ready by 2020, at a cost of US$7 billion." [19]

3. The international community might be considered a third enemy of Iran. Many world leaders are concerned about Iran's nuclear program, state sponsorship of global terrorism, and threats to choke off Middle East oil supplies by closing off the narrow Strait of Hormuz.

"Iran terror network prolific, US report says"

Jerusalem Post 5/1/14

"State Department annual report focuses on Iran's expansive efforts to fund and funnel arms to Islamist organizations, including Hamas and Hezbollah."[20]

Several prominent countries have imposed strict sanctions upon Iran in an attempt to prevent Iran from becoming a nuclear nation. The P5+1 comprised of the United States, Russia, China, United Kingdom, and France, plus Germany brokered a temporary truce with Iran on January 20, 2014, in the hopes that Iran would forgo any aspirations toward achieving a nuclear weapon.

These are the three primary enemies of Iran today, and any or all of them could be used as instruments of the Lord to execute His judgment upon Elam. Although their motives all differ, preventing Iran from developing or acquiring nuclear weapons unites them in a common cause. Perhaps this is also the concern of the Lord. Perchance He wishes to prevent the rogue Islamic regime of Iran from becoming another nuclear nation.

In theory, a nuclear weaponized Iran could decimate the state of Israel, and Iran has been very vocal about their intentions to destroy the Jewish state. These intentions are elaborated upon in the chapter called "Iran: A Past Friend but Present Foe of Israel." This chapter will also demonstrate why Jeremiah's prophecy concerning Elam still awaits its fulfillment.

The destruction of Israel would put a huge damper on the Lord's end time's plans for the Jewish state. Ezekiel 39:7 declares that the Lord intends to uphold His holy name in the midst of His people Israel. In order to accomplish this monumental task, it requires a country called Israel and a Jewish ethnicity residing therein; both conditions exist presently. If Iran is enabled with nuclear weapons to fulfill its stated intentions, neither would exist in the not so distant future.

Taking it one step further, if no Jew exists inside or outside of Israel, then the Second Coming of Jesus Christ to the planet earth can't occur. The return of Christ is predicated upon Jews saying, "Blessed is He who comes in the name of the Lord," according to Matthew 23:39. This becomes an important point considering that genocidal attempts of the Jews appear to be coming indirectly in Psalm 83 and Ezekiel 38, and directly during the Armageddon campaign.

Iran's Enemies Will Stand in Awe

Jeremiah 49:37 talks about Iran being "*dismayed before their enemies.*" This is not alluding to an embarrassing national episode or the implementation of strict disciplinary sanctions, rather the Hebrew word used for *dismayed* conveys an extremely terrifying scenario.

The word "chathath" is used and it means to be beaten down, shattered, frightened, and / or terrified to the point of standing in awe.[21] What Iran goes through apparently causes its enemies to stand in awe at the magnitude of the disaster.

Some other biblical translations of the word say:

"*I will terrify Elam before their enemies*" (The New Revised Standard Version)

"*I will shatter Elam before their enemies*" (New American Standard Version)

"*I will shatter Elam before their foes*" (New International Version)

7.	And before those who seek their life.

This detail added assertion is obviously not talking about the inhumane primitive practice of cannibalism, nor on the flip side about non-Iranians coveting the Iranian lifestyle. Jeremiah seems to have coined the phrase *those who seek their life, or seek their lives.* A biblical search of these phrases evidences that only Jeremiah uses them in the Bible. Whenever he utilizes these phrases, he always refers to a war scenario.[22]

This declaration hammers home the fact that Iran's enemies are interested in annihilating Iranians. Whoever these enemies turn out to be, they are clearly not seeking a diplomatic solution to resolve their disputes with Iran. No sanctions or temporary truces will satisfy their deep seated concerns. The only resolution to the conflict is war, and that's why there are *"those who seek their life."*

Some possible scenarios to consider in light of the current geo-political environment surrounding Iran's relationship with its enemies are explored below. Each of these scenarios could provoke Iran's enemies to forego diplomacy and opt for war.

1. *The Israel Scenario* – if Iran and / or any of its proxies of Syria, the Hezbollah, or the Hamas commence a missile launching campaign into the Jewish state, Israel could easily be provoked into a war with Iran.

"170,000 rockets are aimed at Israel's cities, says IDF intel head"

Times of Israel 1/29/14

Israel Defense Official: We are Entering an "Era of Fire"

Breitbart News 1/29/14

"Israel is entering an "Era of Fire" in which it is threatened by 170,000 rockets and missiles and in which the Syrian civil war has placed "30,000 global jihad terrorists" at its doorstep, Israel's defense intelligence chief said in a speech Wednesday."[23]

2. *The Arab Gulf States Situation* – If Iran chokes off the exportation of the GCC oil through the Persian Gulf into world markets, the affected Arab states, such as Saudi Arabia, could be provoked into war.

"Saudi Arabia Displays Ballistic Missiles in Likely Signal to Iran"
National Journal 4/30/14

Another possible prompt to war would be a forceful move by Iran to spread its Shiite theology into the predominantly Sunni governed countries. Iran has expressed no qualms about advancing its hegemony throughout the preponderance of the Middle East. Bahrain is a prime example of this Sunni verses Shiite (Shia) clash that occurred in the aftermath of the Arab Spring. Bahrain is ruled by a Sunni minority, but is populated by a Shia majority. Bahrain's 1.2 million population is approximately 70% Shia and 30% Sunni.[24]

3. *The International Alliance Scenario* – Shutting down the Strait of Hormuz to choke off the flow of OPEC oil into world markets would also upset the global community. State sponsored terrorism connected to Iran would be another instigator that could draw a country or countries into war. In either instance, an international coalition could be formed that abandons diplomacy and declares war with Iran. We saw this consequence occur in Iraq during Operation Desert Storm in 1990-1991 and to a lesser degree with the military intervention of the NATO alliance against Libya in 2011.

All of the above scenarios are realistic. Iran has made threats to perform all the above. These threats were mostly issued as a potential retaliatory response to having its nuclear program attacked. The news headlines below evidence the legitimacy and seriousness of Iran's threats.

"Iran: 'Thousands of missiles' to rain on Israel"
World Net Daily 8/28/13

"Iran's leader threatens to level cities if Israel attacks, criticizes US nuclear talks"
Fox News 3/21/13

"Iran's (Supreme) leader (Ayatollah Ali Khamenei) said in a speech that the country would annihilate the Israeli cities of Tel Aviv and Haifa if Iran were attacked by Israel, and criticized the U.S. over nuclear talks."

"Iranian commander: We have targets within America"

The Daily Caller 2/1/14

"A top commander of Iran's Revolutionary Guards (Gen. Hossein Salami)boasted Saturday that his forces have plans in place to attack the United States from within, should the U.S. attack the Islamic Republic."

"Iran threatens Strait of Hormuz, vital oil route"

CBS News 12/28/11

It is imaginable that Israel, or perhaps some other nation or coalition of nations, could strike Iran's nuclear program. Israel has warned the world on numerous occasions that it is prepared to strike Iran's nuclear program. Israel has a modern-day precedent for striking nuclear sites. They attacked the Osirak nuclear reactor in Iraq in 1981 and Syria's al-Kibar nuclear facility in 2007. Israel attacking Iran's Bushehr nuclear site or any other Iranian nuclear facility should not be a shock to anyone. Israel pre-emptively striking Iran could be the mainstream news headline on any given morning.

Should Iran be attacked, there is a good possibility that they will make good on some or all of their retaliatory threats. Such a scenario could escalate into a major regional war and Iranians would be confronted with dangerous enemies seeking to destroy them.

8.   *I will* bring disaster upon them.

This fourth *I will* puts all of the previously explored prophetic details into perspective. The breaking of Elam's bow (#2) at the foremost place of its might (#3) that results in a worldwide scattering of the affected people (#4-5), which shatters Iran as its enemies watch in awe (#6-7) is a disaster that is initiated by the Lord.

Up to this point it was obvious by the preceding *I wills'* and *detail added assertions* that the Lord had the upper hand in this matter and that it was a distressful judgment upon Iran, but here we grasp the severity of the situation! We still don't know why all of the above events (#2-7) happen but now we know that the Lord is defining Elam's judgment as an epic "disaster!"

The Hebrew word Jeremiah uses to describe this specific disaster is "raah" and it shows up hundreds of times in the Old Testament. Below are some of the biblical uses of the term. Upon reviewing these other usages, it becomes clear that this disastrous episode in Iran's future will probably rank among one of the worst events in Iran's history!

> *evil, misery, distress, injury:*—adversities, adversity, afflictions, calamities, calamity, disaster, discomfort, distress, distresses, evil, evil deeds, evildoing, great wickedness, harm, hurt , ill, injure, injury, misery, misfortune, misfortunes, pain, situation, sorrow, trouble, troubles, wicked, wicked deeds, wickedly, wickedness, woe, wretchedness, wrong, wrongdoing.[25]

What could Iran be guilty of to warrant a distress of this magnitude? Has Elam ever experienced a disaster of this enormity? The answer to the second question is apparently not. The answer to the first question concerning why this judgment comes upon Iran will be explored in the next detail added assertion.

9   My fierce anger,' says the LORD.

Elam is guilty of fiercely angering the Lord. If this prophecy remains unfulfilled, this means that something Iran does or is presently doing enrages the Lord. Before discussing the issues that are known to provoke the Lord to anger, let me get a bit personal with the reader.

As a Christian I am deeply disturbed that the God of the Bible, that I love and have committed my faith in, has to deal with some extremely egregious problem coming out from Iran. No kind-hearted child would want to see their earthly father, who is imperfect, be fiercely angered, and the Lord is our Heavenly Father, the role model of perfection. I agree with Moses the prophet, John the apostle and Jesus Christ the messiah when they declare;

> *Moses the prophet,* "And the LORD passed before him and proclaimed, "The LORD, the LORD God, merciful and gracious, longsuffering, and abounding in goodness and truth." (Exodus 34:6)

> *John the apostle,* "You are worthy, O Lord, To receive glory and honor and power; For You created all things, And by Your will they exist and were created." (Revelation 4:11)

> *Jesus Christ the messiah,* "For God so loved the world that He gave His only begotten Son, that whoever believes in Him should not perish but have everlasting life. For God did not send His Son into the world to condemn the world, but that the world through Him might be saved." (John 3:16-17)

These Scriptures evidence that the Lord would prefer to have a personal, everlasting, loving relationship with every Iranian rather than be upset with any of them. A testimony to the Lord's longsuffering and abundant mercy is today's back story of the Iranian Christians. Even though the rogue Islamic regime of Iran is provoking the Lord to *fierce anger,* millions of Iranians are forsaking the god of the Koran and becoming believers in the God of the Bible.

Romans 2:4 tells us that it is the Lord's goodness, forbearance, and longsuffering that leads people to repentance. These Christian converts understand this, and many of them want to preach this good news message worldwide.

How Has Iran Fiercely Angered the Lord?

This is not the first biblical instance that describes the Lord as being fiercely angered, nor will Iran be the last country to infuriate the Lord. Zephaniah points out that during the Armageddon scenario when the Lord judges the nations in Joel 3:2 that the Lord will be fiercely angered again.

> "Therefore wait for Me," says the LORD, "Until the day I rise up for plunder; My determination *is* to gather the nations To My assembly of kingdoms, To pour on them My indignation, All My *fierce anger*; All the earth shall be devoured With the fire of My jealousy." (Zephaniah 3:8; *emphasis added*)

The Lord does not randomly execute judgments upon nations. Something the nation does provokes the Lord to anger, which leads to the nation's deserved judgment. A few historical examples are below.

1. *Sexual Immorality*: many Bible teachers believe that the destruction of Sodom and Gomorrah resulted from its advanced stages of sexual immorality. (Genesis 18-19).
2. *Wickedness*: It is commonly taught that Nineveh was destroyed because of its advanced stages of wickedness. (Nahum 1-3).
3. *Oppression of the Jews*: The judgment against Canaan was caused because they continually cursed the Jews. This episode ended the twenty years of harsh oppression of the Jews in the Promised Land by the Canaanites. (Judges 4-5). The destruction of Pharaoh and his Egyptian army at the Red Sea during the time of Moses at the exodus is another example of this. (Genesis 14-15).

These are just a few historical examples of what a nation or population should avoid morphing into if it wants to stay on the good side of God's graces. In Iran's case, sexual immorality is not the present problem. Homosexuality and adultery are strictly prohibited in Iran.

Wickedness is a possible problem, but even though Iranians at large worship the pagan false god of Allah they still advocate moral behavior, apart from the repression of women, Christians and political dissidents. However, the most probable reason the Lord is angry with Iran is because of its declared intentions to harm the Jews. A constant barrage of venomous rhetoric and existential threats emanating out from Iran against Israel have become commonplace.

God's Divine Gentile Foreign Policy

The Lord has longstanding foreign policy in place that is driven by the way the Gentiles treat the Jews. It dates back about 4,000 years ago to the time of Abraham and is still effectually intact. Below are the Scriptures that contain the Lord's Gentile foreign policy and what Iran needs to be concerned about today.

"I will make you (Abraham) a great nation; I will bless you And make your name great; And you shall be a blessing. I will bless those who bless you, And I will curse him who curses you; And in you all the families of the earth shall be blessed." (Genesis 12:2-3; *emphasis added*).

Herein lays all Gentile foreign policy: those who bless Abraham will likewise be blessed, but those cursing him, will be cursed! It is commonly understood contextually, that these verses extrapolate from Abraham to his Hebrew descendants through the genealogies of Isaac, Jacob, and Jacob's twelve sons, who formed the twelve tribes of Israel. Hence, the Genesis 12:3 principle applies to the Jewish descendants of these twelve tribes today. Moreover, there is no valid reason to conclude that this Gentile foreign policy isn't still applicable.

At the time the Genesis 12:3 foreign policy was issued, the world was populated with people. Out from the masses, one was divinely called, and that was Abraham. In essence, he became the first Hebrew, and many translate the word *Hebrew* to mean *to pass over.*[26] Hence, they regard it to mean *the man who passed over.* Abraham, which in the Hebrew language means, "father of multitudes," passed over from ungodly men, to become a man of God. The common understanding from that point forward was that humanity was comprised of Abraham and his Hebrew descendants, and everybody else called Gentiles.

By seeking the destruction of today's Israel, Iran is following in the same failed footsteps of Pharaoh and his Egyptian army and the Canaanites of old. The case was made earlier in this chapter that any nation or coalition of nations that seeks the destruction of the modern-day Jewish state stands in the way of the Lord's big plans for little Israel.

The Lord intends to uphold His holy name in the midst of His people Israel (Ezekiel 39:7), and if Iran can destroy Israel, then the Lord's fierce anger is nothing more than a major embarrassment for Him. Is the Lord just blowing off some steam, or will He accomplish His sovereign plans through Israel and judge Iran for its plans to curse Israel?

" 'Death to Israel' chants mark Iran anniversary"

Al Arabiya 2/11/14

"Iran can now build and deliver nukes, US intel reports"

Times of Israel 1/30/14

> "Iran now has all the technical infrastructure to produce nuclear weapons should it make the political decision to do, Director of National Intelligence James Clapper wrote in a report to a Senate intelligence committee."

10   And *I will* send the sword after them Until I have consumed them.

This fifth *I will* implies that the judgment of Elam is carried out through the means of a war, (*I will send the sword*), rather than the result of a natural disaster like a significant earthquake. The use of the word *sword* commonly represents a military campaign as a biblical typology. Examples of this are found in Jeremiah 9:16, Ezekiel 11:8-10, 25:13, Nahum 3:15 and elsewhere.

This sentence also instructs us that a decisive victory will be achieved over Elam. It won't be comparable to the Hezbollah-Israeli conflict of 2006 that seemed to end up in a stalemate. The use of the word *consumed,* leaves no possibility for a draw in this fight. This won't be a technical knock-out because of an accidental head butt as in the sport of boxing, because Elam will be knocked-out for the ten-count from a devastating war.

Lastly, the Lord promises to "*send the sword after them.*" This strongly suggests that the instrument of the Lord's choice in this matter is not His own mighty hands, but those of Iran's enemies. The Lord personally collapsed the Red Sea to destroy Pharaoh and his army at the time of the exodus, and He will again utilize His own might to defeat the Ezekiel 38 invaders, but in this episode, He empowers Iran's enemies to accomplish His judgment upon Elam.

Perhaps this is another reason the Israeli Defense Forces exist in fulfillment of Bible prophecy? In my *Psalm 83 - the Missing Prophecy Revealed, How Israel Becomes the Next Mideast Superpower* book, I point out that the IDF today exists in fulfillment of Bible prophecy.

The Earthquake Option

Considering the important fact that Iran is a highly seismic country sitting on many powerful earthquake faults, it would be remiss not to mention that an earthquake may come into play as part of Jeremiah's prophecy about Elam. It appears relatively clear in Jeremiah 49:37 that the Lord will use a military option (*the sword*) to execute Elam's judgment, but this does not nullify the possibility that an earthquake could be triggered during the episode.

This possibility is nowhere mentioned in Jeremiah 49:34-39 as it is in other prophecies like Ezekiel 38:19, the Gog of Magog war, but it deserves an honorable mention here. What follows is a quote taken from my prior commentary on Jeremiah 49:34-39 in my *Psalm 83 - Missing Prophecy Revealed* book.

The Natural Disaster Option

Iran has a history of seismic activity. It has experienced a multitude of significant earthquakes, dating back as far as the 7.3 Silakhor quake on January 23, 1909, with an estimated 6,000 fatalities. At least 40,000 were killed in the 7.4 Mangil-Rudbar quake of June 20, 1990. Iran has experienced about ten 6.0 or greater quakes already in the twenty-first century.

Wikipedia states the following:

"Iran is one of the most seismically active countries in the world, being crossed by several major fault lines that cover at least 90% of the country. As a result, earthquakes in Iran occur often and are destructive."[27]

In light of Japan's Fukushima nuclear disaster that resulted from the 9.0 Tohoku earthquake and subsequent tsunami in March of 2011, it is possible that Iran could experience a natural disaster brought on by an earthquake as well. Jeremiah says; "I will bring disaster upon them, My fierce anger," says the LORD." Matthew 24:7 predicts earthquakes will occur worldwide in the end times. Luke 21:11 declares that there will be many great earthquakes.

Summary

Iran fiercely angers the Lord, which results in a divine judgment. This judgment appears to manifest as a major disaster in the central western region of the country that was formerly known as Elam. The disaster is apparently the result of a war conducted between Iran and its enemies.

Iran is presently making enemies as a result of its threats to destroy Israel, incite global terrorism, spread its hegemony over the region and choke off world oil supplies through the Persian Gulf. These enemies include Israel, the GCC, and several members of the international community. Although these enemies have differing concerns about the dangers Iran poses to them, they are all united in a quest to prevent Iran from possessing nuclear weapons.

At some point, Iran seems to cross a political red line ending diplomatic attempts to prevent a war through sanctions and temporary truces. When diplomacy fails, a war begins. The catastrophic results of this war have the potential to cause Iran's enemies to stand in awe of their conquest. The victory appears to be decisive because these enemies of Iran are empowered by the Lord to execute His fierce anger on Iran.

Chapter 5

The Ancient Prophecy of Elam
Part 3 (Jeremiah 49:38)

"I will set My throne in Elam, And will destroy from there
the king and the princes,' says the LORD. (Jeremiah 49:38)

"UAE leader: Israel would destroy Iran if attacked"
Haaretz News 12/6/11

"White House No visa for Iran's UN ambassador pick"
Fox News 4/11/14

The first five *I wills'* and passage breakdowns #1-10 of Jeremiah's prophecy concerning Elam were completed in the previous two chapters. This chapter explores the sixth *I will*, which comprises passage breakdown #11.

> 11   *I will* set My throne in Elam, And will destroy from there the king and the princes,' says the LORD.

The sixth *I will* and its correlating detail added assertion are included together in #11, because the detail added helps to interpret what the Lord plans to do at this juncture of Jeremiah's prophecy. In correlation with the first five *I wills'* in Jeremiah 49:35-37, the Lord plans to set up His throne in Elam.

This specific declaration, "I will set My throne in Elam," is difficult to interpret literally because according to the Scriptures, the Lord's throne presently exists in *Heaven*. However, in the future it will be established in *Jerusalem*. The verses below identify these literal locations.

"Thus says the LORD: "*Heaven is* (the present location of) My throne, And earth *is* My footstool. Where *is* the house that you will build Me? And where *is* the place of My rest? (Isaiah 66:1; *emphasis added*)

"Then it shall come to pass, when you (Jews) are multiplied and increased in the (Promised) land (of Israel) in those days," says the LORD, "that they will say no more, 'The ark of the covenant of the LORD.' It shall not come to mind, nor shall they remember it, nor shall they visit *it*, nor shall it be made anymore. "At that time *Jerusalem* shall be called *The Throne of the LORD*, and all the nations shall be gathered to it, (during the millennial kingdom) to the name of the LORD, to Jerusalem. No more shall they follow the dictates of their evil hearts." (Jer. 3:16-17; *emphasis added*)

"Then I heard *Him* speaking to me from the temple, while a man stood beside me. And He said to me, "Son of man, *this is* the place of My throne (in Jerusalem during the millennium) and the place of the soles of My feet, where I will dwell in the midst of the children of Israel forever." (Ezekiel 43:6-7; *emphasis added*)

Merriam-Webster's Online Dictionary defines "throne" as a noun which means "the special chair for a king, queen, or other powerful person." It further defines that it can also be the chair of state of a sovereign or high dignitary (as a bishop), the seat of a deity, or represents royal power and dignity: sovereignty.[28]

The Hebrew word used for "throne" in Jeremiah 48:38 is *kisse*, and it means a seat of honor, a throne, an official seat, or authority.[29] Since there is no other scriptural support for a literal throne of the Lord being set up inside of Iran, the probable use of the word in this instance is an *official seat* of *honor* that is endowed with sovereign *authority* over the territory of Elam. Other biblical uses of the word as an official seat established by a king for a dignitary are located in 1 Kings 2:19 and Esther 3:1.

In the overall context of the prophecy, it appears as though the Lord will establish His sovereign authority over the territory of Elam. In a real time application it suggests that the present radical Islamic regime in Iran could be dethroned, at least partially in its stronghold in the territorial location of ancient Elam. This can be deduced from the realization that the current Iranian Islamist leadership that adheres to the tenets contained in the Koran cannot maintain its sovereignty alongside the throne of the God of the Bible! It is like mixing oil and water or putting a square peg into a round hole, because Jehovah and Allah are not the same god.

Admittedly, this is one of the more difficult verses in Jeremiah's prophecy to understand because the reference to the throne of God is difficult to interpret literally. On the surface it seems simple. Whenever a ruling body is dethroned a replacement government typically ensues. A few possibilities as to how this might happen are enumerated below. Upon reading these prospects it is important to remember that the detail added in this verse is the elimination of the "king and the princes" of Elam.

1. *A Vassal ruler* could be put in charge of the area by a conquering enemy. The prophecy involves enemies, and historically, whenever an enemy conquers an area they often remove the king and his court and usurp his authority. As the victor, an enemy has the right to relocate their throne into the area, or simply extend their sovereignty over the area via a vassal. Perhaps the Lord will use some individual from one of the conquering enemies as His tool to execute sovereignty over the affected area.

A biblical example of this was King Cyrus of Persia, who we are informed in Isaiah 44:28-45:5 was anointed by the Lord to rule over the Medo-Persian Empire after they conquered the Babylonians in approximately 536 BC. In this instance, the Lord used a Gentile ruler as His vassal earthly king. Cyrus was given an official seat of authority in Shushan, the capital of ancient Elam. This was a throne used to execute the will of the Lord.

Some believe that this governing transition fulfilled Jeremiah 49:38, but I explain why this is most likely not the case in the chapter called "Does the Prophecy of Elam Await Fulfillment?" Besides, if the Lord established His throne in Elam sometime after 536 BC through the Persians, where did it disappear to between now and then? The territory of Elam today is strongly Islamic which implies that the God of the Bible has yet to establish His throne there.

2. *An international body* could take control over the area to manage the disaster. This type of scenario occurred when Saddam Hussein was ousted from presidential power in Iraq at the hands of an international coalition led by the United States. The conquering coalition established temporary authority over Iraq until elections could take place, and the country could get back on its feet. This could result if Elam's disaster turns out to be a humanitarian crisis and the Lord wants to remedy the situation for the future return of the refugees. Jeremiah 49:39 declares that the captives of Elam will be brought back to their native land someday.

3. *A regime change* could take place in Iran as a result of Elam's disaster. A modern-day example of this occurred in Egypt. As a result of the Arab Spring, the presidential dictatorship of Hosni Mubarak was replaced by an Egyptian military junta until democratic elections could take place. As a result of Egypt's first ever democratic presidential election, the military submitted to the Islamist leadership of the Muslim Brotherhood leader Mohammad Morsi. Shortly thereafter,

Morsi was deposed and arrested as a result of a second military coup.

Presently, Egypt is torn between becoming a secular or Islamist nation. At the time of the authoring of this chapter, the fate of Egypt is still being determined, but ultimately Isaiah 19:4 predicts that Egypt will be governed by a cruel master.

Iran Survives to Participate in Ezekiel 38

It is important to note that whatever manifests as the Lord's throne in Elam in fulfillment of passage breakdown #11, it does not prevent the surviving portion of Iran from participating in the Ezekiel 38 prophecy under the banner of Persia. Ezekiel's Persia prophecy appears to be distinct from Jeremiah's, and will probably occur sometime after Elam's disaster. These differences are sequenced and explained in the chapter titled "Are Jeremiah 49 and Ezekiel 38 the Same Prophetic Events?"

Do the prophecies concerning Iran in Jeremiah 49:34-39 and Ezekiel 38 predict a national dissection within Iran between the former territories of Elam and Persia? Will the Iran of tomorrow geographically and / or geo-politically be different from the one of today? Historically these were two separate territories, but today they are collectively part of Iran.

A few examples of a nation being separated in modern history would be East and West Germany, North and South Korea and North and South Viet Nam. Maybe an East and West Iran may result in the aftermath of the fulfillment of Jeremiah's prophecy concerning Elam.

Perhaps after Elam's judgment, the Iranian army (IRGC) that enlists in the Magog invasion looks more like the Libyan army in weakness than the Turkish army in strength. All appear to be members alongside Russia in the Ezekiel 38 invasion.

Russia, listed as Magog, and Turkey, identified as Meshech and Tubal, are grouped together in Ezekiel 38:2-4. They appear to be the lead members of the Magog coalition. Iran, bannered as Persia, is seemingly lumped into the honorable mention category of Ezekiel

38:5 alongside Ethiopia and Libya. Libya and Ethiopia possess much weaker armies than Russia and Turkey. Is there a reason that Ezekiel groups Persia with Libya and Ethiopia rather than with Russia and Turkey?

Presently, the Iranian military is more comparable in rankings to the armies of Russia and Turkey rather than those of Libya and Ethiopia. The 2014 world army rankings by http://*www. globalfirepower.com*[30] have Iran currently ranked #22 among world armies, with Turkey #8 and Libya #78. Russia is presently rated #2 behind top ranked America, making Russia the greatest military power within the Magog alliance.

Ethiopia is ranked #40, but during Ezekiel's time, Ethiopia, identified by the name "Cush," may have represented the modern-day locations of Lower Egypt, Ethiopia, Sudan, South Sudan and Somalia. Cush was the grandson of Noah and his descendants are generally thought to have settled in these areas.

America's potential role in Ezekiel 38:13 as the "young lions of Tarshish" is explored in my teaching DVD entitled "*America and the Coming Mideast Wars.*" This DVD points out that America is not a participant of the Magog invaders, but is probably one of the protestors of this epic battle.

Israel's IDF is positioned at #11, but they will probably improve their rankings after their victory in Psalm 83. This appears to occur prior to the fulfillment of Ezekiel 38. This DVD points out that the IDF exists in fulfillment of Bible prophecy in order to defend the existence of the Jewish state in the concluding Arab-Israeli war of Psalm 83.

The Destruction of Iran's King and his Court

Jeremiah 49:38 concludes by predicting the destruction of the king and his court. The prophecy calls for the destruction "*from there of the king and the princes.*" The word used for "*from there*" seems to be geographically specific. It possibly alludes to the destruction or deposing of the local leadership in the west central province of Iran, formerly Elam, or it could extend further into the supreme Islamic leadership of Iran.

Perhaps as a result of Elam's disaster the ruling rogue Islamic regime gets replaced by a military junta as in Egypt. Many Iranians, like their Egyptian counterparts, are hoping for a more secular government as was the case before the Islamic revolution occurred in 1979. However, if this is the case why does Iran become part of the predominantly Muslim coalition of Ezekiel 38? Apart from Russia, the other members of the Magog alliance are mainly Muslim. The answer could be that maybe Jeremiah 49:34-39 and Ezekiel 38 are part of the same prophecy. This possibility is addressed and dispelled in the chapter entitled "Are Jeremiah 49 and Ezekiel 38 the Same Prophetic Events?"

Some other Bible translations are listed below. They might suggest that the ousting of the king and princes deals with the specific local rulers of the affected area of ancient Elam rather than the broader Islamic leadership of Iran. The Hebrew word used for *princes* is "sar" and it can also allude to political officials rather than royal princes.[31]

"I will set my throne in Elam, and destroy their king and officials, says the LORD." (Revised Standard Version)

"I will set my throne in Elam and destroy her king and officials," declares the LORD." (New International Version)

"I will set My throne in Elam And destroy out of it king and princes,' Declares the LORD. (New American Standard Version)

"I will set my throne in Elam, and will destroy from thence king and princes, saith Jehovah." (American Standard Version)

Summary

If Jeremiah's prophecy concerning Elam is about to find fulfillment, then Iran will no longer be negotiating the terms of its nuclear program, but the terms of its surrender, or at least partial surrender, in Elam. A devastation that eliminates the king and his court, and is subsequently replaced by the throne of the victor, strips that ruling body of its governing authority over the affected territory.

Whatever is meant by the Lord's promise to establish His throne in Elam, it can't allow Islam to share the glory. Since Islam is currently the dominant religion in the territory of Elam, something must happen to remove its stronghold from that specific region. It is doubtful that this verse has found fulfillment in the past because if it has, the Lord's throne has been abandoned and replaced by the rogue Islamic regime of Iran.

Chapter 6

The Prophecy of Elam
Part 4 (Jeremiah 49:39)

'But it shall come to pass in the latter days: I will bring back the captives of Elam,' says the LORD." (Jeremiah 49:39)

"Church growing in Iran despite repression"

Christian Today 3/24/12

"Thousands of Syrian refugees converting to Christianity"

Catholic World News 3/31/14

"Christian Aid Mission, a Protestant organization based in Virginia, is reporting that thousands of Syrian refugees are converting to Christianity in Turkey, Lebanon, and Iraq. Literally thousands of Syrians from traditional Muslim backgrounds are turning to Jesus Christ," the organization stated. "It's not an inflating of the numbers, nor is it an optimistic estimate."

This chapter concludes the verse-by-verse commentary of Jeremiah 49:34-39. By way of review, the three prior chapters explored the desolation of Elam and the worldwide dispersion of the Elamites. Additionally, the potential enemies of Elam were identified along with their differing motives for disliking Elam. Lastly, it was hypothesized that a new God ordained government will someday replace the present Islamic ruling regime in Elam.

12   But it shall come to pass in the latter days:

In this last verse the order is reversed from the pattern of the first five verses and the detail added assertion precedes the final *I will* of the Lord.' The important added detail is the timing of the prophecy. Jeremiah 49:34-39 finds fulfillment in the *latter days*.

Some, like Bible prophecy expert Jack Kelley, teach that only Jeremiah 49:39 and not the entire prophecy happens in the latter days.[32] Others, like Bible prophecy teachers Dr. Arnold Fruchtenbaum, Joel Rosenberg, Bill Koenig and myself, believe the entire prophecy takes place in the latter days. I explain why in the chapter entitled "Does the Prophecy of Elam Await Fulfillment."

Whichever is the case, most would agree that at least this specific verse is speaking about the end times. The Hebrew words for *latter days* are "acharith yom." They are used in tandem together at least eleven times in the Bible and these are the specific Scriptures; Deuteronomy 4:30, 31:29, Isaiah 2:2, Jeremiah 23:20, 30:24, 48:47, 49:39, Ezekiel 38:16, Daniel 10:14, Hosea 3:5, Micah 4:1. In each instance they allude to events that take place in the end times.

The *latter days, last days, latter years,* or *time of the end* are expressions often used in the Bible to attest to the fact that the present earth will expire. Humanity can't proceed along its Christ rejecting course forever with impunity. The wrath of the Lord is coming, but according to Revelation 20:4, this period of wrath is followed by a blessed thousand year messianic kingdom period.

The earth will be restored to its original Garden of Eden like condition during this period, according to Ezekiel 36:35 and Isaiah 51:3, to cite only two of the several references throughout the Scriptures. In the millennium, the whole world will be filled with the knowledge of the Lord, according to Isaiah 11:9. This kingdom period was the high point of all Old Testament prophecy, and is when the final *I will* of Jeremiah 49:39 finds fulfillment.

The Good News for Elam

> 13   *I will* bring back the captives of Elam,' says the LORD.

When the dust settles, after the wrath of God is complete and the dispersed Iranian refugees no longer live under the threat of war in their homeland, they will be brought back safely into Elam. The theme of displaced peoples returning safely back to their homeland during the millennial kingdom applies to several Middle East ethnicities. This includes Israelis, Egyptians, Assyrians, Jordanians, Iranians, and more.

That's the good news for these Middle Easterners, but the bad news is that in order to become a returning refugee you must first become a displaced refugee. At various times and by varying means, these populations are all involved in one or more of the final battles of the end times! As a result, many of them are exiled into foreign lands.

Jeremiah 49:35-36 says that Iran will be attacked and Iranians will be dispersed worldwide. As the Scriptures below point out, there will be no shortage of additional Middle Eastern refugees in the end times. In every instance, similar to Iran, their dispersions results from divine judgments upon their homelands.

Egypt, Syria and Jordan are no exceptions. These are three prominent members of the Psalm 83 Arab confederacy and they all warred against Israel in the Arab-Israeli wars of 1948, 1967 and 1973. These three notorious nemeses of Israel appear to participate in the final Arab-Israeli battle described in Psalm 83. This seems to be when their respective national destructions take place. As a result of their desolations, a refugee crisis arises and exiles are scattered abroad.

Interestingly, the Arab states of Psalm 83 confederate to destroy Israel so that the longstanding Palestinian refugee crisis will end. Psalm 83:4 clearly calls for the destruction of the Jewish state. The confederates must believe that if Israel is wiped off the map, the Palestinian refugees can then have their own homeland. The irony is that in the process the Arab states are defeated by the IDF, and an even greater refugee crisis results as multitudes of Egyptians, Jordanians and Syrians find themselves living in captivity.

Below is an excerpt taken from my book called *Psalm 83: the Missing Prophecy Revealed, How Israel Becomes the Next Mideast Superpower*. These verses identify the casualties and captives that result from the judgments associated with the Psalm 83 prophecy. These Scriptures also include judgments on other countries and terrorist populations besides Egypt, Jordan and Syria. Afterward, the good news prophecies concerning the regathering of the refugees from Egypt, Jordan and Syria will be presented.

Arab War Casualties from Psalm 83[33]

There appear to be hordes of Arab casualties resulting from Psalm 83. Listed below are some of the Scriptures that I believe identify the Arab casualties suffered as the apparent result of the Psalm 83 war.

The Killed and Wounded Arabs of Psalm 83

- *Jordan* – Primarily alluding to passages about Ammon, Moab, and Edom. Ammon represents modern-day northern Jordan, Moab—central Jordan, and Edom—southern Jordan. Ezekiel 25:13 and Ezekiel 25:9-10; Jeremiah 48:8, 42, and 49:2; Isaiah 15:4; and Amos 2:2-3.
- *Egypt* – Isaiah 19:18; and Ezekiel 29:5, 8, and 30:4, 8. (*These Ezekiel verses could be part of Egypt's third judgment by the Antichrist as written about in the chapter of my Psalm 83 book called "Egypt's Desolation, Deportation, and Conversion."*)
- *Syria* – Isaiah 17:1, 9, 14; Jeremiah 49:26-27; and possibly Amos 1:3-5.

(*Note: Psalm 83:8 identifies Assyria (Assur) rather than Syria (Aram). So some prophecies concerning Syria, such as Isaiah 17, could occur independently from Psalm 83. But it is the author's opinion that Isaiah 17 will occur during Psalm 83 or at least in the close proximity of time to Psalm 83*).

- *Saudi Arabia* – Ezekiel 25:13, primarily alluding to passages about Dedan, which is modern–day northwestern Saudi Arabia. The Saudis are seemingly represented under the banner of the Ishmaelites in Psalm 83:6.

- *Palestinians* – Primarily alluding to passages about Gaza, Philistia, Philistines, and the Edomites. Jeremiah 49:10; Ezekiel 25:16; and Obadiah 1:18.
- *Lebanon* – Primarily alluding to passages about Tyre and Sidon. Ezekiel 28:13; Amos 1:10; and Joel 3:4 (possibly).

The Arab POWs and Refugees from Psalm 83
- *Jordan* – Isaiah 11:14; Jeremiah 48:7, 44-47, 49:3, 5-6; Ezekiel 25:3-4; and Amos 1:15.
- *Egypt* – Ezekiel 29:12-13. (This may be more related to the desolation by the Antichrist in Daniel 11:42-43 as per the chapter in my *Psalm 83* book called *"Egypt's Desolation, Deportation, and Conversion."*)
- *Syria* – Isaiah 17:3, 9, 11:16; and Amos 1:5.
- *Saudi Arabia*- Jeremiah 49:8.
- *Palestinians* – Jeremiah 49:11, 20; Obadiah vv. 19-20; and Amos 1:8.
- *Lebanon* – Obadiah v. 19 alludes to captives as far as Zarephath, which would be located in modern-day southwestern Lebanon.

The Returning Middle Eastern
Refugees Will Become Believers

Here is the good news for the Egyptian, Jordanian, and Syrian remnants that survive Psalm 83. These captives can rejoice with the returning Iranians because they will be returning to their respective homelands to dwell within the utopian conditions of the messianic kingdom once it's established. They will all be believers in Christ at that time, not Allah, because the prerequisite for entering into the coming millennial age is faith in Christ.

By then, the prophecy written by Zephaniah will have been fulfilled and Allah and all other false gods will be eliminated.

"The LORD *will be* awesome to them, (contextually referring to the Jordanians) For He will reduce to nothing all the gods (including Allah) of the earth; *People* shall worship Him, (the God of the Bible) Each one from his place, Indeed all the shores of the nations." (Zephaniah 2:11; *emphasis added*)

These saved Middle Easterners that survive the Tribulation period and make it into the messianic kingdom don't presently accept Christ as their Savior, because if they did, they could be Raptured as part of the Bride of Christ before the wrath of God is poured out during the Tribulation Period. Believing refugees that survive the Tribulation period are among those that get left behind in the Rapture. Anyone who believes in Christ before He Raptures His church will not be left behind according to 1 Corinthians 15:51-52 and 1 Thessalonians 4:15-18.

This is called a Pre-Tribulation Rapture and my teachings on this topic are presented in the commentary section of chapter seventeen in my book called "*Revelation Road, Hope Beyond the Horizon.*"

There are many Middle Eastern believers today and that number continues to grow. Even though they are believers, they may witness some of the final battles leading up to Armageddon that occur before the tribulation begins, such as Psalm 83, Ezekiel 38 and the judgment of Elam (if it's a pre-trib event). This is because we don't know the exact timing of the Rapture. The Rapture could occur before, during, or after any or all of the Pre-tribulation prophecies. All that a believer is assured of today is that he or she is not appointed to the wrath of the Lord that is poured out during the Tribulation period.

"Much more then, having now been justified by His (Christ's) blood, we (who believe) shall be *saved from wrath through Him.*" (Romans 5:9; *emphasis added*)

"And to wait for His Son from heaven, whom He raised from the dead, *even* Jesus who *delivers us from the wrath* to come." (1 Thessalonians 1:10; *emphasis added*)

"For God *did not appoint us to wrath*, but to obtain salvation through our Lord Jesus Christ, who died for us, that whether we wake or sleep, we should live together with Him." (1 Thess. 5:9-10; *emphasis added*)

The Returning Middle Eastern Refugees Will Be Blessed

The returning refugees will be blessed because they are believers. They will live in Garden of Eden like conditions characterizing the messianic kingdom, and because they are returning to their cherished homelands.

Jordanians

When it comes to the Jordanians, the descendants of Ammon (Ammonites) and Moab (Moabites) will be restored, but the descendants of Edom (Edomites) may not. Obadiah 1:18 declares that the Edomites will have no survivors. This point is also emphasized in Jeremiah 49:17-18 and Ezekiel 25:13-14.

> "The house of Jacob (IDF) shall be a fire, And the house of Joseph (IDF) a flame; But the house of Esau (the Edomites) *shall be* stubble; They shall kindle them and devour them, And *no survivor* shall *remain* of the house of Esau," For the LORD has spoken." (Obadiah 1:18; *emphasis added*)

The Edomites have ethnical representation within today's Palestinians. I devote an entire chapter to understanding who the Edomites are in my *Psalm 83, Missing Prophecy Revealed* book. The chapter is called, "Whodomites, Who are the Edomites Today."

Addressing the benevolent plight of the Moabites, they appear to be returning to what would today be considered central Jordan. Notice the timing of *the latter days* with application to Moab below. These are the same Hebrew words used by Jeremiah 49:39 concerning the return of the Elamites.

> "Yet I will bring back the captives of Moab In *the latter days*," says the LORD. Thus far *is* the judgment of Moab. (Jeremiah 48:47; *emphasis added*)

The Ammonite remnant will also be returning to their native territory of northern Jordan. Jer. 49:2 warns that there will be a war that leaves the capital of Jordan in ruins. As a result of the war Israel will gain sovereignty over at least northern Jordan. Jer. 49:3 says that there will be Arab prisoners captured from this war. Jer. 49:5 says that there will also be refugees driven out of Jordan. Then Jeremiah issues the good news for the Ammonites below.

> "But afterward I will bring back The captives of the people of Ammon," says the LORD" (Jer. 49:6)

Jeremiah says that "afterward" the captives of Ammon will return to their homeland. This Jeremiah 49:1-6 prophecy concerning Ammon is similar to the Jeremiah 49:34-39 prophecy regarding Elam, in that they are both spoken about in Jeremiah 49 and that their respective prophecies are forthcoming. This means they are both events that find fulfillment in the latter days. It seems clear that Jeremiah's prophecy about the Ammonites is applicable to the same generation, and so it should be the same case for his predictions about Elam.

Syrians

The Syrian and Egyptian refugees will also have something to cheer about according to Isaiah 19.

> "In that day there will be a highway from Egypt to Assyria, and the Assyrian will come into Egypt and the Egyptian into Assyria, and the Egyptians will serve with the Assyrians. In that day Israel will be one of three with Egypt and Assyria—a blessing in the midst of the land, whom the LORD of hosts shall bless, saying, "Blessed *is* Egypt My people, and Assyria the work of My hands, and Israel My inheritance." (Isaiah 19:23-25)

The Syrians will receive the accolade of being called the "work of My hands." This implies that these refugees will be fashioned in a special manner, specifically by the hands of the Lord, probably to play an important role within the millennium. Presently, Syria is suffering from a disastrous revolution that has created millions of refugees. Somehow, the Lord will work all this suffering into something good for the Syrians. Romans 8:28 tells us that turning negatives into positives for believers is a specialty of the Lord.

> "And we know that all things work together for good to those who love God, to those who are the called according to *His* purpose." (Romans 8:28)

When attempting to discern the biblical predictions concerning Syria, it is important to note the following:

1. About the time of Isaiah's ministry, which spanned between 740-701 BC, Assyria encompassed much of modern-day Syria and Northern Iraq.

2. Although the name of Syria is directly derived from Assyria and the land was integrated into the Assyrian Empire at the time of Isaiah, Syrians in general maintain a separate Arab identity from the true descendants of the ancient Assyrians.[34]

3. Prior to the historic conquest of Damascus by Assyria in 732 BC, much of today's Syria was referred to as Aram and the indigenous peoples were called the Arameans.

Egyptians

Egyptians in the millennium have some bitter-sweet news to contend with. The *good news* for Egyptians was presented alongside the Assyrian scenario already. While Assyria will be called "the work of My hands," Egypt is called "Blessed" and classified as "My people" according to Isaiah 19:25.

The *bad news* for Egypt is that they will be the lowliest among all the kingdoms throughout the millennium, according to Ezekiel 29:15. Egypt experiences a desolation that causes forty years of Egyptian exile according to Ezekiel 29:12-13. Then comes the *good news,*

"I will bring back the captives of Egypt and cause them to return to the land of Pathros, to the land of their origin, and there they shall be a lowly kingdom. It shall be the lowliest of kingdoms; it shall never again exalt itself above the nations, for I will diminish them so that they will not rule over the nations anymore." (Ezekiel 29:14-15)

Pathros is the Hebrew name for Upper Egypt, the territory of the Nile River valleys of the delta, between Cairo and Aswan.[35] The forty year period of Egyptian exile seems to carry over into the millennium. It probably starts during the Tribulation period as part of Daniel 11:42-43, when the Antichrist invades Egypt. If this is the case, then forty year period could possibly extend up to three decades into the millennium because the Tribulation period only last seven years and the millennium begins shortly thereafter.

Egypt appears to face two end time judgments; the first resulting from Psalm 83 and the second from the invasion of the Antichrist. Isaiah 19:1-18 appears to describe Egypt's judgment for its participation in Psalm 83 as an enemy of Israel. I explore Egypt's end time's judgments in greater detail in my *Psalm 83, Missing Prophecy Revealed* book.

Iranian Refugees Return to Restored Fortunes

Some Bible translations interpret Jeremiah 49:39 as restored fortunes, rather than returning refugees.

"But in the latter days I will restore the fortunes of Elam, says the LORD." (Revised Standard Version)

"Yet I will restore the fortunes of Elam in days to come," declares the LORD." (New International Version)

'But it will come about in the last days That I will restore the fortunes of Elam,'" Declares the LORD. (New American Standard Bible)

The Hebrew words they interpret as *restore the fortunes* are "shub" and "shebuth," and they imply a return from captivity into a homeland replenished with fortunes. Simply restoring the fortunes of a territory doesn't help the displaced people from that area. What good are restored fortunes if you can't possess them because you are in trapped in exile? I believe the best way to interpret Jeremiah 49:39 is as follows,

> "But it will come about during the millennial reign of Christ that the Lord will take responsibility for making sure that the Iranians (Elamites) are brought back to their homeland and that they are entreated to an abundant and resourceful life in the messianic kingdom."

Considering that the throne of the One that created the universe will be established, in some capacity, in Elam as part of the fulfillment of Jeremiah 49:38, it is safe to presume that Elam will be restored to a plentiful place. It is destined to become a territory where the faithful remnant of returning Iranians can enjoy the "abundant life" that comes from Jesus Christ. The "abundant life" is a promise for all believers, now, then and forever.

> "The thief (Satan) does not come except to steal, and to kill, and to destroy. I (Jesus Christ) have come that they (believers) may have life, and that they may have *it* more abundantly." (John 10:10; emphasis added)

Summary

Iranians, Egyptians, Jordanians, Syrians and other Middle Easterners are going to find themselves in a refugee or prisoners of war crisis, as a result of desolations upon their homelands from wars before and during the Tribulation. Fortunately, a remnant of each will survive and recognize, as many of their countrymen already do, that Jesus Christ is the Messiah! Unfortunately, they learn this lesson the hard way as these others are left behind after the Rapture to endure the tough trials of the Tribulation period.

These Middle Easterners will learn what a Diaspora is truly all about, but unlike the prolonged Diaspora of the Jews, theirs will be short lived. It appears as though the generation that experiences the judgment will be the same that experiences the establishment of the thousand year messianic kingdom.

The exiled Iranians that accept Christ as their personal Savior can look forward to returning to their homeland and experiencing an abundant life during the millennium. However, not all of their countrymen will be so smart and become so blessed. Many of the Islamic leaders, IRGC soldiers, and civilians will become casualties of the wars of Elam (Jer. 49) and Persia (Ezek. 38). If they survive those episodes, they then must face the time of the Antichrist and the accompanying wrath of the Lord poured out within the Tribulation period.

With this information at hand in these latter days, we believers had best redeem the time and do all that we can to pray for and reach out to every Middle Easterner that we now know, or will come to know, before they get left behind.

> "How then shall they (Middle Easterners) call on Him (Jesus Christ) in whom they have not believed? And how shall they believe in Him of whom they have not heard? And how shall they hear without a preacher? And how shall they preach unless they are sent? As it is written: *"How beautiful are the feet of those who preach the gospel of peace, Who bring glad tidings of good things!"* (Romans 10:14-15)

Chapter 7

Does the Prophecy of Elam Await Fulfillment?

Part 1 – The Historical Arguments

"Strike Iran Now to Avert Disaster Later"

Wall Street Journal 12/11/13

"A conventional-weapons attack is preferable to the nuclear war sure to come."[36]

It was Monday evening on December 2, 2013, when I heard the renowned biblical scholar Dr. Arnold Fruchtenbaum utter the words that I had hoped to hear;

"*No, it could not have been partially fulfilled in the past; it all refers to the same event.*"

Dr. Fruchtenbaum was responding to my question concerning the prophetic status of Jeremiah 49:34-39. I had asked him a series of initial questions that culminated in a final two tiered question;

1. "Could Jeremiah 49:34-38 have already been fulfilled in the past?"

2. "Is Jeremiah 49:39 the only remaining part of the prophecy to be fulfilled?"

The reasons that I was gladdened to hear his answer are because;

- I'm in full agreement with his assessment that *it all refers to the same event*,

- He is my friend and mentor,

- Many Iranian Christians hope that the event has not found historical fulfillment because they plan on leaving Iran when the prophecy occurs. (They see themselves potentially among the exiles referenced in Jeremiah 49:36).

Moreover, he is one of the first Bible prophecy experts to have written about Jeremiah's prophecy concerning Elam, which earns him an additional level of respect. His prior writings and our entire conversation will be presented in the chapter called "Does the Prophecy of Elam Await Fulfillment? Part Three."

Jeremiah 49:34-39: Is it Prophecy or History?

The past four chapters approached Jeremiah 49:34-39 as a Bible prophecy that remains entirely unfulfilled. In order to adequately demonstrate that the prophecy still awaits full completion, it is important to discuss the three primary views about Jeremiah's prophecy. The next three chapters will address these views, which are as follows:

1. The prophecy has found full historical fulfillment,
2. The prophecy has found partial historical fulfillment,
3. The prophecy remains entirely unfulfilled

Presuming that the prophecy lacks any fulfillment, then the logical question becomes, when will the prophecy happen? There are several timing possibilities listed below. In the chapter titled, "Is the Ancient Prophecy of Elam a Pre-Tribulation Event?," I explain why the event probably occurs before the "Tribulation Period." Since Jeremiah 49:34-39 has been vastly overlooked by the majority of the prophecy experts, these potential time frames are primarily formulated by the author. The timing prospects for this prophecy are; that it is a:

1. Pre-Tribulation (Pre-trib) event that occurs either before Psalm 83 or Ezekiel 38,
2. Pre-Trib event that occurs in concert with either Psalm 83 or Ezekiel 38,
3. Pre-Trib event that occurs after either Psalm 83 or Ezekiel 38,
4. Tribulation event, but not part of the Armageddon Campaign,
5. Tribulation event that is part of the Armageddon Campaign.

Concerning the Psalm 83 and Ezekiel 38 wars, an upcoming chapter in this book entitled, "Psalm 83 or Gog of Magog; what's Next?," explains the sequence and differences between the two prophecies. They are two separate prophecies, so Jeremiah 49:34-39 could be part of either, but should not overlap into both. In my estimation, Jeremiah 49:34-39 remains entirely unfulfilled and is a stand-alone prophecy. It does not appear to be part of either Psalm 83 or Ezekiel 38.

One of the glaring reasons that I don't include Jeremiah's prophecy concerning Elam in Psalm 83 or Ezekiel 38 is because Elam is not mentioned as a participant in either prophecy. Elam's omission appears to be intentional by both Ezekiel and Asaph, the author of Psalm 83. Both prophets were familiar with Elam and the Elamites, but each opted to leave them out of their respective prophecies.

Asaph and Ezekiel provided extensive lists of the belligerents in their respective prophecies. Ezekiel identified a nine member coalition, (Magog, Rosh, Meshech, Tubal, Persia, Ethiopia, Libya, Gomer and Togarmah); and Asaph listed a ten member confederacy, (Edom, Ishmaelites, Moab, Hagarenes, Gebal, Ammon, Amalek, Philistia, Tyre and Assyria). You will notice that Elam is absent from both groups.

Perhaps Asaph omitted Elam because the Elamites are not Arabs, and his prophecy primarily deals with a concluding war that is fought mostly between the Arabs and Jews. Asaph also left Persia out of his ten member confederacy, possibly for the same reason. Persians are not Arabs, and the two differing ethnicities have a long history of warring against each other. The Persians conquered the Arabs (Babylonians) about 539 B.C. More recently, the Persians (Iranians) fought against the Arabs (Iraqis) in between 1980-1988 A.D.

The Prophecy Has Found Full Historical Fulfillment View

This view is the subject of the rest of this chapter. Thus far in my research of Jeremiah 49:34-39, I have only uncovered two historical fulfillment arguments worthy of honorable mentions. The first of the full fulfillment arguments teaches that Jeremiah 49:34-39 was completely accomplished by the Persian Empire at the time of Esther somewhere between 486–465 BC. For the purposes of this chapter, this view will be labeled as the "*Bad News for Elam and the Elamites.*"

This observation has been advanced by James B. Jordan.[37] The Preterists, who believe that all Bible prophecies have already found historical fulfillment, will undoubtedly gravitate toward this view. This teaching will be critiqued at the end of this chapter.

The second full fulfillment argument primarily pertains to *the people of Elam* (the Elamites) in Jeremiah 49:34-38, whereas Jeremiah 49:39 applies to *the territory of Elam*. Separating the Elamites from their land is a convenient way for this teaching to deal with the inherent problem of Jeremiah 49:39. Verse 39 contains the phrase, "in the latter days." This expression requires an end time's fulfillment of at least verse 39. In order to skirt around this timing problem, the Elamites must be removed from Jeremiah 49:39. For this chapter's purposes this view will be called "*Good News for Elam, but Bad News for the Elamites.*"

Both of these full historical fulfillment views teach that all of Jeremiah 49:34-39 has been completely accomplished as far as the Elamite people are concerned. Presuming that this assessment is correct, those Christians living inside Iran today that are hoping this prophecy remains unfulfilled, will undoubtedly be disappointed. If either of these historical fulfillment assessments are correct, these Iranian Christians will need to expeditiously establish an alternative exit strategy out of Iran. Hopefully for them, it will be the miraculous Rapture described in 1 Corinthians 15:51-53 and 1 Thessalonians 4:15-18.

Good News for Elam, but Bad News for the Elamites

For obvious reasons, the *Good News for Elam, but Bad News for the Elamites* view favors the RSV, NIV, NASB Bible translations that say the fortunes of Elam, rather than the captives of Elam, will be restored. Below is a quote that summarizes the historical fulfillment view.

> "*Is this passage (Jer. 49:34-39) referring to past historical events or events which are yet to happen? In general, this historical event is interpreted as having taken place already. (Note that in addition to Jeremiah 49:39, this phrase, "I will restore the fortunes", is found in Jeremiah 48:47 in reference to Moab and in 49:6 in reference to the Ammonites.) The Elam and the Babylon empires were conquered by the Medo-Persian empire under king Cyrus who replaced the Elamite king and set his throne in Elam (Jeremiah 49:38). Thus, Elam became another conquered country under Cyrus' rule showing this prophecy was fulfilled already. The phrase, "latter days" is used in connection with the fortunes of Elam, not people returning to Elam. As mentioned previously, Elam was once a prosperous agriculture area. Now it is desolate, but in the latter days it will become an area of fortune again with a great agriculture harvest. I can remember being in Iran in the 1970's and talking with an agriculture expert who had surveyed the land. He said that with irrigation this area could become one of the greatest distribution centers of agriculture in the world. This is yet to happen, "in the days to come", for the fortunes of Elam.*"[38]

This is one of several views presented by Allyn Huntzinger in his book called *Persians in the Bible*. Huntzinger was a missionary in Iran from 1963-1979. Huntzinger's missionary efforts ended with the advent of the 1979 Iranian Revolution.

Allyn Huntzinger can be considered a pioneer when it comes to presenting the views of Jeremiah 49:34-39. He published his book in 1977, when commentaries on Jeremiah's prophecy concerning Elam were almost non-existent and certainly non-exhaustive. I have spoken with Allyn Huntzinger as part of my research for this book. Allyn has informed me that he doesn't favor the historical fulfillment view, but felt the need to include it in his book.[39]

The above quote from this second view presented by Huntzinger implies that when King Cyrus of Persia conquered Elam and Babylon around 539 BC, Jeremiah 49:34-38 found historical fulfillment. This means that the Elamites must have been dispersed worldwide in fulfillment of Jeremiah 49:36 over 2500 years ago. Moreover, it suggests that the territory of Elam, upon its end time's restoration, *could become one of the greatest distribution centers of agriculture in the world.*

These presumptions beckon several important questions.

1. Were the Elamites scattered worldwide by King Cyrus? (Jer. 49:36)
2. Was the Lord fiercely angered at Elam during the time of King Cyrus? (Jer. 49:37)
3. Did the conquest of Elam result in a catastrophic disaster? (Jer. 49:37)
4. How is the land restored? (Jer. 49:39)
5. Why is it restored?
6. For whom is it restored; Persians or Elamites?

It is true that Persia conquered the territory of Elam and subsequently established its capital in Shushan, which was the historic capital city of Elam.[40] However, it does not appear true that Cyrus, or the subsequent Persian kings, forced the Elamites into a worldwide exile. Moreover, there is no biblical basis to presume that the Elamites had fiercely angered the Lord during the time of the Persian Empire period. Neither did Elam's conquest involve a disaster of the size and scope predicted in Jeremiah 39:37.

"Cyrus the Great," as he is commonly referred to, was a noble king and was well known for his policies of toleration. This fact is pronounced in "The Cyrus the Great Cylinder," which was excavated in 1879, by the Assryo-British archaeologist Hormuzd Rassam. This baked-clay cylinder, which was written in the Akkadian language with cuneiform script, is thought to be the first charter of right of nations in the world. It is a priceless artifact that is kept today in the British Museum in London.[41]

Rather than force the Elamites into exile, Cyrus employed Elamite and Babylonian scholars to correspond across his kingdom, making Persian, Elamite, and Babylonian the official languages of this cosmopolitan empire.[42] Evidence of this is located on an inscription to Cyrus the Great that was placed on a pillar in Palace P at Pasargadae.[43] The caption reads "I am Cyrus the Great an Achaemenid."[44] The engraving is written in the languages of Persian, Elamite and also in Akkadian, which is one of the great cultural languages of world history, also called Babylonian-Assyrian.

Furthermore, the conquest of Cyrus the Great had more to do with events pertaining to Israel and Babylon, rather than Elam. Cyrus was anointed by the Lord to conquer Babylon and to be a blessing to the Jews.[45] The chapter called "Iran, A Past Friend but Present Foe of Israel" explains this further.

The above facts strongly suggest that the Elamites were not dispersed worldwide by Cyrus. In addition to this historical information, there is also a biblical basis to conclude that Jeremiah 49:34-39 has not found full or partial fulfillment. Scriptures that refute the full and partial fulfillment arguments such as Ezra 4:9, Acts 2:9 and Isaiah 11:11 will be presented and explained in the next chapter.

How and Why is the land of Elam restored? (Jer. 49:39)

The *Good News for Elam, but Bad News for the Elamites* argument doesn't explain how and why the land becomes restored. If Jeremiah 49:39 has no Elamite captivity being restored, then how is the land becoming resourceful and why does it need to become productive again? Is the Lord planning to perform a supernatural Garden of Eden type miracle in Elam, and for whom?

Another important question concerning Elam's land restoration, is whom is it being restored for? If there are no returning Elamites, then what people group is going to roll up their sleeves and get their hands dirty tilling the soil of Elam? It won't be the Jews because during the Messianic Kingdom, they will be cultivating the land allotted to their patriarch Abraham in Genesis chapter 15. This expansive territory is west of the Euphrates River that courses through Iraq and Syria. Elam is east of the Euphrates.

> "To your (Abraham) descendants (the Jews) I have given this land, from the river of Egypt to the great river, the River Euphrates." (Gen. 15:18; emphasis added)

Perhaps it would be the Persians, but they suffer a costly defeat during the Gog of Magog invasion, according to Ezekiel 38:18-39:6, and we don't read anything in the Bible about their future from that point forward. The Persians may not even make it into the Messianic Kingdom.

The only way Jeremiah 49:39 makes any sense is to include the Elamites into the end time's equation. It must be the Elamite captives that returns home and restores their ancient homeland of Elam. The point below was made in the prior chapter concerning this matter.

The Hebrew words used in Jeremiah 49:39 for *bring back the captives*, or in some translations, *restore the fortunes* are "shub" and "shebuth," and they imply the return of an indigenous people from a Diaspora into a homeland that can be re-cultivated with Lord's blessings.

Lastly, the previous quote suggested that the territory of Elam is desolate today, but that is not the case. The Bushehr nuclear plant is located there and the area is filled with Iranian military installations. Below is a list of some of the cities and their current corresponding populations in what was once the territory of ancient Elam.[46] These are some of the cities and population counts that could be adversely affected by the impending disaster of Elam.

- Ahvaz . . . . 1,432,965[47]
- Shiraz 1,227,000
- Kermanshah. 794,863
- Khorramabad. 334,945
- Dezful 235,819
- Bushehr. 170,000

Bad News for Elam and the Elamites

The Bad News for Elam and the Elamites view is summed up in the following quote from James B. Jordan.[48]

> "So, when were these things (Jeremiah 49:34-39) fulfilled? They were fulfilled in the events of the book of Esther. Haman organized the Persian Elamites who hated the Jews to attack them. But God reversed the fortune of His people. The Jews were allowed to put to the sword those who hated them. Many of the Elamites converted to the true faith (Esther 8:17) before the massacre of the wicked Elamites happened (Esther 9). Thus, as predicted, the four winds of evangelism came first, and then the sword of destruction. After that, Esther and Mordecai became great in the land, and God's throne was set up there."

This quote beckons the following important questions.

1. If Elamites were defeated and dispersed during the time of Esther, then why does Ezra 4:9 refer to them after the time of Esther?
2. Was Elam struck at the foremost of its might during the time of Esther? (Jer. 49:35)
3. Were the Elamites scattered worldwide during the time of Esther? (Jer. 49:36)
4. Was the Lord fiercely angered at Elam during the time of Esther? (Jer. 49:37)
5. Did the conquest of Elam at the time of Esther result in a catastrophic disaster of Elam? (Jer. 49:37)
6. Was Elam made desolate at the time of Esther?
7. Was the Lord's throne established in Elam at the time of Esther? (Jer. 49:38)
8. Were the king and the princes destroyed from Elam at the time of Esther? (Jer. 49:38)
9. Was Elam's fortunes restored sometime after the time of Esther? (Jer. 49:39)
10. Did the Elamites return from exile sometime after the time of Esther? (Jer. 49:39)

Before answering the above questions, I encourage the reader to read the full exposition of James B. Jordan entitled, "*The Oracle Against Elam* (Jeremiah 49:34-39)." The quote above needs to be understood in the larger context of James B. Jordan's entire teaching on the topic. The article can be located on the Internet at this website address: *http://www.biblicalhorizons.com/biblical-chronology/8_03/*

In his quote, James B. Jordan clearly makes a connection between Persians and the Elamites. It is important to note that Elam is spoken about at least 27 times in the Bible, but it is not mentioned once in the book of Esther. Neither does the book of Esther mention the words Elam or Elamites. However Shushan, which was located in ancient Elam, is mentioned at least 17 times in the book of Esther. Thus by association, James B. Jordan connects Elam and the Elamites to some degree with the Persian dominance over the territory.

The book of Esther was written probably about 444-434 B.C., and it describes the events that occurred around the midpoint of the reign of the Persian Empire, which spanned approximately between 550-330 B.C.[49] Thus, the book of Esther is concerned more with the undertakings of the Persian Empire than it is with the Elamites or the territory of Elam.

Presuming that James B. Jordan is correct to make the *Persian Elamite* connection, then it is safe to suggest that the answer to question number 3 above is YES. The Persians planned to commit an act of genocide against the Jews. This would *fiercely anger* the Lord. But, although the Lord would be justifiably angry at the Persians, would He also be upset with the Elamites? Perhaps the answer remains YES, because Esther 9:2 alludes to cities and peoples throughout all the Persian provinces that wished to harm the Jews. This would likely have included the Elamites. Esther 8:9 informs that there were one hundred and twenty-seven total provinces.

> "The Jews gathered themselves together in their cities throughout all the provinces of the king Ahasuerus, to lay hand on such as sought their hurt: and no man could withstand them; for the fear of them was fallen upon all the peoples." (Esther 9:2, ASV)

Likewise the answer to question number 6 concerning the Lord's throne being established in Elam could possibly be YES. Esther's cousin Mordecai[50] was bestowed with great honor by the king of Persia, and the Jews became benefactors of this blessing.

> "And Mordecai went forth from the presence of the king in royal apparel of blue and white, and with a great crown of gold, and with a robe of fine linen and purple: and the city of Shushan shouted and was glad. The Jews had light and gladness, and joy and honor. And in every province, and in every city, whithersoever the king's commandment and his decree came, the Jews had gladness and joy, a feast and a good day. And many from among the peoples of the land became Jews; for the fear of the Jews was fallen upon them. (Esther 8:15-17, ASV)

However, the possible YES answers seem to end with these two questions, leaving seven remaining unanswered questions above without positive YES answers. In order for James B. Jordan's interpretation to be correct, all the additional questions require YES answers. However, the NO answers are given below.

1. *Was Elam struck at the foremost of its might during the time of Esther?* (Jer. 49:35)

The answer to this question would appear to be NO. The foremost of Persian might should have been located in Shushan to protect the Persian King Ahasuerus and his royal court. Although eight hundred people were killed by the Jews in Shushan according to Esther 9:6, 15, the Jews did not conquer Shushan and send the Persian King and his court into captivity. In fact, the very last verse in the book of Esther confirms this. The verse declares that King Ahasuerus still maintained his kingship in the aftermath.

> "For Mordecai the Jew *was* second to King Ahasuerus, and was great among the Jews and well received by the multitude of his brethren, seeking the good of his people and speaking peace to all his countrymen." (Esther 10:3)

2. *Were the Elamites scattered worldwide during the time of Esther?*
(Jer. 49:36)

The answer to this question would appear to be NO. There is no historical or biblical evidence that demonstrates this prediction was fulfilled during the time of Esther. In fact, Ezra 4:9 refers to the Elamites during the reign of King Artaxerxes who reigned after King Ahasueres. King Ahasuerus was the Persian King during the time that Esther was a queen.

3. *Was the Lord fiercely angered at Elam during the time of Esther?*
(Jer. 49:37)

This question was answered above as a possible YES, but this historical view requires a full, not a partial, fulfillment of Jeremiah 49:34-39. In order for this view to be taken seriously all of these nine questions require a YES answer, and that isn't the case.

4. *Did the conquest of Elam at the time of Esther result in a catastrophic disaster of Elam?* (Jer. 49:37)

The disaster predicted to occur in Jeremiah 49:37 would apparently leave the territory of Elam desolate and in need of restoration. These restored fortunes to Elam are prophesied to happen in the latter days according to Jeremiah 49:39. The territory of Elam does not appear to have ever experienced this type of severe disaster. This is attested by the fact that the land is inhabited by Iranians today and remained populated by at least Persians, Jews, and Elamites even after the time of Esther.

Moreover Jeremiah 49:37 says that the disaster will leave the Elamites dismayed before the eyes of their enemies. There was only one possible enemy at the time of Esther, and that was the Jews, who were desperately attempting to survive the genocidal decree of the Persians. There do not appear to be any additional enemies (plural) of the Elamites at the time of Esther. Therefore, on these two counts the answer to this question is a resounding NO!

5. Was Elam made desolate at the time of Esther?

It is safe to say that this answer is also NO due to the reasons just given in the prior question.

6. Was the Lord's throne established in Elam at the time of Esther?
(Jer. 49:38)

This answer was already given as a possible YES, but technically, King Ahasuerus was not dethroned at the time. Even though Esther 10:3 says that Mordecai the Jew became second in the overall hierarchy of the empire, King Ahasuerus remained in charge of his.

7. Were the king and the princes destroyed from Elam at the time of
Esther? (Jer. 49:38)

There is no mention of an Elamite king in the book of Esther. Only the Persian King Ahasuerus is identified throughout the biblical book. Esther 10:3 proves that King Ahasuerus survived and maintained authority over his kingdom. The answer to this question is also NO!

8. Was Elam's fortunes restored sometime after the time of Esther?
(Jer. 49:39)

The answer to this question is NO. There does not appear to have been a need for the restoration of Elam's fortunes at the time of Esther. The area was not destroyed and the Elamites were not taken into worldwide captivity. Jeremiah 49:36 predicts that a global dispersion of the Elamites occurs, and that does not appear to have happened yet.

9. Did the Elamites return from exile sometime after the book of
Esther? (Jer. 49:39)

The answer to this question is NO. The answer given for the prior question also answers this question. The Elamites were not sent into global exile at the time, and therefore they will not be returning because of the events in the book of Esther. Although Elamite exiles will return to restored fortunes in Elam in the latter days according to Jeremiah 49:39, it has nothing to do with what occurred at the time of Esther.

Summary

No historical evidence exists that substantiates the possibility that Jeremiah's prophecy concerning Elam has found a past fulfillment. Scriptures like Ezra 4:9, Acts 2:9, Isaiah 11:11, Ezekiel 32:4 and Jeremiah 25:25, which will be presented in the next chapter, will also rule out a historical fulfillment during the Babylonian, Greek, and Roman Empire periods.

Moreover, there is no reason to remove the Elamite captivity from Jeremiah 49:39. The Elamites are the logical benefactors of a restored Elam, just like the Jews will be the reestablished occupants of the greater Israel during the Messianic Kingdom era.

At least from the historical fulfillment argument, the Iranian Christians can still hope in the judgment of Elam as a viable exit strategy out from repressive Iran.

Chapter 8

Does the Prophecy of Elam Await Fulfillment?

Part 2 – The Partial Fulfillment Argument

"*From my research it appears that the only part of Jeremiah's prophecy that remains a question mark is verse 39. The Elamites were defeated and scattered among the nations just as Jeremiah predicted. The nation ceased to exist and there's been no mention of them since.*"[51] Jack Kelley - 10/26/13

This quote from Bible prophecy expert Jack Kelley represents the partial fulfillment interpretation of Jeremiah 49:34-39. This view teaches that all of Jeremiah 49:34-38 has been completely accomplished, but Jeremiah 49:39 still remains unfulfilled, or as Kelley says *remains a question mark*.

The potential problems with the partial fulfillment argument will be explored in the second half of this chapter. Beforehand, a commentary that reflects this perspective will be provided by yours truly. Although the partial fulfillment view is not my preferred interpretation, I'm undertaking this expositional exercise in order to be thorough.

The fact of the matter is that there are very few comprehensive commentaries concerning Jeremiah 49:34-39 in existence. Among the handful that are readily available, most of them favor the entirely unfulfilled interpretation. Jack Kelley is one of the few to explain the partial fulfillment view. Although I don't agree with this interpretation, I applaud him for addressing Jeremiah 49:34-39.

The Partial Fulfillment
Hypothesis of Jeremiah 49:34-39

CAVEAT: Below is my complimentary attempt to provide a commentary of Jeremiah 49:34-39 from the partial fulfillment perspective. PLEASE NOTE THAT THIS IS NOT MY PREFERRED VIEW! This interpretation is being provided because it is an alternative view that has been proposed, and I anticipate this view, or variations of it, will be forthcoming after this book gets published.

Below is a list of the predictable events that might follow the release of a book like this. This list is presented from the vantage point of personal experience. My last book called *Psalm 83: The Missing Prophecy Revealed, How Israel Becomes the Next Mideast Superpower*, resulted in the following sequence of events. The *Psalm 83* book, like this one, also explored a vastly overlooked Bible prophecy.

- People will ask their pastor or favorite Bible teacher how they interpret the overlooked prophecy. These questions often arise during Q and A sessions at Bible prophecy conferences.
- The pastor or Bible expert diligently reviews the biblical text of the prophecy to analyze the specific details of the subject prophecy.
- The biblical scholar turns to his or her favorite commentaries before responding publicly.
- The Bible expert responds by either, endorsing one of the proposed views provided in this book, or by introducing an alternative interpretation.
- Alternative teachings usually stimulate an academic controversy.

Jeremiah 49:34-39 Speculation for An Altered View

"The word of the LORD that came to Jeremiah the prophet against Elam, in the beginning of the reign of Zedekiah king of Judah, saying," (Jer. 49:34)

Jeremiah receives the prophecy around 596 B.C. Zedekiah ruled the Southern Kingdom from 597 to 586 B.C. At that time, the Babylonian Empire had emerged as the world's dominant superpower.

The prophet appears to intentionally inscribe the information sequentially in chapter 49. He inserts his report immediately after alerting that King Nebuchadnezzar would be used to judge Kedar and the kingdoms of Hazor in Jeremiah 49:28-33. Kedar was probably located in what is today the desert area of Northwest Saudi Arabia. Hazor is thought to be located nearby to Kedar.

The timing of the issuing of the prophecy and the strategic location of the information suggests that the judgment of Elam could find some association with the escapades of King Nebuchadnezzar during the Babylonian era. The Babylonians conquered Elam around 612 B.C.[52] and maintained sovereignty over the territory until the Persians conquered Elam around 559 B.C.

> "Thus says the LORD of hosts: 'Behold, I will break the bow of Elam, The foremost of their might.'" (Jer. 49:35)

The Elamites had a long history of warmongering dating back to events recorded in Genesis 14:1-9. They were also expert archers as per Isaiah 22:6. This Scripture informs that when the judgment of Elam occurs, the Elamites will be soundly defeated. The conquest will render useless their bows, which were their preferred weapons of warfare. They will be struck at the chief place of their might, which possibly represented their capital city of Susa. (Sushan in Hebrew).

> "Against Elam I will bring the four winds From the four quarters of heaven,And scatter them toward all those winds; There shall be no nations where the outcasts of Elam will not go." (Jer. 49:36)

The conquest of Elam will result in the Elamites experiencing a period of worldwide exile. The four winds idiom, coupled with the statement that there shall be no nations where the Elamites will not go, also supports the idea of a global dispersion. It pictures the outcasts of Elam being blown about into the nations like chaff before the wind.

Since this vast scattering did not completely occur during the time of the Babylonian empire, it could involve a process over a prolonged period of time. Additionally, the four winds of heaven phrase might find association with a similar expression used in Daniel 7:2-3.

"Daniel spoke, saying, "I saw in my vision by night, and behold, *the four winds of heaven* were stirring up the Great Sea. And four great beasts came up from the sea, each different from the other." (Daniel 7:2-3; *emphasis added*)

The four great beasts of Daniel's vision are commonly taught to represent the coming four Gentile empires of Babylon, Persia, Greece, and Rome. These empires rose and fell from power between 605 B.C. to 313 A.D. The four winds from heaven stir up the Great Sea, which represents the world, and as a result, these Gentile empires emerge sequentially over time. In theory, as each empire arose, more and more Elamites were dispersed.

"For I will cause Elam to be dismayed before their enemies And before those who seek their life. I will bring disaster upon them, My fierce anger,' says the LORD; 'And I will send the sword after them Until I have consumed them." (Jer. 49:37)

This verse says that Elam will have multiple enemies, which seems to support the possibility that the Babylonians were not Elam's sole adversary. The enemies could include the Persians, Greeks, and the Romans over time. When the Persians conquered Elam, the Elamites were dismayed to witness King Cyrus relocate his throne to Susa, the former capital city of Elam.[53]

Moreover, the Elamites are guilty of fiercely angering the Lord. This could be connected to the attempted genocide of the Jews by the Persians. This event is described in the biblical book of Esther. The Persians ruled over one hundred and twenty-seven provinces according to Esther 8:9. Esther 8:5 tells us that the Persian plan was for all these provinces to annihilate their cohabiting Jewish populations. It appears safe to conclude that a remnant of Elamites dwelt within these Persian provinces at the time, and that they participated in this genocidal campaign. Attempting to terminate the Jews in alliance with the Persians would fiercely anger the Lord.

Jeremiah says that the sword, which represents war, will be used to consume the Elamites. The Elamites were conquered through wars by the Babylonians around 612 B.C., as well as the Persians about 559 B.C.

"I will set My throne in Elam, And will destroy from there
the king and the princes," says the LORD." (Jer. 49:38)

In possible fulfillment of this prophecy, King Cyrus the Great of
Persia relocated his throne to Susa, which was in Elam. Isaiah 44:28
and 45:1 declare that Cyrus was anointed by the Lord to conquer
the Babylonians and facilitate the return of the Jews into Israel. This
is confirmed by these additional Scriptures, 2 Chronicles 36:22-23,
Ezra 1:1-2, 7-8 and elsewhere.

Throughout the Persian Empire era, Shushan (Susa) was used
as a Persian capital city. The usurpation of power by the Persian
kings resulted in the dethroning of the Elamite king and princes
during the corresponding period.

"But it shall come to pass in the latter days: I will bring back
the captives of Elam," says the LORD." (Jer. 49:39)

Jeremiah's prophecy concludes with good news for the Elamites.
They will be able to return to their ancient homeland in the end
times. After approximately 2600 years of prolonged global exile
and general loss of ethnic identity, the fortunes of the Elamites will
be restored. If this interpretation is correct, the Diaspora of the
Elamites far surpasses in duration the 1878 year Diaspora of the
Jews.

The Potential Pitfalls of the
Partial Fulfillment Argument

This alternative commentary requires that Jeremiah 49:34-
39 finds fulfillment over a prolonged period of time. Typically,
judgments upon populations in the Bible do not occur over extended
periods, but are expeditiously executed. Examples would be the
judgments on Sodom and Gomorrah, Nineveh, and Jerusalem
in 70 A.D. by the Romans. The destruction of Jerusalem by the
Romans resulted in the commencement of the Jewish Diaspora.

*"There's no record of a re-emergence of the Elamites since the
Persian conquest 2500 years ago."*[54] - Jack Kelley

Since Jack Kelley is one of the few contemporary Bible prophecy teachers that advocate for a partial fulfillment of Jeremiah 49:34-39, his view will be analyzed more closely in the remainder of this chapter. Kelley is well-respected for his prophetic expertise and I enjoy reading his articles and biblical commentaries. Unfortunately, his commentary on Jeremiah 49:34-39 is thus far condensed into a sole article with minimal detail.

In general, the partial fulfillment view tends to amalgamate the Elamites into Persians. This process of cultural and ethnical integration primarily occurs during the Persian Empire era, but could linger on afterward. It presumes that the majority of Elamites were sent into global exile due to their defeat by the Persians, even though there is historical and biblical evidence to the contrary. In this scenario, the ethnicity of the Elamites that remained in Elam becomes blurred, and the identity of those in exile becomes mostly lost.

In theory, a contrast between the Jews and Elamites could be made to help explain the logic of this Elamite identity crisis. Whereas the Jews maintained their *Jewishness* during their 2000 years of Diaspora and know who they are today; the Elamites forfeited their *Elamishness* during their 2500 years of exile and have generally lost track of their ethnicity.

The partial fulfillment interpretation beckons several tough questions like;

- If the Elamites lost their ethnic identity centuries ago during their dispersion, then who is returning to restored fortunes in Jeremiah 49:39?

- If it's the Persians, then why are there no Bible prophecies predicting restored fortunes for the Persians in the latter days?

- Since the former territory of Elam is currently inhabited, and does not exist in a desolate condition, then why are the fortunes of Elam in need of restoration in the latter days? (Jer. 49:39)

These are just a few logical geo-political questions, but some biblical questions also exist like;

- If the Elamites were in global exile, and their identity lost during the Persian Empire period, then why are the Elamites listed in Ezra 4:9 and Acts 2:9 during the "Day of Pentecost? (The Day of Pentecost occurred about three hundred years after the collapse of the Persian Empire). The reference in the book of Ezra places Elamites living in Elam after the second body of Jewish exiles returned from Babylon to Jerusalem 459 B.C. Ezra's reference of the Elamites occurred during the reign of the Persian King Artaxerxes who ruled between 465-425 B.C.[55]

- If Elam's disaster occurred in a past desolation, then why is Elam listed in Isaiah 11:11 as a land that Jews are regathered out of for a second time? (Many Bible teachers believe Isaiah 11:11 alludes to the regathering of the Jews into Israel today).

From the partial fulfillment perspective there are four main window periods of time that Jeremiah 49:34-38 could have happened. They are during the;

- Babylonian Empire (605-539 B.C.),
- Medo-Persian Empire (539-330 B.C.),
- Greek Empire (330-63 B.C.),
- Roman Empire (63 B.C.-313 A.D.)

Among these four, the one that receives most credence is the Medo-Persian Empire period. These four sequential periods will each be briefly reviewed to see if Jeremiah 49:34-38 occurred during these time frames.

The Babylonian Empire (605-539 B.C.) and Elam

Jeremiah issued the prophecy of Elam about 596 B.C., when the Babylonian Empire was burgeoning. This means that all conquests of Elam prior to this date of issuance can be disregarded as a fulfillment of Jeremiah 49:34-39. The prophecy was inserted into the final six verses of Jeremiah chapter 49. The first thirty-three verses of the same chapter dealt with prophecies concerning Ammon, Edom, Damascus, Kedar and the kingdoms of Hazor.

Ammon, Edom, and Damascus have not yet experienced their judgments as of yet. I believe Jeremiah's predictions for them find fulfillment in correlation with the war prophesied in Psalm 83. However, Jeremiah 49:28-30 clearly declared that the prophecies regarded with Kedar and the kingdoms of Hazor were going to happen during the reign of King Nebuchadnezzar, within the Babylonian Empire period. In essence, Jeremiah's generation would experience the judgments forecasted for Kedar and Hazor.

> "Against Kedar and against the kingdoms of Hazor, which Nebuchadnezzar king of Babylon shall strike. Thus says the LORD: "Arise, go up to Kedar, And devastate the men of the East! Their tents and their flocks they shall take away. They shall take for themselves their curtains, All their vessels and their camels; And they shall cry out to them, 'Fear *is* on every side!' "Flee, get far away! Dwell in the depths, O inhabitants of Hazor!" says the LORD. "For Nebuchadnezzar king of Babylon has taken counsel against you, And has conceived a plan against you." (Jeremiah 49:28-30)

Considering that Kedar and Hazor were struck during Jeremiah's generation, it would seem feasible that Elam could have also been destroyed during that same period. After all, the judgment of Elam was written in the verses that immediately followed the prophecy concerning Kedar and the kingdoms of Hazor. However, Jeremiah 49:34-39 says nothing about Nebuchadnezzar or the Babylonians. The only hint given about Elam's fate is in Jeremiah 49:37, which informs that enemies will be involved in Elam's disaster.

The Bible Knowledge Commentary of the Old Testament, authored by John F. Walvoord and Roy B. Zuck, provides the following interpretation of Jeremiah 49:34-39.

> "*Though there is some evidence that Nebuchadnezzar defeated the Elamites about 596 b.c., his subjugation at that time did not fulfill this message. Elam became a central*

part of the Persian Empire that later conquered Babylon. Jeremiah's statement about Elam's destruction seems to take on eschatological dimensions as God said He would set His throne in Elam to supervise her destruction. Yet Elam's destruction will not be total because God will restore her fortunes... in days to come."

This commentary makes a good point. The Elamites survived the onslaughts of the Babylonian Empire. Elamites existed when Persia conquered Babylon. Moreover, the Elamites existed throughout the Persian Empire era also. The prior chapter pointed out that engravings written in Persian, Elamite and Akkadian, have been discovered that date back to the time of King Cyrus the Persian.

Medo-Persian Empire (539-330 B.C.) and Elam

Interactions between the Persians and the Elamites were explored in the prior chapter. The explanations provided in that chapter were utilized to disqualify the full historical fulfillment view of Jeremiah 49:34-39. The same arguments apply in this section.

By and large the Elamites were not sent into worldwide exile during that period. Perhaps some Elamites were dispelled then and maybe more departed during the subsequent Greek and Roman empires, but it doesn't appear that Jeremiah 49:35 was fulfilled during the reign of the Persians.

Jack Kelley believes Jeremiah 49:34-38 appears to have happened during this period of time. He writes the following:

"Elam's capital city, Susa, was one of the world's first post flood cities, and was a regional center off and on for many centuries before being destroyed by Ashurbanipal, the last of the great Assyrian Kings, in 647 BC. As was the custom of Assyrian kings, he removed many of the surviving Elamites from their homeland. He took them to the former Northern Kingdom of Israel, which had been conquered by Assyria 74 years earlier, where they were resettled among the Israelites who remained there.

That Was Only The Beginning. But this did not fulfill Jeremiah's prophecy, which wouldn't even be given for at least another 50 years. Susa was rebuilt, only to be conquered again, this time by the Persian King Cyrus. It was rebuilt again and renovated by King Darius the Great to serve as the capital of the Persian Empire. Susa was mentioned in Daniel 8:2 as the location where the prophet received a vision recorded in Daniel 8 of the subsequent conquest of the Persian Empire by Alexander the Great. This prophecy was fulfilled two hundred years later when Susa surrendered without a battle to Alexander.

Daniel 8:2 identifies Susa as being in the province of Elam, indicating it was already a part of the Persian Empire at the time. From this brief history it appears that all but the last verse of Jeremiah's prophecy was fulfilled in the Assyrian and Persian conquests. By the way, Daniel was buried in Susa and his tomb has been preserved to this day because he has always been highly revered among the Persian people."[56]

This quote overlooks several important facts and/or probabilities;

- King Cyrus reigned between 539-530.[57] He was the first king of the Persian empire. He primarily ruled over his empire though policies of tolerance and peace, rather than mandatory expulsion. Cyrus enabled several populations to return to their homelands, including many Jews that were allowed to return to Israel. At the same time he employed, rather than exiled, Elamites within his burgeoning cosmopolitan empire.

Below is a quote from Cyrus's infamous cylinder pertaining to his peaceful nature;

"The famous Cyrus Cylinder (538 BC), which records his capture of Babylon and his program of repatriating his subject peoples in their homelands, includes this statement: "May all the gods whom I have resettled in their sacred cities daily ask Bel and Nebo for a long life for me.""[58]

- Elamites were definitely dwelling within some of the 127 Persian provinces at the time of Esther during the reign of King Ahasuerus between 486-465 B.C.[59] We know this from a reference to the Elamites in Ezra 4:9. Ezra alludes to the Elamites during the reign of King Artaxerxes (465-425), who succeeded King Ahasuerus. If they existed during the reign of King Artaxerxes, they obviously existed during the rule of King Ahasuerus his predecessor.

- Elamites existed in Elam at the time of Pentecost around 33 A.D. If the Elamites had forfeited their ethnic identity to the Persians, then why were they identified in Acts 2:9 during the Day of Pentecost? The Elamites at Pentecost could have been Jews from Elam, or Elamite converts to Judaism. Regardless, the reference to the Elamites implies that they existed well into 1st century A.D.

  Unlike the Elamites, other ancient ethnic groups like the Midianites and Canaanites are absent among those at Pentecost in Acts 2:9. These two people groups were conquered by the Jews in the accounts described in Psalm 83:9-11, and in chapters 4 through 8 in the book of Judges.[60] In the aftermath of their respective defeats, their ethnic identities appear to have gradually disappeared.

  If Kelley's argument is correct, then just as there were no Midianites or Canaanites present in Acts 2:9, then neither should there have been any Elamites in existence at that time. In his article he writes, "*There's no record of a re-emergence of the Elamites since the Persian conquest 2500 years ago.*"[61]

- Isaiah 11:11 predicts that Jews will be regathered from Elam. The regathering Isaiah alludes to is commonly taught to have begun in 1948 when Israel became a restored nation.

Greek Empire (330-63 B.C.) and the
Roman Empire (63 B.C.-313 A.D.) and Elam

During the Greek Empire period, Elam was referred to as Cissia or Susiana.[62] During both the Greek and Roman Empires, the Elamites existed according to Acts 2:9.

"Then they were all amazed and marveled, saying to one another, "Look, are not all these who speak Galileans? And how *is it that* we hear, each in our own language in which we were born? Parthians and Medes and *Elamites*, those dwelling in Mesopotamia, Judea and Cappadocia, Pontus and Asia, Phrygia and Pamphylia, Egypt and the parts of Libya adjoining Cyrene, visitors from *Rome*, both Jews and proselytes." (Acts 2:7-10; emphasis added).

Summary

The partial fulfillment hypothesis concerning Jeremiah 49:34-39 is not commonly taught, and has several obvious flaws. This view fails to demonstrate when Elam was desolated by a disaster of the severity that necessitated a mass exodus of Elamites from their homeland. It also falls short in clearly evidencing when the global exile of the Elamites occurred. Moreover, this teaching reclassifies the Elamites mostly as Persians even though the two ethnicities were distinct.

The prophecy promises to restore the fortunes of the devastated territory. It also assures that the affected population will be able to safely return from exile in the latter days. Presently, Elam is neither uninhabited nor desolate.

In a nutshell, this interpretation beckons more questions than it offers solid answers. Perhaps as the prophecy experts become more acquainted with Jeremiah's prophecy concerning Elam, the partial fulfillment theory might receive more support. Maybe then some Bible scholar can answer the many open ended questions presented in this chapter.

Chapter 9

Does the Prophecy of Elam Await Fulfillment?

Part 3 – The Future Fulfillment Argument

```
"Bolton: Israel has until Aug. 21
to stop Bushehr"
```
World Tribune 8/16/10

WASHINGTON — A former senior U.S. official, (Ambassador John Bolton), has warned that Israel has less than a week to attack Iran without generating massive nuclear fallout.[63]

This chapter will present the future fulfillment argument of Jeremiah 49:34-39. The biblical commentary provided in chapters three through six treated the prophecy of Elam as an entirely unfulfilled event, but this chapter clarifies why this view appears to be the preferred explanation.

The general consensus among the handful of individuals that have written about Jeremiah 49:34-39 is that the prophecy of Elam remains entirely unfulfilled. However, the unfulfilled interpretation can scarcely be considered the overwhelming popular view, simply because of the lack of exposition available. Moreover, among the sparse commentaries available to review, most of them are limited to short articles, isolated speaker presentations, personal conversations, and/or a few random paragraphs in a couple of books.

Several quotes from expositors that favor the future fulfillment view will be presented first, followed by my reasons for supporting this position.

Bible Prophecy Expert
Dr. Arnold Fruchtenbaum's View

One of my favored and most trusted commentaries was alluded to earlier in the book from Dr. Arnold Fruchtenbaum. Concerning Jeremiah 49:34-39, he writes the following in his book entitled, *The Footsteps of the Messiah;*

> "*Although Persia or Iran (ancient Elam) is not an Arab state but a Persian one, its future will be examined here because it shares the same religion (Islam) with Moslem Arabs. Peace will come between Israel and Iran by means of destruction, according to Jeremiah 49:34-39. In verses 34-38 Jeremiah described the destruction of Elam, with the inhabitants being completely dispersed all over the world. But then verse 39 declares: 'But it shall come to pass in the latter days, that I will bring back the captivity of Elam, says Jehovah.'*
>
> *The destruction of Iran will be partial, and the dispersion will be temporary. Eventually the inhabitants will return and resettle Iran. The future of Iran is similar to that of Egypt, but the length of time they will be in dispersion is not revealed. So peace will come between Israel and Iran via destruction, dispersion, and then a conversion and a return. There will be a saved nation of Elam (Persia or Iran) in the (Millennial) Kingdom.*"[64]

Dr. Fruchtenbaum points out that at least Jeremiah 49:39 represents a forthcoming event. He acknowledges that the dispersion described in Jeremiah 49:34-38 "*will be temporary.*" However, from his comment about a temporary dispersion, he could be simply acknowledging that it won't be a permanent condition. This did not sufficiently answer the question, at least for me, as to whether or not he thinks that Jeremiah 49:34-38 has already found a past fulfillment.

This uncertainty prompted me to ask Dr. Fruchtenbaum about his view on the entire timing of Jeremiah's prophecy on Elam. While we were together at a Pre-Trib Rapture prophecy conference in Dallas, Texas on December 3, 2013, I seized the opportunity to briefly discuss this subject matter with him. From the best of my recollection the conversation went something like this;

SALUS: "Dr. Fruchtenbaum, in your book called *The Footsteps of the Messiah* you state that Jeremiah 49:34-39, concerning Elam, is an end time's prophecy. Is that still your view?"

DR. FRUCTHENBAUM: "Yes, that's correct. The prophecy speaks about a fulfillment that occurs in the latter days."

SALUS: "Yes I concur that Jeremiah 49:39 alludes to a regathering of Elamites in the latter days, but is it possible that Jeremiah 49:34-38 could have had a partial past fulfillment in Elam's history, but only the Elamite regathering remains as a pending event?"

DR. FRUCTHENBAUM: *After pausing a moment to reflect, he responded with a high degree of certainty,* "No, it could not have been fulfilled in the past; it all refers to the same event. There is no partial fulfillment."

Before I conclude our conversation, let me take the reader into my mindset at the time of this conversation. The resounding authority with which Dr. Fruchtenbaum spoke on this prophecy resonated deeply within me.

Years ago as a new Christian, at the not so ripe age of 37, I cut my prophetic teeth on his sound biblical teachings. I read his books and listened to his cassette teaching tapes almost daily. Even today, whenever I conduct a phone radio interview, I have his *Footsteps of the Messiah* book next to me. I keep his book close at hand as a reference resource, just in case the interviewer asks me a prophetic question that I may lack a ready, comprehensive answer for. I do this because I am confident, that in most cases, Dr. Fruchtenbaum's book contains a sound response.

Throughout the years that followed, Dr. Fruchtenbaum and I became friends. We shared several personal meetings together, which served as an integral part of my Christian discipleship. In fact, it was at one of those gatherings that he encouraged me to write a book about Psalm 83. That result of that conversation was the book, *Isralestine the Ancient Blueprints of the Future Middle East.* Soon after its release in 2008, mainstream Bible prophecy teachers like Hal Lindsey, Chuck Missler and Dr. David Reagan began teaching about Psalm 83 as a prophecy for our time.

There are two important things to note about Dr. Fruchtenbaum's teachings. *First,* many consider him to be one of the world's foremost authorities in the field of Bible prophecy. *Second,* he will always refrain from presenting biblical newspaper exegesis in correlation with Bible prophecy. It is easier to achieve sainthood from the Pope than to get Arnold to connect Bible prophecy with today's news headlines.

So, with all of the above in mind, the reader can understand my desire to emphasize how qualified his interpretation of this prophecy is. After listening to his credible and confident comments on Jeremiah's prophecy concerning Elam, I felt compelled to make the concluding comments below.

SALUS: Arnold, do you realize that the Bushehr nuclear plant is smack dab in the heart of ancient Elam, and it is a strategic site for Israel to strike?

DR. FRUCHTENBAUM: Yes, I am aware of this.

SALUS: Were you also aware of the fact that the Bushehr plant was loaded with Russian fuel rods in August of 2010, and at that time, former U.S. Ambassador John Bolton said once those rods were installed, Israel's window to strike Iran could be closed? His comments expressed his sincere concerns that a strike upon Bushehr could create a nuclear disaster.

DR. FRUCHTENBAUM: Yes, I am familiar with his comments and concerns.

SALUS: In addition to Bolton's trepidations, subsequent studies have been conducted that suggest a strike upon Bushehr could create a nuclear disaster far exceeding that of Chernobyl in April, 1986, and Fukushima in March, 2011. Perhaps this is the disaster spoken of in Jeremiah 49:37

that necessitates the worldwide dispersion of the affected Iranians in ancient Elam as per Jeremiah 49:36.

DR. FRUCTHENBAUM: Yes, I know Bill; this could prove to be very interesting.

From my perspective, his concluding comment may have been his way of suggesting, without being guilty of committing newspaper exegesis, that Jeremiah's prophecy concerning Elam could be related to Iran's nuclear program. Wow, is it possible? Does Jeremiah's prophecy actually hint of today's top headlines concerning the potential disaster of a strike upon Iran's nuclear facility in Bushehr?

As any end time's Bible prophecy nears its fulfillment, it should not be a surprise to read news headlines that may allude to the stage-setting of the prophetic event. For instance, look at the possible predictive correlations below.

"Report: Putin Wants to Regain 'Superpower' Status"

Newsmax 2/13/14

Ezekiel 38 alludes to a prophecy concerning a coalition spearheaded by Russia that attempts to destroy Israel in the latter years in order to possess great booty and plunder from the Jewish state. The prophecy describes a powerful Russia that only the Lord Himself can destroy. Ezekiel 38:18-23 describes the destruction of the Gog of Magog confederacy, not by America, the E.U. or the I.D.F., but seemingly solely by events outsourced from the Lord.

Many prophecy pundits today are carefully watching Russian advances, including the takeover of Crimea in March of 2014. Russian president Vladimir Putin, although he may not specifically be the infamous Gog of the prophecy, is definitely a person of possible prophetic interest today. He has suggested that one of the biggest tragedies of the 20th century was the collapse of the Soviet empire, and that one of the biggest triumphs of the 21st century would be its reemergence.

"Syrian Official: If Damascus is Attacked, Tel Aviv Will Burn"

Israel National News 8/28/13

Isaiah 17 predicts the complete destruction of the world's oldest and most continuously inhabited city of Damascus. The modern day capital city of Syria will someday cease to exist (Isaiah 17:1). The prophecy seems to identify an overnight destruction (Isaiah 17:14) that is caused by the Israeli Defense Forces (Isaiah 17:9) as an act of self-defense (Isaiah 17:14). Over the past few years, threats from Syria to attack Tel Aviv, Israel, have been matched by retaliatory threats from Israel to destroy Damascus, Syria.

Bible Prophecy Expert Joel Rosenberg's View

Another highly respected Bible prophecy teacher that believes Jeremiah 49:34-39 remains entirely unfulfilled is bestselling author Joel Rosenberg. Below are some quotes that were taken from a Rosenberg presentation entitled "What is the Future of Iran in Bible Prophecy." The entire presentation can be watched on YouTube.[65]

Concerning the timing that Jeremiah's prophecies take place, Rosenberg says,

> *"This prophecy clearly states that the Lord will direct the course of events that will conclude the modern history of Iran."*

> *"Concerning a time reference, we learn from Jeremiah 49:39, that these prophecies will take place in the last days. These are end time's prophecies."*

Concerning the worldwide dispersion of the Elamite exiles in Jeremiah 49:36, Rosenberg says below that it is "going to happen." In other words it has not happened historically.

> *"One thing that's going to happen in the last days is that God is going to scatter the people of Iran, and cause many of them to spread out all over the planet, and there's no nation to which the outcasts of Iran won't go."*

Rosenberg posits a potential correlation with the scattering of Jer. 49:36 and the ongoing Iranian Diaspora that began at the time of the takeover of the Islamic Regime in 1979. He informs,

"The Islamic Revolution of 1979 set a convulsion in Iran and around the world, and many Iranians that were studying abroad realized that they couldn't return to Iran. Many people within the country decided what a madman the Ayatollah Khomeini was and they decided to flee, and they spread out around the globe. When you talk to Iranians living in America, many of them will say that 1979 was the fulfillment of this portion of Jeremiah's prophecy. For the first time in human history more than five million Iranians were scattered throughout the world. One out of every fifteen Iranians doesn't live in Iran for one reason; the Islamic Revolution of 1979."

Regarding the fierce anger of the Lord, coupled with the promise to send the sword after the Iranians, described in Jeremiah 49:37, Rosenberg says,

"The prophecy says that God has fierce anger toward Elam. Why would he have fierce anger? Perhaps, it's because the Iranian leadership is slaughtering people. Perhaps, it's because they are executing Christian pastors."

"God is so clear about what he is going to do in these few verses. First, He's going to scatter the Iranians all over the world, and then in the last days He's going to act. He's going to bring the sword against them, that tends to mean scripturally, military action against them humanly speaking, but not always, sometimes the Lord Himself supernaturally intervenes against the nations; as He did against Egypt."

Rosenberg finds Jeremiah 49:38 *"most interesting,"* concerning the establishment of the Lord's throne in Elam. He believes that this could be alluding to Iran becoming a sending nation of evangelizing missionaries into the world. This has been occurring on a large scale since 1979, and Rosenberg expects this trend to continue throughout the last days.

Lastly, concerning a potential prophetic correlation between Jeremiah 49 and Ezekiel 38 and 39, Rosenberg states,

> *"Now we don't know if Ezekiel 38 and 39 are the same set of events that will bring Jeremiah 49 to fulfillment, but many Iranian believers believe that. And, I (Rosenberg) think it's a plausible case, although I would not state my whole existence on it. Clearly these two passages, Jeremiah 49 and Ezekiel 38 and 39, describe supernaturally directed destructions of the Iranian government, supreme leader, and military. And then, the Holy Spirit it's described in Ezekiel 39, will be poured out in a way that I (Rosenberg) believe will bring many into the kingdom. And, I (Rosenberg) think that's consistent with the prophecies of Jeremiah 49."*

In the chapter entitled, "Are Jeremiah 49 and Ezekiel 38 the Same Prophetic Events?" I explain why I don't think Jeremiah and Ezekiel are describing the same prophecies.

Bible Prophecy Expert Bill Koenig's View

Another individual of contemporary prophetic prominence, that advocates the entirely unfulfilled view, is White House correspondent Bill Koenig. Koenig, who maintains an active website filled with daily news headlines at *http://www.watch.org*, believes that Jeremiah 49:34-39 could be signaling a strike upon Iran's nuclear program.

Bill Koenig and I are good friends, and have shared speaking platforms and appeared on several Christian television programs together. Bill has said the following,

> *"Jeremiah 49:34-39 appears to be an end time's prophecy for our time. The prophet seems to be signaling that a strike upon Iran's nuclear program could occur and result in a disaster of epic biblical proportions. The disaster appears*

to result in the dispersion of many Iranian exiles into the nations of the world. There is no history of such a significant disaster ever occurring throughout Iran's ancient history. The verdict is still out on this prophecy, but I for one am keeping a watchful eye on this prophecy."

The Bible Knowledge Commentary: Old Testament Commentary

Bible prophecy experts John F. Walvoord and Roy B. Zuck seem to be advocating a future fulfillment of Jeremiah 49:34-39. They write the following in their book entitled, *The Bible Knowledge Commentary: Old Testament,*

"Though there is some evidence that Nebuchadnezzar defeated the Elamites about 596 b.c., his subjugation at that time did not fulfill this message. Elam became a central part of the Persian Empire that later conquered Babylon (cf. Dan. 8:2). Jeremiah's statement about Elam's destruction seems to take on eschatological dimensions as God said He would set His throne in Elam to supervise her destruction. Yet Elam's destruction will not be total because God will restore her fortunes... in days to come"[66]

Bible Prophecy Expert John McTernan's View

Another noted contemporary Bible prophecy teacher echoing this similar view is John McTernan. He believes that Jeremiah 49:34-39 remains entirely unfulfilled also. He writes the following in an article posted on his website *http://www.defendproclaimthefaith.org.*

"The prophecy speaks of the people being driven off the land and scattered into all the world. This has never happened in recorded history. It also speaks of the God of Israel setting His throne in Elam. This has never happened. This is all future because this prophecy was never fulfilled. It appears that with Elam now the focus of world attention, God is about to fulfill it."

"*In verse 39, Jeremiah wrote that in the "Later-Day" God would bring the people back to Elam. This means that during the reign of the Lord Jesus, God is going to show His mercy and bring the Elam/Iranians back into the land. Awesome events are about to break over Elam. They have a nuclear reactor and are making plans to destroy Israel. Elam is preparing for the Mahdi and world conquest. The prophecy recorded in Jeremiah 49:34-39 is waiting to be fulfilled. It appears the time to judge Elam/Iran and Islam is at hand. The throne of the Lord Jesus will be over Elam.*"[67]

Bible Prophecy Expert Sean Osborne's View

Sean Osborne is also a friend and an excellent researcher. Sean Osborne has assisted me on various topics of research on Bible prophecy in the past. He was quoted in an earlier chapter of this book regarding Jeremiah's prophecy concerning Elam. Osborne has written a comprehensive article on the Jeremiah 49:34-39 that presents the entirely unfulfilled view. This recommended reading is available at this website link: *http://eschatologytoday.blogspot. com/2010/09/jeremiah-49-will-coalition-of-nations.html*. Below is a quote from this September 15, 2010, article that was updated on April 27, 2014.

"*At this point there exists very strong evidence for the existence of a coalition of nations prepared to move militarily against the nuclear weapons aspirations of the Islamic Republic of Iran in what I believe will be a highly probable literal fulfillment in our day of Jeremiah 49:34-39.*"

The Author's Reasons That Support the Entirely Unfulfilled View

All of the quotes above add credence to the view that Jeremiah 49:34-39 remains entirely unfulfilled. Below are some of my reasons for subscribing to this view.

Jeremiah's Prophecy Involves the Final Generation

One convincing factor that favors the entirely unfulfilled view is the worldwide regathering of the Elamites in the end times described in Jeremiah 49:39. Not only does the verse specifically state that the prophecy finds a latter day fulfillment, but its writing format is highly indicative of other similar last days biblical passages.

There are several other comparative Scriptures in the Bible that refer to the regathering of displaced exiles back into their historic homelands. Like the Iranians, these other populations return from captivity to restored fortunes. In addition to the Iranians, the list includes the Israelis, Jordanians, Egyptians, Syrians and Assyrians. In most cases, with the exception of the Israelis, these Scriptures seem to refer to the following:

1. A specific generation, rather than a sequence of successive generations, that is forced into exile due to a desolation or a disaster,

2. A dispersion that occurs in the end times,

3. A national Christian conversion of the displaced remnant,

4. A regathering of indigenous peoples to their homelands during the millennial reign of Christ.

Comparing the Dispersions of Egyptians and Elamites

For example, a quote earlier in this chapter from Dr. Arnold Fruchtenbaum stated, "*The future of Iran is similar to that of Egypt, but the length of time they will be in dispersion is not revealed.*" What was meant by this comment can be determined from another quote taken from Dr. Fruchtenbaum's same book concerning Egypt.

"*Only when the Egyptians worship the same God as Israel, through Jesus the Messiah, will peace finally come (to Egypt). For the first forty years of the (Millennial) Kingdom, the land of Egypt will be desolate and the Egyptians will be dispersed all over the world. But afterwards, the Egyptians will be regathered, becoming a kingdom again.*"[68]

Fruchtenbaum's quote about Elam, in correlation with Egypt, comes from the fact that Egypt and Elam are both recipients of end time's disasters. Egypt's desolation also leads to a dispersion and is explained in Ezekiel 29:1-12.

"I will make the land of Egypt desolate in the midst of the countries *that are* desolate; and among the cities *that are* laid waste, her cities shall be desolate forty years; and I will scatter the Egyptians among the nations and disperse them throughout the countries." (Ezekiel 29:12)

Ezekiel attaches a forty year period to Egypt's dispersion, whereas Jeremiah does not reference the duration of the Elamite diaspora. Ezekiel predicts that Egypt will be a desolate country in the midst of other *countries that are desolate*. It would not be far-fetched to consider that Elam may be among those territories that are desolate at the time. We find out that Egypt's 40 years of desolation and dispersion is an end time's event from Ezekiel's follow up verses.

"Yet, thus says the Lord GOD: "At the end of forty years I will gather the Egyptians from the peoples among whom they were scattered. I will bring back the captives of Egypt and cause them to return to the land of Pathros, (*in Egypt*) to the land of their origin, and there they shall be a *lowly kingdom*. It shall be the *lowliest of kingdoms*; it shall never again exalt itself above the nations, for I will diminish them so that they will not rule over the nations anymore. No longer shall it be the confidence of the house of Israel, but will remind them of *their* iniquity when they turned to follow them. *Then they shall know that I am the Lord GOD.*""" (Ezek. 29:13-16; *emphasis added*)

Although Ezekiel doesn't specifically state that the prophecy happens in the "latter days" as Jeremiah 49:39 does, these verses are filled with other timing clues. For instance, Ezekiel declares that Egypt will be the lowliest of kingdoms, and that it will never again be exalted above other nations. Presently, Egypt is far from being the lowliest of all kingdoms. It is the most populated Arab state, and it possesses the highest ranked military in the Arab world.

Egypt has a population of approximately 84,605,000, which is more than twice that of Algeria, the next largest populated Arab country. Algeria hosts a populace of about 38,295,000.[69] Egypt's military is ranked 13th and Saudi Arabia is ranked 26th.[70]

These Ezekiel verses also specify that the Lord is responsible for the regathering of the Egyptians. Also, the last sentence informs us that the regathering takes place when the dispersed Egyptians know the Lord. In other words, these are Egyptian believers in the Messiah, Jesus Christ, and because of their faith in Christ, the nation of Egypt exists during the millennial reign of Christ. This point is emphasized by Dr. Fruchtenbaum in his above quote concerning Egypt's future in the millennium.

Fruchtenbaum's quote suggests that the forty years of Egyptian dispersion overlaps into the millennium. I believe his assessment is correct, because the desolation appears to be brought about by the invasion of Egypt by the Antichrist in Daniel 11:42-43. Many teach that the timing of this invasion is during the second half of the seven years of tribulation. The millennium is set up in the immediate aftermath of the tribulation period.

Isaiah 19 provides more information about Egypt, Assyria and Israel in the Messianic Millennium.

"In that day Israel will be one of three with Egypt and Assyria—a blessing in the midst of the land, whom the LORD of hosts shall bless, saying, "Blessed *is* Egypt My people, and Assyria the work of My hands, and Israel My inheritance." (Isaiah 19:24-25)

Comparing the Dispersions
of Jordanians with Elamites

Jeremiah 49 addresses the returns of two sets of exiles. Jeremiah 49:1-6 references the Ammonites, who are Northern Jordanians today, and Jeremiah 49:34-39 alludes to the Elamites, whose modern day equivalents are the Iranians of West Central Iran. The chapter opens with a serious prophetic judgment about the Jordanians. Jordan is currently considered to be one of the most moderate Arab states. However, this was not the case throughout most of modern history, nor does it appear to be the case in the future. Jordan demonstrates its hostility toward Israel when it enlists in the Psalm 83 confederacy.

> "Therefore behold, the days are coming," says the LORD, "That I will cause to be heard an alarm of war In Rabbah of the Ammonites; It shall be a desolate mound, And her villages shall be burned with fire. Then Israel shall take possession of his inheritance," says the LORD." (Jeremiah 49:2)

This passage is self-explanatory from the perspective of literal interpretation. Jordan will be involved in a war with Israel, which Jordan will lose decisively! In the aftermath of Israel's conquest over this Arab country, Israel will capture some of its land that sits within the boundaries allotted to the Hebrew patriarch Abraham. According to Genesis 15:18, the borders of this land include Jordan, which sits within the allocated land between the Nile River in Egypt, and the Euphrates River in Iraq and Syria.

Jordan is one of the countries listed in the Psalm 83 prophecy. Although Jordan has been defeated by Israel in the Arab-Israeli wars of 1948, 1967, and 1973, Israel has never captured Jordan. Israel annexed some territory in 1967 that had been under Jordanian control, but this prophecy refers to a final battle between Jordan and Israel.

Jeremiah 49:3 declares that Jordan is severely plundered and their pagan god, Islamic clerics, and political leaders go into captivity. Jeremiah 49:5 forecasts that even the Jordanians will go into exile. However, the following verse issues good tidings to the faithful believing remnant of Jordanians.

> "But afterward I will bring back The captives of the people of Ammon," says the LORD." (Jer. 49:6)

This sequence of events clearly apply to a single generation; the generation that goes to war with Israel and ends up in captivity as a result. Since this prediction has yet to occur, and we are living in the last days, it is presumably safe to suggest that this is a latter day prophecy.

Since this prophecy, along with the Elam prophecy, are all located in Jeremiah chapter 49, the pendulum swings strongly in favor of the entire Elam prophecy also being end time's generationally specific.

More evidence concerning Jordan's judgment taking place in the latter days exists in Jeremiah 48 and Zephaniah 2. Jeremiah 48 addresses Moab's end time's judgment. Moab, also a confederate member of Psalm 83, is modern day central Jordan.

> "Woe to you, O Moab! The people of Chemosh (*Ancient Moabite God, that would represent Allah today*) perish; For your sons have been taken captive, And your daughters captive. "Yet I will bring back the (*Jordanian*) captives of Moab In the latter days," says the LORD. Thus far *is* the judgment of Moab." (Jer. 48:46-47; *emphasis added*)

Again we see that a faithful remnant of Jordanians, after learning the hard way, will forfeit their faith in the false god of Allah for a saving faith in Jesus Christ the Messiah! This point is hammered home in the next sequence of verses!

> "I have heard the reproach of Moab, And the insults of the people of Ammon, With which they have reproached My people (*Israel*), And made arrogant threats against their borders (*of the Jewish state*). Therefore, as I live," Says the LORD of hosts, the God of Israel, "Surely Moab

shall be like Sodom, And the people of Ammon like Gomorrah— Overrun with weeds and saltpits, And a perpetual desolation. The residue of My people (*Israel*) shall plunder them, And the remnant of My people (*Israel*) shall possess them." This they (*Jordanians*) shall have for their pride, Because they have reproached and made arrogant threats Against the (*Jewish*) people of the LORD of hosts. The LORD *will be* awesome to them, (*Jordanians & Jews*) For He will reduce to nothing all the gods of the earth; (*Especially Allah*) *People* shall worship Him, Each one from his place, Indeed all the shores of the nations." (Zephaniah 2:8-11; *emphasis added*)

No Historical Fulfillment Records of Jeremiah 49:34-39

Previous chapters in this book have gone to exorbitant lengths to demonstrate that it is extremely difficult, if not virtually impossible, to prove that Jeremiah 49:34:39 has found either full or partial historical fulfillment. Unless there is some smoking gun evidence to the contrary, then this prophecy remains entirely unfulfilled!

The ramifications of Jeremiah 49:34-39 remaining unfulfilled are staggering. It almost reeks of sensationalism and newspaper exegesis, when you read today's mainstream headlines about Iran's burgeoning and relatively unchecked nuclear program. But in this modern era, news is a 24/7 phenomena, and the flow of relevant potential prophetic information is constant. Prior to 1980, before CNN was launched, news reports were restricted to several hours daily. But now, that's all changed and worthy news headlines emanate almost hourly on Fox, CNN, MSNBC and over the Internet.

The Sound Scriptural and Geo-Political Evidence for a Future Fulfillment

It has already been pointed out that the Elamites survived throughout all of the primary four Gentile Empires of the Babylonians, Persians, Greeks, and Romans. This is why the

Elamites are mentioned at the "Day of Pentecost" in Acts 2:9. Furthermore, Elam is mentioned in the Bible in Isaiah chapter 11 in conjunction with the 1948 A.D. regathering of Israel.

> "It shall come to pass in that day That the Lord shall set His hand again the second time To recover the remnant of His people (*the Jews*) who are left, From Assyria and Egypt, From Pathros (*Egypt*) and Cush (*lower Egypt & Northern Ethiopia*), From Elam (*Iran*) and Shinar (*Iraq*), From Hamath (*Syria*) and the islands of the sea. He will set up a banner for the nations, And will assemble the outcasts of Israel, And gather together the dispersed of Judah From the four corners of the earth (*Worldwide*)." (Isaiah 11:11-12; *emphasis added*).

There are different interpretations for the timing of the "second time" of this verse. Some suggest that the first time was the Old Testament exodus from Egypt and the second commenced in 1948. Another view, and the one I prefer, is that the first time was the regathering from Babylon and the second was 1948. There is another view that suggests the first time was in 1948 and the second will be at the end of the tribulation period.

The reason I support that Babylon was first and 1948 was the second time view, is because both occurred sequentially after Isaiah's time. These two regatherings were extremely significant and found a preponderant Jewish population residing outside of their homeland of Israel at the time.

The last view presumes that a preponderance of Jews will be dispersed worldwide during the tribulation period, and I don't believe that will be the case. Zechariah 13:8 informs us that two-thirds of the Jews will not leave Israel, but will be killed inside the land of Israel. Egypt, as the first regathering, doesn't make sense to me because the Jews had already been regathered into Israel long before Isaiah wrote his eleventh chapter.

Regardless of which view one holds, the weight of the evidence suggests that Isaiah 11:11-12 alludes to the present regathering of the Jews into Israel, which has been ongoing officially since

1948. If this is the case, then Elam is mentioned in the modern day because of Isaiah's reference to the regathering of the Jews from there in 1948. Jews existed in ancient Elam even until 1948. Isaiah could have inserted the term Persia, Media, or some other ancient name that would have alluded to modern day Iran, but he chose to refer to Elam.

Summary

There exists a strong possibility that one of today's top news stories, Iran's nuclear program, was eluded to about 2600 years ago by Jeremiah the prophet. If so, the Bushehr nuclear plant located in West Central Iran could be destroyed. This could then create a humanitarian crisis that could kill many Iranians and necessitate the evacuation of tens of thousands in the affected area.

Independent studies have been conducted by the Arab Gulf states and other non-Arab entities that demonstrate convincingly, that the Bushehr nuclear facility is a disaster waiting to happen. An earthquake, or a military strike, could be all that it takes to create an epic biblical disaster.

"Iran's other nuclear timebomb"
National Post 3/31/14[71]

This timely National Post article warns that "*a city of over a million people in southwest Iran, sits in one of the most active seismic regions in the world, at the intersection of three tectonic plates.*" It points out that over a million people could be affected by a disaster in Bushehr. It further quotes;

> "*It* (the Bushehr nuclear plant) *is built with a 40-year-old design that has shown its limitations; the emergency coolant system is also 30 years old; it is running on two different technologies;* (German & Russian) *according to the International Atomic Energy Agency, the* (Iranian) *staff is not properly trained to face any kind of accident.*"

The entire report is so potentially vital to the prophecy of Jeremiah 49:34-39 that it has been quoted further in an appendix within this book. I encourage the reader to read the appendix entitled, "Iran's Other Nuclear Nightmare" after reading this chapter.

Lastly, it is interesting to note that there are many Iranians already dispersed into the nations of the world that will probably receive the upcoming distressed Iranians with open arms. Family members and friends already scattered abroad currently exist to embrace these future exiles from Elam. They empathize first hand with their humanitarian plight. The Iranian diaspora has been ongoing since the takeover of the Islamic regime in 1979. A dated report from 1999 provided the following estimates. These rounded off numbers reflect the approximated Iranian populations residing in each respective country.

Iranians of the Diaspora[72]

- Afghanistan 20,000
- Australia 53,500
- Austria 15,000
- Belgium 8,000
- Canada 120,000
- China 10,000
- Cyprus 5,000
- Denmark 10,000
- Eastern Europe 30,000
- Egypt & N. Africa 20,000
- Finland 2,000
- France 62,000
- Germany 110,000
- Greece 20,000
- India 60,000
- Iraq 250,000
- Israel 30,000
- Kuwait 100,000
- Lebanon 30,000
- Norway 6,000
- Pakistan 140,000

- Philippines, Korea & Japan 30,000
- South Africa. 10,000
- Spain & Portugal. 15,000
- Sweden 20,000
- Switzerland 6,000
- Syria 50,000
- The Netherlands 10,000
- The Commonwealth of
  Independent States (CIS). 60,000
- Turkey. 800,000
- UAE, Bahrain & Other Arab Gulf States 350,000
- United Kingdom 80,000
- United States 1,350,000
- Central & South America & Elsewhere 30,000
- **TOTAL. 3,912,500**

Chapter 10

Iran: A Past Friend but Present Foe of Israel

"Ayatollah: Kill all Jews, annihilate Israel"

World Net Daily 2/5/12

Iran lays out legal case for genocidal attack against 'cancerous tumor'(of Israel)[73]

O nce upon a time, a few millennia ago; the government of Iran was very pro-Israel. This is definitively not the case today! Presently, the Iranian leadership harbors an unhealthy and unholy hatred of the Jews and their Jewish state. This enmity is fueled by the Islamic mindset of the current Iranian leaders. This disposition will disappear when the prophecies of Jeremiah 49 and Ezekiel 38 find fulfillment. These two powerful prophetic episodes, which should happen soon and sequentially, will loosen the stranglehold of Islam and of the Mullah's in Iran.

This chapter explores why the Lord judges Iran severely in the future. It also takes a peek into the past when Iran, under the banner of Persia, was formerly friendly to Israel. Someday, Iran will again be an ally of Israel's, as it was during the time of King Cyrus the Great. We know this from Jeremiah 49:38-39, which declares that the Lord will set up His throne in Iran and regather the Iranian exiles back to their homeland in the latter days. It would be utterly nonsensical to think that Iran could harbor any hatred toward Israel when the Lord's throne is established there.

It is interesting to note that Iran is the only Gentile nation in the world that is promised to host the throne of the Lord. Today, some Americans seem to erroneously think that the Lord sits in heaven draped in the American flag, singing the Star Spangled Banner, but there is no biblical reference to the Lord's throne being established anywhere on US soil. Only Jerusalem (Jer. 3:17) and Elam (Jer. 49:38) can boast that someday the Lord will establish His throne in their respective locations.

The Lord appears to already be giving the world a sneak preview of the establishment of His throne in Iran, at least spiritually speaking, through the throngs of Christian conversions currently occurring within Iran. A concerted, three-fold spiritual campaign is underway in Iran against the backdrop of severe Islamic repression. This peaceful Christian crusade includes an undeniable supernatural component.

- Free Bibles are being smuggled into Iran under high risk of persecution to the non-profit peddler.
- Satellite television programs, like Iran Alive Ministries and TBN's Nejat TV are effectively penetrating through the ethereal airways, and reaching over the heads of the mullahs into the households of millions of Iranians.
- In coordination with the above, Iranians are receiving and responding to healings, miracles, visions and dreams that are being outsourced from the Lord. This unexplainable phenomenon is occurring in apparent fulfillment of a prophecy in the book of Joel. Peter quoted this prophecy in Acts 2:17-21 during the time of Pentecost.

"And it shall come to pass afterward That I will pour out My Spirit on all flesh; Your sons and your daughters shall prophesy, Your old men shall dream dreams, Your young men shall see visions. And also on *My* menservants and on *My* maidservants I will pour out My Spirit in those days. "And I will show wonders in the heavens and in the earth: Blood and fire and pillars of smoke. The sun shall be turned into darkness, And the moon into blood, Before the coming of the great and awesome day of the LORD.

And it shall come to pass *That* whoever calls on the name of the LORD Shall be saved. For in Mount Zion and in Jerusalem there shall be deliverance, As the LORD has said, Among the remnant whom the LORD calls." (Joel 2:28-32)

This prophecy is exposited upon further in the last chapter of this book.

Iran in Past Bible Prophecies

Iran is the subject of several Bible prophecies. Not only is Iran part of the future prophecies of Jeremiah 49:34-39 and Ezekiel 38 and 39, but it was also part of other significant ancient biblical predictions. These past prophecies were fulfilled during the Medo-Persia empire period. They included:

1. The emergence of the second Gentile Empire (Medo-Persian) in Daniel 2:31-45. (550–330 BC)[74] This empire was represented by the chest and arms of silver in the prophecy.
2. The rise of the Persian king Cyrus the Great of Isaiah 44:28 and 45:1 (600-529 BC)[75]
3. The fall of the second Gentile Empire (Medo-Persian) at the hands of the third Gentile Empire (Greek) in Daniel 2:36-45 (333 B.C.to 149 BC)[76] This empire was represented by the belly and thighs of bronze in the prophecy.

At various times during the fulfillment of these prior prophecies, their attitude toward the Jewish people was vastly different than that of the present rogue Islamic regime. In the past, there were periods of friendship and mutual respect for each other. However, the extreme disdain toward Israel among Iranian leaders in modernity reached an unprecedented height after the 1979 Islamic Revolution.

The present hatred of the Iranian leadership toward Israel is somewhat reminiscent of their Persian ancestors during the time of Esther, around 483-473 BC. At that time, the Persians were misled by their Prime Minister Haman into thinking that the Jews were rebellious and subversive subjects of the Persian kingdom. He convinced King Ahasuerus to issue a genocidal decree against the Jews in Esther chapter three. While Haman was primarily concerned with destroying the Jews dwelling within the one hundred and twenty-seven Persian provinces, the current goal of the Iranian leadership threatens to destroy both the Jews and the state of Israel.

The first supreme leader that emerged as a result of the Iranian Revolution was Ayatollah Ruhollah Khomeini, who in 1979 called America the "Great Satan," and later branded Israel as the "Little Satan." There is no shortage of Anti-Semitic quotes made since the revolution, and the current Ayatollah is one of Iran's greatest critics of Israel. Ayatollah Seyed Ali Hosseini Khamenei has made numerous Anti-Semitic comments:

- "The Zionist regime is a true cancer tumor on this region that should be cut off." "And it definitely will be cut off."[77]
- "We will support and help any nations, any groups fighting against the Zionist regime across the world, and we are not afraid of declaring this."[78]
- "The fake Zionist (regime) will disappear from the landscape of geography,"[79]
- "Israel is a 'rabid dog' of the region bent on besmirching the Islamic Republic's reputation"[80]

Such disturbing comments would never have emanated from the lips of Cyrus the Great, who was greatly revered for his policies of peace. The Bible tells us that Cyrus was so pro-Israel that promptly after conquering Babylon around 539 B.C., he issued a decree to rebuild the Jewish temple that had been previously destroyed in 586 B.C. by the Babylonians.

> "Now in the first year of Cyrus king of Persia, that the word of the LORD by the mouth of Jeremiah might be fulfilled, the LORD stirred up the spirit of Cyrus king of Persia, so that he made a proclamation throughout all his kingdom, and also *put it* in writing, saying, Thus says Cyrus king of Persia: "All the kingdoms of the earth the LORD God of heaven has given me. And He has commanded me to build Him a house [temple] at Jerusalem which *is* in Judah. Who *is* among you

of all His people? May his God be with him, and let him go
up to Jerusalem which *is* in Judah, and build the house of
the LORD God of Israel (He *is* God), which *is* in Jerusalem.
And whoever is left in any place where he dwells, let the men
of his place help him with silver and gold, with goods and
livestock, besides the freewill offerings for the house of God
which *is* in Jerusalem." (Ezra 1:1-4; *emphasis added*)

Whereas Cyrus recognized the God of Israel and Israel's right to
exist in their ancient homeland, the present Iranian regime refuses
to do either. This point is critical because prophetic similarities
exist between now and the time of Cyrus.

During Cyrus's reign, the predicted seventy years of Hebrew
captivity had concluded, and it was time for the restoration of Israel.
The same prophet, Jeremiah, that issued the prophecy of Elam,
foretold of the seventy year Diaspora into Babylon.

The Babylonian Diaspora

"And this whole land [of Israel] shall be a desolation *and*
an astonishment, and these nations shall serve the king of
Babylon seventy years. 'Then it will come to pass, when
seventy years are completed, *that* I will punish the king
of Babylon and that nation, the land of the Chaldeans,
for their iniquity,' says the LORD; 'and I will make it a
perpetual desolation." (Jeremiah 25:11-12)

The Return (Aliyah) from Babylon in to Israel

"For thus says the LORD: After seventy years are completed at
Babylon, I will visit you and perform My good word toward
you, and cause you to return to this place. For I know the
thoughts that I think toward you, says the LORD, thoughts
of peace and not of evil, to give you a future and a hope. Then
you will call upon Me and go and pray to Me, and I will listen
to you. And you will seek Me and find *Me*, when you search
for Me with all your heart. I will be found by you, says the
LORD, and I will bring you back from your [Babylonian]

captivity; I will gather you from all the nations and from all the places where I have driven you, says the LORD, and I will bring you to the place [Israel] from which I cause you to be carried away captive." (Jer. 29:10-14; *emphasis added*)

Presently, another Aliyah, even more expansive and notable than the one in Jeremiah 29 is underway, and it was also prophesied by the same prophet, Jeremiah, in addition to several other prophets. Below are just three promises to restore the Jews into their homeland of Israel.

"Therefore, behold, *the* days are coming," says the LORD, "that they shall no longer say, 'As the LORD lives who brought up the children of Israel from the land of Egypt,' but, 'As the LORD lives who brought up and led the descendants of the house of Israel from the north country and from all the countries [worldwide] where I had driven them.' And they shall dwell in their own land." (Jer. 23:7-8; emphasis added).

"Therefore say to the house of Israel, 'Thus says the Lord GOD: "I do not do *this* for your sake, O house of Israel, but for My holy name's sake, which you have profaned among the nations wherever you went. And I will sanctify My great name, which has been profaned among the nations, which you have profaned in their midst; and the nations shall know that I *am* the LORD," says the Lord GOD, "when I am hallowed in you before their eyes. For I will take you from among the nations, gather you out of all countries, and bring you into your own land. (Ezekiel 36:22-24)

"It shall come to pass in that day *That* the Lord shall set His hand again the second time To recover the remnant of His people who are left, From Assyria and Egypt, From Pathros and Cush, From Elam and Shinar, From Hamath and the islands of the sea. He will set up a banner for the nations, And will assemble the outcasts of Israel, And gather together the dispersed of Judah From the four corners of the earth." (Isaiah 11:11-12)

These three predictions explain the monumental nature of the present regathering of the Jews into Israel. Jeremiah 23:7-8 declares that the Hebrew exodus out of Egyptian bondage at the time of Moses, which was truly a miraculous feat, will pale in comparison!

Ezekiel informs us that the regathering takes place when Israelis are in a condition of unbelief. He says that they are not being assembled into Israel for their sake, but for the sake of the Lord's holy name. He further states that the Lord had to take matters into His own hands concerning His holy name because during the Diaspora, the Jews were generally profaning His holy name. Even today, many Jews don't believe in the God of the Bible, and even less accept that Jesus Christ is the Messiah.

Isaiah 11:11-12 has been included because it mentions a worldwide regathering of Jews to Israel. This includes Iranian Jews that are returning from Elam. This means that the territory of Elam had to exist when Israel was restored as a nation on May 14, 1948. This topic was previously addressed in the chapter called "Does the Prophecy of Elam Await Fulfillment? Part 3 – *The Future Fulfillment Argument*."

Why the Lord Judges Iran
Severely in the End Time's

The striking prophetic similarity between King Cyrus of the past, and the Iranian Supreme Leader Ayatollah Khamenei of the present, is that both leaders witnessed the restoration of the Jews back into their historic homeland of Israel. Khamenei was born in 1939, nine years prior to the rebirth of Israel in 1948, and throughout his life he has witnessed the return of several million Jews back into the Jewish state.

One might think that Khamenei would be amazed by the unprecedented process of Jewish Aliyah into Israel. However, he is intolerant and indignant to Israel, and indifferent to the miraculous spectacle that is occurring before his eyes. This could never have been said of King Cyrus.

Whereas King Cyrus fully acknowledged Israel as the Jewish state, Ayatollah Khamenei and his government obstinately refuse to follow in the wise footsteps of their famous Persian predecessor. The rogue Islamic regime of Iran vehemently opposes the existence of Israel. Khamenei believes that Israel is an occupying force of a state that belongs to the Palestinians. He calls for the destruction of Israel in order to facilitate a country called Palestine.

"Iran rejects two-state solution for Palestine"

Al Jazeera 10/2/11

> "Our claim is freedom of Palestine, not part of Palestine. Any plan that partitions Palestine is totally rejected," Khamenei told the gathering. "Palestine spans from the river [Jordan] to the [Mediterranean] sea, nothing less."[81]

The prophecies of Jeremiah 49, and especially Ezekiel 38 and 39, will topple the reigning Islamic regime if it remains in place when these epic events take place. The devastation that accompanies these ancient predictions leaves no reason to believe that the ruling Mullahs can remain in control in the aftermath. Iran should become one of the most downtrodden countries in the world after these biblical battles.

It is doubtful that the present Anti-Semitic Islamic leadership of Iran will be overthrown, or voted out prior to the fulfillment of these two prophecies. Their hatred of the state of Israel will probably worsen and motivate them to bring harm to Israel. Some form of aggression against Israel, whether it is a preemptive attack upon Israel, or a retaliatory response to an attack from Israel, could be what fiercely angers the Lord in Jeremiah 49:37. Regardless, Iran's certain involvement in Ezekiel 38 will force the Lord to stomp out the Islamic regime once and for all. This is probably why nothing good in the Bible is said about Persia's future after Ezekiel 38 occurs.

The severity of Iran's judgment is measured out proportionately to its aggressions toward Israel. Iran, under the banner of Persia, wants to destroy Israel according to the motives of Ezekiel 38:11-13. Because of this, Persia will bring its own destruction upon itself. Iran's destruction will be executed by the hand of the Lord according to Ezekiel 38:18-39:6.

Summary

About two thousand miles and a grueling forty to fifty-hour bus ride separates Israel from Iran geographically, but geopolitically and spiritually, the two nations may as well be located on different planets. In fact, it would not be far-fetched to suggest that Iran's present leadership would prefer that Israel existed on a different planet instead of earth.

Although a wide territorial expanse separates these two nations, Israel's land-based *Jericho-III* missile can reach Iranian targets anywhere in the country. Below is a relative assessment worth mentioning from military intelligence expert Sean Osborne.

> *"Even though Jericho-III range and performance data is classified Top Secret, the entire delivery system is officially classified as a true ICBM because it could accurately strike targets well over 7,100 miles distant according to USAF intelligence reports. That range means it could deliver a nuke to almost anywhere on Earth via a great circle trajectory.*
>
> *Estimates on the Jericho-III performance data are based upon real performance data from Israel's Shavit satellite launch vehicle (SLV), which the Jericho-III nuclear delivery vehicle is based upon. Jericho-III will carry either a single warhead with a 1+ megaton yield or three MIRV warheads of the 350kT yield. Accordingly, a Jericho-III is believed to capable of delivering an extremely high-speed strike anywhere in the Middle East region within 30 minutes. The extremely high speed of the delivery vehicles makes the warhead virtually immune to any anti-missile system in Iran's arsenal."*[82]

Osborne suggests that the Jericho-III can reach Iran within 30 minutes. This is an important observance, because at some point Iran will probably attempt to wipe Israel off of the globe. This was the stated intention of former Iranian president Mahmoud Ahmadinejad, and is still the aspiration of Ayatollah Khamenei.

"Israel should be wiped off map, says Iran's president" (Ahmadinejad)
The Guardian 10/26/05

Jeremiah 49:34-39 foretells that Iran is going to do something that fiercely angers the God of the Jews. It is possible that the present Islamic regime in Iran may have already crossed that red line. According to Jeremiah's prophecy, a disaster in Iran is forthcoming. Some of us suspect that this disaster could involve an Israeli strike upon Iran's nuclear program, namely at the location of the Bushehr nuclear reactor. Such an attack could result in a nuclear disaster.

Ezekiel 38 and 39 suggests that Iran's current hatred of Israel won't subside until Persia is soundly defeated for its participation in the Gog of Magog invasion. Something drives Iran to join in the Russian invasion of Israel in the latter years.

Both of these prophecies may occur during the reign of the current Islamic administration. Neither of these prophecies could have occurred historically at the time of King Cyrus of Persia, because he was a friend to Israel. Cyrus did not anger the Lord, nor did he invade Israel. However, Iran's present rogue regime is flirting with disaster because of its anti-Semitic sentiment toward Israel. Unless there is a dramatic change in Iran's foreign policy toward Israel, the prophecies of Jeremiah 49 and Ezekiel 38 and 39 could occur together, or separately in the near future.

Fortunately for a remnant of surviving Iranians, the future will be bright like it was at the time of King Cyrus. In fact, it will be even better than in the past because the King of Kings, Jesus Christ, will be reigning upon the earth during the period of Iran's restoration.

Christ's primary throne will be headquartered in Jerusalem, but perhaps His throne mentioned in Jeremiah 49:38, will serve as His vacation palace. Kings of the past often traveled to a secondary location for some R and R (rest and recovery, or rest and recreation). Perhaps King Jesus will follow suit. If this is the case, then the restored fortunes promised to Iran in Jeremiah 49:39 could turn what is about to become a war zone into a fantastic destination to visit in the millennium.

Chapter 11

Psalm 83 or Ezekiel 38; what's Next?

"Israel Building Fence Along West Bank"

CNN 6/18/02

"Israel Builds Security Wall Along Lebanese Border"

Israel National News 4/30/12

"Israel finishes building border fence with Egypt"

Egypt Independent 4/12/13

"With Golan fence, Israel closer to surrounding itself with barriers"

Washington Post 6/6/13

The news headlines above clearly point out that Israel is not currently dwelling securely today. The tiny Jewish state is protecting its northern, eastern, and southern borders with security fences. Israel's western border is protected by the Mediterranean Sea.

Someday, when Israel does dwell securely, the prophecies described in Ezekiel 38 and 39 will occur. Interestingly, the security fences that Israel has constructed have nothing to do with Ezekiel 38, but everything to do with Psalm 83. In fact, none of the Ezekiel 38 invaders share common borders with Israel.

Ezekiel 38:8-13 mandates that Israel must be dwelling securely, without walls, bars, or gates, and in the center of the land, probably alluding to the Genesis 15:18 land mass. This territory extends from the Nile River in Egypt to the Euphrates River, which courses through parts of Iraq and Syria.

> "On the same day the LORD made a covenant with Abram, saying: "To your descendants I have given this land, from the (*Nile*) river of Egypt to the great river, the River Euphrates." (Gen. 15:18)

This point about Israel dwelling securely is so important that much of the latter part of this chapter is devoted to this topic. Additionally, for Ezekiel 38 to find fulfillment, the Jewish state must be in receipt of great spoil. In my estimation, Israel today is not fulfilling these prerequisite conditions.

Israel is unable to dwell securely as a result of their surrounding Psalm 83 hostile Arab neighbors. Walls, bars, and gates exist in Israel today in order to protect them from being terrorized by certain members of the Psalm 83 confederates, such as Hamas, Hezbollah, and the Palestinians. Additionally, the goal of the Ezekiel 38 invaders is to destroy Israel and take their plunder and great spoils. Israel doesn't presently appear to possess all of the great spoil that Russia and their coalition will someday covet and attempt to confiscate.

Why Psalm 83 is Important to Iran

If you are reading this book cover to cover, you realize that the content primarily pertains to the prophecies of Jeremiah 49 concerning Elam, and Ezekiel 38 regarding Persia. These prophecies directly affect Iran, because ancient Elam and Persia make up modern day Iran.

Conversely, Psalm 83 is a prophecy that only indirectly affects Iran, because Iran is not identified in the Psalm. Iran is adversely affected through the devastating effects that Psalm 83 will have upon its proxies, Hezbollah and Syria, and partial proxies, Iraq and Hamas. These Arab populations are directly involved in Psalm 83.

This chapter invites the reader to compare and contrast the differences between Psalm 83 and Ezekiel 38. Understanding these two distinct prophecies helps to envision why Iran's hatred toward Israel in the end times manifests into hostility. This chapter will also enable the reader to decipher why Psalm 83 seems to precede Ezekiel 38 chronologically.

Psalm 83 can be read in the appendix of this book entitled "The Text of Psalm 83 and Ezekiel 38:1-39:20." The Psalm deals with a climactic, concluding Arab-Israeli war. The Middle East wars between the Arabs and Jews in 1948, 1967 and 1973 have served as a precursor to this final war. The growing consensus among many Bible prophecy experts that believe Psalm 83 is an impending prophecy, is that Egypt, Jordan, Syria, Iraq, Lebanon, Saudi Arabia, the Palestinians, Hamas, Hezbollah and possibly Al Qaeda, confederate one final time to wipe Israel off of the map.

> "They have said, "Come, and let us cut them off from *being* a nation, That the name of Israel may be remembered no more." (Psalm 83:4)

This chapter doesn't devote much time to interpreting all eighteen verses in Psalm 83 because this has been accomplished in my book called "*Psalm 83: The Missing Prophecy Revealed, How Israel Becomes the Next Mideast Superpower.*"

In the end analysis, Israel wins the war as the IDF earns the Jewish state a decisive victory. In the aftermath of an Israeli conquest over the Psalm 83 confederates, the stage seems to become finally set for the fulfillment of Ezekiel 38 and 39. Israel can dwell securely, tear down their security walls, and become increasingly prosperous by capturing some Arab lands and spoils of war. Israel supports a healthy economy presently, but after Psalm 83 the country stands to be even wealthier.

Psalm 83 and Ezekiel 38 are Different Prophecies

Some Bible teachers believe that Psalm 83 and Ezekiel 38 are the same prophecies. This line of thinking ignores several important distinctions.

One important distinction between these prophecies is found in their *differing motives*. Psalm 83:12 declares that the Arab confederates want to destroy Israel in order to take over the Promised Land. Ezekiel 38:12-13 states the Ezekiel invaders will seek to destroy the Jewish state and confiscate plunder and great spoil.

Another significant difference between Psalm 83 and Ezekiel 38 may be understood by identifying the purpose of the exceedingly great army of Ezekiel 37:10. The Ezekiel invaders are destroyed divinely according to Ezekiel 38:18-39:6, but the Psalm 83 Arab confederates appear to be defeated by the Israel Defense Forces, according to Ezekiel 25:14, Obadiah v. 18, and elsewhere. Thus, the two prophecies describe *differing defeats*. Psalm 83 is a war won by the IDF. However, Ezekiel 38 is an invasion that is conquered supernaturally by the Lord. The Magog coalition appears to be too formidable for the IDF, America, or anybody else to stop. Thus, the Lord has to take matters into His own hands.

Interestingly, an exceedingly great army of Israel is mentioned in Ezekiel 37:10. This reference seemingly segues into the Ezekiel 38-39 prophecy. Logically, a reader might assume this army plays an instrumental role in the war of Ezekiel 38 because it's identified in the chapter that precedes it. However, Ezekiel 38:18-39:6 teaches that this army plays little to no part in Ezekiel's invasion. These verses specify that the Lord divinely defeats the Ezekiel invaders. There is no mention of an Israeli army, apart from perhaps playing a role in the burying of the dead soldiers for seven months, and the burning of the enemies' weapons for seven years. (Ezekiel 39:9-16).

The Ezekiel 37:10 army is the subject of an entire chapter in my *Psalm 83* book. This amazing army appears to be the tool empowered by God to defeat the Psalm 83 Arab confederacy. If so, the fact that the army of Ezekiel 37:10 is referenced prior to the Ezekiel 38-39 war passages infers that chronologically Psalm 83 probably precedes Ezekiel 38.

Psalm 83 and Ezekiel 38 clearly involve *different coalitions*. This difference is easily observed. Both prophecies describe coalitions that go to war with Israel. However, these coalitions are entirely different from each other. Although both confederacies consist of primarily Muslim nations, no Ezekiel invaders are listed in Psalm 83 and vice versa.

These two images below display the differences between the Psalm 83 confederacy and the Ezekiel 38 coalition. Psalm 83 comprises an inner circle that surrounds modern day Israel. The circle shape represents this inner circle. The ancient names in Psalm 83:6-8 are superimposed over their modern day equivalents. The lower image evidences that the Ezekiel 38 coalition forms an outer ring of nations that surround the Psalm 83 inner circle.

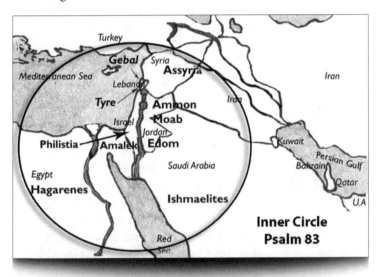

Pictures provided by Lani Harmony at *http://www.laniharmony.com*

Lastly, the wars are fought on *different battlefields*. The Ezekiel invaders charge from the north according to Ezekiel 38:15, 39:2. The Psalm 83 confederates have Israel surrounded and seemingly attack from all sides.

Ezekiel 38 Has Preconditions Still Outstanding

The fact that Israel today does not currently meet all of the requirements identified in Ezekiel 38:8-13, means that Ezekiel 38 still has preconditions that have not been fulfilled as of yet. A Bible prophecy cannot be considered imminent until all the prophetic prerequisites are met. The verses below put forth the predicted events of Ezekiel's prophecy. The details describe an Israel that only partially exists presently.

"After many days you will be visited. In the *latter years* you will come into the land of *those brought back from the sword* and gathered from many people on the mountains of Israel, which had *long been desolate*; they were brought out of the nations, and now all of them *dwell safely*. You will ascend, coming like a storm, covering the land like a cloud, you and all your troops and many peoples with you." Thus says the Lord GOD: "On that day it shall come to pass that thoughts will arise in your mind, and you will make an evil plan: You will say, 'I will go up against a land of *unwalled villages*; I will go to a peaceful people, who *dwell safely*, all of them dwelling *without walls*, and *having neither bars nor gates'*—to take plunder and to take booty, to stretch out your hand against the waste places that are again inhabited, and against a people gathered from the nations, who have acquired livestock and goods, *who dwell in the midst* of the land. Sheba, Dedan, the merchants of Tarshish, and all their young lions will say to you, 'Have you come to take plunder? Have you gathered your army to take booty, to carry away silver and gold, to take away livestock and goods, to take great plunder?" (Ezekiel 38:8-13; *emphasis added*).

These Ezekiel passages specify the following:

- Israelis must be regathered from the nations in the latter years into a re-established sovereign Jewish state.
- Jews will be brought back from the sword, to dwell in the midst (center) of the land, which had long been desolate.
- Israelis must be a peaceful people dwelling securely at the time.
- Israel's security is characterized by the absence of walls, bars and gates.
- The nation possesses an abundance of gold and silver and has acquired livestock (agricultural) and (commercial) goods.
- The Jewish state needs to possess a great bounty of plunder and booty.

These Ezekiel passages begin by stating that the Jews will be regathered from the nations of the world to the "mountains of Israel." This does not imply that all Jews will migrate into the mountainous areas of Israel; rather, it alludes to the Jewish people forming a sovereign state. Although the Bible often refers to mountains in a literal, geographical sense, it may also allude to the leadership or government of a nation in the typological sense. In this instance, the inference is an independent Jewish entity over which a sovereign government presides.[83] Since this government is associated with "the mountains of Israel," we can safely surmise that the location of this restored sovereign Jewish state is Israel.

Moreover, the Jews are coming out from persecution into a desolate land. This was the case after the persecution of the holocaust. The Jews returned after experiencing a genocidal attempt by the Nazis into a land that had been predominantly desolate for centuries. Mark Twain visited Israel in 1867, and published his impressions in *Innocents Abroad*. He described a desolate country – devoid of both vegetation and human population:

> *"A desolate country whose soil is rich enough, but is given over wholly to weeds… a silent mournful expanse…a desolation… we never saw a human being on the whole route…hardly a tree or shrub anywhere. Even the olive tree and the cactus, those fast friends of a worthless soil, had almost deserted the country."*[84]

Furthermore, the prophet depicts the Israelis dwelling in a condition of security. Ezekiel declares that the Israelis are "a peaceful people who dwell safely (yashab betach), all of them dwelling without walls."

This means that as a nation they "all" "dwell safely." He uses the Hebrew words Yashab Betach three times in Ezekiel 38:8, 11, and 14 to highlight this point.[85] Deuteronomy 12:10, 1 Samuel 12:11 and Ezekiel 28:26 use these Hebrew words in tandem to identify the sovereign State of Israel dwelling in a condition of military security.[86] This biblical precedence points out that it is a safety which is achieved militarily, because the defeated enemies no longer pose a threat to Israel. Ezekiel's description of a nation dwelling without walls, bars, nor gates, also emphasizes a genuine condition of national security.

Throughout time, humans constructed fortified walls to prevent enemy intrusions and to enforce separation between two diverse population groups. The Chinese built the Great Wall around 200 BC to protect China's northern borders from intruders. Hadrian's Wall, constructed in 122 AD, was a defensive fortification located in Roman Britain during the rule of Emperor Hadrian. The Germans erected the Berlin wall in 1961 in order to separate the Communistic political system of the East from the capitalism spreading in the West.

Likewise, Israel has today constructed its own fortified walls intended to prevent the terrorist element of the Palestinian population from intruding into Israel proper. The main wall, called the Separation Wall, serves as Israel's barrier from the West Bank. This wall reaches up to twenty-five feet in some places and spans approximately 403 miles. As such, Israel today is not "a nation dwelling without walls" as described in Ezekiel 38:11.

Note that Ezekiel references "a people gathered from the nations, who have acquired livestock and goods." Israel acquires livestock, representing agricultural wealth, and goods, representing commercial wealth. This condition of restored fortune will resemble the period of Israel's history around 1000 BC, when King Solomon reigned over the nation.[87] As was the case then, Israel should become one of the wealthiest—if not the wealthiest—of the world's nations.

In his next verse, Ezekiel informs us that Israel's restored fortune is what the Russian-Iranian led coalition aspires to attain. Sheba and Dedan, which likely represent the modern nations of Yemen and Saudi Arabia, along with other merchant and military populations, question the coalition's motivation and in so doing, enlighten us as to its true intention. The Russian-Iranian coalition targets the livestock, goods, and other "great plunder" acquired by Israel.

> "Sheba, Dedan, the merchants of Tarshish, and all their young lions will say to you, "Have you come to take plunder? Have you gathered your army to take booty, to carry away silver and gold, to take away livestock and goods, to take great plunder?"" (Ezek. 38:13).

The Bible appears to suggest that the nation of Israel accomplishes these "prerequisite" conditions, at least in part, via a military solution. The Israeli Defense Forces will become engaged in a serious regional conflict. In victory, they will become primed for the future events of the Russian-Iranian coalition destined to form against them. Turning back a few pages from the Ezekiel passages quoted above to Ezekiel Chapter 28, we discover that God will come to the defense of Israel. These passages inform us when Israel will dwell securely.

> "And there shall no longer be a pricking brier or a painful thorn for the house of Israel from among all who are around them, who despise them. Then they shall know that I am the LORD GOD. Thus says the LORD GOD: "When I have gathered the house of Israel from the peoples among whom they are scattered, and am hallowed in them in the sight of the Gentiles, then they will dwell in their own land which I gave to My servant Jacob. And they will *dwell safely* there, build houses, and plant vineyards; yes, they will *dwell securely*, when I execute judgments on all those around them who despise them. Then they shall know that I am the LORD their God." (Ezek. 28:24–26; *emphasis added*)

Simply paraphrased: "Yes, they will dwell securely (yashab betach), when I (God) execute judgments on all those (Arab nations) around them who despise them." Ezekiel reminds us that the national security Israel so desperately seeks today occurs via the judgments executed "on all those around them who despise them."

Surprisingly, "all those (Arab nations) around them who despise" the emerging Jewish State of Israel, are conspicuously absent from the Gog of Magog coalition. Unlike the Psalm 83 Arab states, not one of the Ezekiel invaders shares common borders with Israel. Why not? This particular question has longed baffled many prophecy buffs, because the Arab nations surrounding the Jewish state are Israel's most observable enemies, and they clearly represent "all those around them who despise them."

The adversaries of Israel, identified in Psalm 83, will seek to cut the Jews off from being a nation by forming their own coalition. Unfortunately for them, their fate is described in Ezekiel 28:24–26 as "all those around them who despise them." They are those upon whom God will execute devastating judgments prior to the formation of the Russian-Iranian coalition. But how will these judgments be executed? The answer to this question is one of the central themes of my *Psalm 83, Missing Prophecy Revealed* book. The IDF will become an "exceedingly great army," and defeat the surrounding enemies of Israel that despise the Jewish state!

We can safely presume that the execution of the judgments upon the surrounding Psalm 83 nations, those countries that despise Israel, will occur before the Gog of Magog coalition forms. We deduce this by recollecting that the Russian-Iranian led coalition will attempt to invade a militarily secure Israel. This condition of security becomes a reality subsequent to the judgments executed upon the surrounding Psalm 83 nations.

Some people believe the secure Israel that the Ezekiel invaders attack results when the Antichrist confirms the seven-year peace treaty with Israel in Daniel 9:26-27. Although Israel will temporarily become secure at that time, this is probably a subsequent period of national security for the Jewish state. This is because the seven-year treaty begins the seven years of tribulation, i.e. Daniel's Seventieth Week," and the Gog of Magog invasion seemingly precedes this period. I qualify this statement in the chapter called, "Is the Ancient Prophecy of Elam a Pre-Tribulation Event?"

Additionally, the Israel that becomes a peaceful country dwelling securely in Ezekiel 38:8, 11, 14, seems to obtain this peace and safety in the strict interpretation of the Hebrew words "yashab betach." The Tandem biblical uses of these words in Deuteronomy 12:10, 1 Samuel 12:11, and Ezekiel 28:26 describe a condition of national security that is obtained militarily, rather than politically.

Because of the judgments executed upon the Arabs who despise Israel, the Jewish state will attain the autonomy required to set the stage for the Ezekiel 38 invasion. The world will be forced to internationally esteem Israel as the sovereign Jewish State, and the Arab-Israeli conflict we witness today, will finally be resolved. As such, Israel will be a nation of peace achieved via their military might. It is the "exceedingly great army" of Israel foretold in Ezekiel 37:10 that is the instrumental tool utilized in the execution of the judgments against the surrounding Arab nations. In the aftermath of their IDF victory, the Jewish State will probably seize some conquered Arab territory, and exploit vast amounts of the Arab spoils of war. Israel could then resemble the Israel described in Ezekiel 38:8-13.

Before further developing the theme of the Israeli conquest "on those around them who despise them," let us first appreciate the reason for the restoration of the nation Israel as the Jewish state, which occurred May 14, 1948. Many people, including numerous Christians that subscribe to "Replacement Theology, believe the existence of Israel is the result of a UN moral obligation to the Jews after the horrendous holocaust event. However, Israel's existence is a miraculous fulfillment of several Bible prophecies. One of the evidences of this is the Ezekiel 38 prophecy. The Lord intends to use this most massive Mideast invasion of all time, to uphold His holy name through Israel and the Israelis, so that mankind will recognize that He is the Holy One in Israel. We are told this in the verses below.

> "So I [God] will make My holy name known in the midst of
> My people Israel, and I will not let them profane My holy
> name anymore. Then the nations shall know that I am the

LORD, the Holy One in Israel. Surely it is coming, and it shall be done," says the LORD GOD. "This is the day of which I have spoken." (Ezek. 39:7–8; *emphasis added*)

With the exclusive divine help of their God Jehovah, the Jews defeat the Gog of Magog coalition during the events described in Ezekiel 38:18-39:6. Then in Ezekiel 39:7, we see that through these events, God makes His "holy name" known to all the rest of the world nations. Similarly, in Ezekiel 36:22–24, we learn that the Restoration of the Nation Israel as the Jewish State serves the same greater purpose.

"Therefore say to the house of Israel, "Thus says the LORD GOD: 'I do not do this for your sake, O house of Israel, but for My holy name's sake, which you have profaned among the nations wherever you went. And I will sanctify My great name, which has been profaned among the nations, which you have profaned in their midst; and the nations shall know that I am the LORD,' says the LORD GOD, 'when I am hallowed in you before their eyes. For I will take you from among the nations, gather you out of all countries, and bring you into your own land.'" (Ezek. 36:22–24; *emphasis added*)

Furthermore, it is noteworthy that God intends to be "hallowed" by the Jewish people in the sight of the international community. The Hebrew word for "hallowed" is qadash, and it is the same word utilized in Ezekiel 36:23 and Ezekiel 28:25, concerning Israel's enemies that despise them. In both instances, it emphatically highlights the restoration of the sovereign Jewish state of Israel as an epic and holy event.

Miraculously, in modern history, the call of Zionism has tugged adamantly upon the hearts of the Jewish people, who for centuries lived dispersed throughout the nations of the world. Israel became a nation in 1948, and the Jewish people have responded to the Zionistic inclination implanted within them, both individually and corporately. Many of them have answered the sacred call, and have migrated back into the land that 1,878 years prior had bid them a hostile farewell.

Yes, the Jews have returned and "all those (predominantly Arabs) around them who despise them" have attempted to prevent the prescribed process. Therefore, I invite you to reread Ezekiel 28:24–26 with this hallowed understanding.

What we can glean from all of this is that God is presently preparing to make His Holy Name known throughout the nations of the world. He is gathering the Jewish people and forming them into an exceedingly great army. The execution of judgments on many Arabs will be a humbling and hallowing event in the world's future history. Gentiles will be provided with ample reasons to consider the biblical significance of the Jews, the nation of Israel, and most importantly, the holy name of their God Jehovah.

The Ezekiel invasion required the existence of the "Chosen People", and their possession of the "Promised Land." These are both critical components of the unconditional Abrahamic Covenant. When the Lord divinely defeats the Gog of Magog invasion, He can whole-heartedly declare that He is the covenant-making, promise-keeping LORD; the Holy One in Israel!

What the world is currently witnessing in the theater of the Middle East is the stage being set for the marquee event, whereby the holy name of God features prominently before the international audience. The Arab-Israeli conflict, the Arab Spring, the Syrian revolution, the civil strife in Egypt, the Iranian nuclear concerns, Russian aggressions against its neighbors, Turkey's newfound disdain toward Israel, and many other events are but the opening acts in God's grand show.

Due to the strengthening relationship between Russia and Iran, prophetic scholars are rightfully discerning the world's nearness to the fulfillment of the events described in Ezekiel 38 and 39. They will indeed occur soon, however, not necessarily next. Prior to this, the nation of Israel must display sovereignty, peace, security, and fortune. "All those around them who despise them" presently oppose these four conditions.

The LORD will soon execute judgments upon these enemies! These judgments will be fashioned in the manner prescribed by God, who is presently poised to sanctify His Holy Name. Approximately four thousand years ago, God spelled out His international foreign policy through Abraham, as contained in Genesis 12:3.19. He promises blessings to those who bless the Jewish descendants of Abraham, and curses those who curse them.

The same recipe for Jewish disaster that the surrounding Arab nations concoct will be redirected against them in like fashion. This punishment will highlight the curse-for-curse-in-kind component of the Abrahamic Covenant.[88] According to Psalm 83, the Arab Kingdom will come against the Jewish Kingdom in an apparent fulfillment of the prophecy of Jesus Christ.

> "For nation will rise against nation, and [Arab] kingdom against [Jewish] kingdom. And there will be famines, pestilences, and Earthquakes in various places. All these are the beginning of sorrows." (Matthew 24:7–8; *emphasis added*)

In World War I and World War II, nation rose against nation. This set the stage for the restoration of the nation Israel and the reestablishment of the Jewish Kingdom. The Arab nations bordering Israel have proven their dissatisfaction with the re-emergence of the Jewish Kingdom in their area of the world. They will ultimately confederate in the fulfillment of Psalm 83, and in that unified condition, will represent the sentiment of the broader Arab Kingdom. They [the Arab Kingdom] have said, "Come, and let us cut them off from being a nation, That the name of Israel [the Jewish Kingdom] may be remembered no more." (Psa. 83:4)

When the Jewish Kingdom prevails militarily over the Arab Kingdom, the fulfillment of Ezekiel 28:24–26 will occur, as God executes the "judgments on all those around them who despise them." The deliverance of these devastating judgments via the mighty means of the Jewish Kingdom will display that the divine foreign policy contained in the ancient decree of the Abrahamic Covenant is still effectually intact. The Abrahamic Covenant will, at that time, nullify all incompatible international foreign policy relating to the Arab- Israeli conflict.

After digesting this information, the reader might consider that there is indeed a God, and that His name is holy. Enormous events on a David-and-Goliath scale continue to unfold in the

Middle East and directly affect our daily lives. Terrorism, primarily born from Middle East mayhem, has extended its ugly embrace around our lives. Try carrying a tube of toothpaste onto an airplane. It has become a major ordeal as tight airport security has become unavoidable. Who among us would have foreseen that a basic element of personal hygiene would become an advanced tactical weapon in the arsenal of terrorism?

Now is the perfect time to consider the significance of the reestablishment of Israel, Jesus Christ (the Messiah and the Son of God), and the holy name of God, our Heavenly Father. Let us continue to delve into the Bible to discover more about the days in which we live. Let us be active participants in keeping His book in its rightful position at the top of the best-seller list.

Summary

In conclusion, the fulfillment of a Bible prophecy mandates that the predictive details line up entirely and exactly with the actual event when it occurs. There can be no overlooking even the slightest detail given. The growing tendency among eschatologists to recognize that current Mideast events are stage setting for the coming Psalm 83 and Ezekiel 38 wars is to be commended. However, newspaper exegesis can often cause us to overlook significant prophetic details, and should be avoided.

Perhaps Ezekiel 38 will come soon and precede Psalm 83, but it is doubtful. There are ten distinct members listed in Psalm 83 that are not listed in Ezekiel 38. These ten represent Israel's most observable modern-day enemies since becoming a nation in 1948. For the plethora of reasons explained in this chapter, I don't believe Ezekiel 38 is an imminent event. However, I do believe Psalm 83 could be the next prophetic Mideast news headline.

Why does Russia assemble together a large coalition to invade Israel? By comparison, it would be like America enlisting Canada and Mexico to attack New Jersey. New Jersey and Israel are about the same size territorially. One possible answer is that Russia needs reinforcements to conquer Israel after it shocks the world by defeating its Arab neighbors of Psalm 83.

Iran's current disdain toward Israel will reach a fever pitch when Hezbollah, Syria, Hamas and Iraq are conquered by the IDF in fulfillment of Psalm 83. Iran is deeply invested militarily, economically and politically in these four proxies. In the aftermath of Psalm 83, Iran should be easily persuaded to join Russia's Ezekiel 38 coalition. Iran's willingness to enlist will be greatly intensified if Jeremiah's prophecies concerning Elam happen before, during or after Psalm 83.

Pray for the Iranians that want no part of the current Islamic regime. Many of them are too impoverished to depart from the Islamic repression dominating their country. With the coming of Psalm 83, Jeremiah 49 and Ezekiel 38, many of these Iranians will be adversely affected and possibly killed. In my estimation, this is why Jesus Christ is presently reaching out to many Iranians through healings, dreams, visions, appearances and miracles in this final hour. The Lord wishes that none would perish, but that all would have everlasting life and that includes the Iranians.

Chapter 12

Overview of the Ezekiel 38-39 Prophecy

"Putin to fulfill Bible prophecy with Ukraine actions"
Examiner.com 3/4/14

"Superpower Russia: We're Back!"
Newsmax 3/4/14

This chapter presents a basic overview of certain parts of Ezekiel 38-39, and is intended to compliment the previous chapter called "Psalm 83 or Ezekiel 38; what's Next?" The entire biblical text of Ezekiel 38-39 can be read in the appendix called, "The Text of Psalm 83 and Ezekiel 38:1-39:20."

The general consensus among many Bible prophecy teachers is that the invaders listed in Ezekiel 38:1-5 include:

- Russia and some of the countries in the Southern Steppes (Magog and Rosh),
- Turkey (Meshech, Tubal, Togarmah and Gomer),
- Iran (Persia),
- Libya, Tunisia, Algeria, Morocco (Put, or Phut),
- Ethiopia, Sudan, Somalia (Cush, or Kush),
- Germany (Some suggest Gomer represents Germany rather than Turkey).

A cruel leader presides over Russia at the time that Ezekiel 38 occurs. In light of Russia's apparent bid to re-emerge as a superpower, some speculate that this ruthless ruler could be Russian President

Vladimir Putin. Whoever he is, we are informed in Ezekiel 38:10 that he devises a maniacal plan against Israel.

> 'Thus says the Lord GOD: "On that day it shall come to pass *that* thoughts will arise in your mind, and you will make an evil plan." (Ezek. 38:10)

The Russian leader's "evil plan" is to assemble a formidable strategic coalition in order to invade Israel for the sake of material gain.

> "You will say, 'I will go up against a land of unwalled villages; I will go to a peaceful people, who dwell safely, all of them dwelling without walls, and having neither bars nor gates'—¹²to take plunder and to take booty, to stretch out your hand against the waste places *that are again* inhabited, and against a people gathered from the nations, who have acquired livestock and goods, who dwell in the midst of the land. ¹³Sheba, Dedan, the merchants of Tarshish, and all their young lions will say to you, 'Have you come to take plunder? Have you gathered your army to take booty, to carry away silver and gold, to take away livestock and goods, to take great plunder?'"(Ezek. 38:11-13)

I point out the tactical aspect of his sinister plan in the chapter entitled "Russia Forms an Evil Plan to Invade Israel," in my book called *Revelation Road, Hope Beyond the Horizon*.

The *Revelation Road* chapter posits the possibility that the Magog coalition is strategically assembled by Russia. Certain countries probably coalesce for one or more of the following reasons.

- *Predominantly Muslim Nations opposed to Israel* -Apart from Russia, the other countries are predominantly Muslim. They are already spiritually united through their common faith. Although schisms exist between Sunni and Shia nations, they all share a common hatred of Israel. Most of the Ezekiel invaders including Iran, Libya, Tunisia, Algeria, Morocco, Sudan and Somalia, currently refuse to recognize Israel as the Jewish state.[89] Turkey recognizes Israel, but relations between the two countries have dramatically deteriorated since 2010.

- *Angry with Israel after Psalm 83* - Presently, these Islamic nations are not fond of Israel. Their disdain toward Israel will increase after the IDF conquers the Muslim confederacy described in Psalm 83.

- *Important Mideast Water Arteries*- The Ezekiel invaders all border the available waterways that Israel will need to export its commerce into world markets. This alignment of nations can blockade these important water arteries. Turkey, Libya, Tunisia and Algeria surround the Mediterranean Sea. Iran can blockade the Persian Gulf. Ethiopia and Somalia can hinder shipments passing through the Red Sea.

For those of you not familiar with the official Old Testament identity of this Russian leader, he is referenced early on in Ezekiel's prophecy.

> "Now the word of the LORD came to me, saying, "Son of man, set your face against Gog, of the land of Magog, the prince of Rosh, Meshech, and Tubal, and prophesy against him, and say, 'Thus says the Lord GOD: "Behold, I am against you, O Gog, the prince of Rosh, Meshech, and Tubal.""" (Ezekiel 38:1-3)

Gog is the lead figure who hails from the land of Magog. Some scholars debate whether or not Gog is an individual or a location within the greater territory of Magog. However, Ezekiel calls Gog a prince and uses the pronoun "he" to identify him. The opinion among some scholars, which I favor, is that Gog represents a title of an individual, rather than a specific name or place. Gog would be likened to a Caesar from ancient Rome, or a Czar from the former Imperial Russia, or a Kaiser from Germany, prior to the Nazi era.

The connection between Magog and Russia runs partially through the Scythians. This association was made centuries ago, by the secular Jewish historian Josephus. He called them an "invading horde from the north."[90] During Ezekiel's time, Magog existed in the proximity of where Russia is today. Wikipedia states, "In the 17th and 18th centuries, foreigners regarded the Russians as descendants of Scythians. It became conventional to refer to Russians as Scythians in 18th century poetry."[91]

Because the name Russia only dates back to around the eleventh century AD, it makes the Magog-to-Russia connection a bit difficult. Most scholars point out that Ezekiel 38:15 declares that Gog personally comes out from the far north, which directionally from Israel is the location of Russia. Many scholars, including Dr. Arnold Fruchtenbaum, Chuck Missler, Dr. Ron Rhodes, Dr. David Hocking, Dr. David Reagan, and Joel Rosenberg, subscribe to Russia being identified as Magog by Ezekiel. In his book, *Northern Storm Rising*, author Dr. Ron Rhodes, presents other good reasons to recognize the connection between Magog and Russia.

Regarding Iran's involvement in the Ezekiel (or Gog of Magog) invasion, refer to Ezekiel 38:5, where Persia is listed. The Iranian-Persian connection is easily made, considering Persia was renamed Iran in 1935 AD.

For an exhaustive look at Ezekiel 38-39, I have footnoted my recommended readings on the subject.[92] Below is a nutshell outline of the Ezekiel 38-39 prophecies.

Ezekiel 38 and 39 Basic Commentary

Ezekiel 38:1-7 lists the nine-member coalition of Gog's hordes, consisting of armies from Magog, Rosh, Meshech, Tubal, Persia, Ethiopia (Cush), Libya (Put), Gomer, and Togarmah.

Ezekiel 38:8-10 appropriates the general timing and battlefield location of the invasion. The prophecy occurs in the latter years, upon the land of Israel. Prerequisites of the invasion require that the nation of Israel be reestablished, that the worldwide re-gathering of the Jews be underway, and that the Israelis live in a condition of national security.

It is safe to assume that the first two requirements have been met. Israel was restored as the Jewish State on May 14, 1948, and Jews have been returning steadily ever since. However, the last prerequisite does not presently exist, in my estimation. Israelis are not dwelling safely in their homeland. They live under constant threat by multiple surrounding enemies. This point was previously presented in the chapter called, "Psalm 83 or Ezekiel 38; what's Next?"

Ezekiel 38:11-13 informs us that Russia's leader prepares an evil plan to invade Israel and capture great plunder. The plunder consists of agricultural and commercial goods, as well as gold and silver. At least four more populations are introduced into the prophecy, apparently as protestors. These are Sheba (Yemen), Dedan (Saudi Arabia), the Merchants of Tarshish (Britain or Spain, or both), and all their Young Lions (United States of America, and / or Central and South America). I explain why I believe the Young Lions of Tarshish probably represents the U.S.A. in my *Psalm 83, Missing Prophecy Revealed* book, in the chapter entitled, "America and the Coming Mideast Wars."

Ezekiel 38:14 through 39:6 informs us the attackers will be many, and they come against Israel primarily from the north. We are reminded the event finds fulfillment in the "latter days," and that the Lord warned of the event well in advance. Moreover, these verses confirm that the invaders are destroyed by the Lord, through an Old Testament type of fire and brimstone battle. This is important to note, because it reminds us that the Israel Defense Forces (IDF) of today are apparently not a dominant factor in this battle.

Ezekiel 39:7-8 provides the Lord's purpose for personally defeating this massive Mideast invasion.

> "So I will make My holy name known in the midst of My people Israel, and I will not let them profane My holy name anymore. Then the nations shall know that I am the LORD, the Holy One in Israel. Surely it is coming, and it shall be done," says the Lord GOD. "This is the day of which I have spoken." (Ezekiel 39:7-9)

It is vital to recognize the significance of what the prophet Ezekiel declares in these verses. They represent the summation of the divine purpose surrounding this prophetic event. He is emphasizing that the God of His people, the Jews, is upholding His Holy Name in the end times through the nation of Israel.

This beckons the question: "Where are God's people of today, *i.e.* the Church, when Ezekiel 38 occurs?" In the Ezekiel 38 prophecy, the Jews are identified three times as the people of God. I briefly discuss below the significance of the Lord calling the Jews, "My people Israel." In my *Psalm 83, The Missing Prophecy Revealed* book, I devote an entire chapter to this important subject.

Perhaps even more imperative, Ezekiel 39:7 notifies the world that the God of the Jews is a promise keeper. The Magog invaders seek to annihilate the race that the Lord appointed virtually impossible to eradicate. Genocidal attempts of the Jews are all doomed to failure unless they meet the stringent requirements specified in Jeremiah 31:35-37.

> "Thus says the LORD, Who gives the sun for a light by day, The ordinances of the moon and the stars for a light by night, Who disturbs the sea, And its waves roar(The LORD of hosts *is* His name): "If those ordinances depart From before Me, says the LORD, *Then* the seed of Israel shall also cease From being a nation before Me forever." Thus says the LORD: "If heaven above can be measured, And the foundations of the earth searched out beneath, I will also cast off all the seed of Israel For all that they have done, says the LORD." (Jer. 31:35-37)

My People Israel

It is also important to note that Ezekiel alludes to the Jewish people as "*My people Israel*," three times in Ezekiel 38 and 39. The first two uses are below.

> "Therefore, son of man, prophesy and say to Gog, 'Thus says the Lord GOD: "On that day when *My people Israel*

dwell safely, will you not know *it?* Then you will come from your place out of the far north, you and many peoples with you, all of them riding on horses, a great company and a mighty army. You will come up against *My people Israel* like a cloud, to cover the land." (Ezekiel 38:14-16; *emphasis added*).

These verses address the Jewish people and their homeland of Israel. The Israelis, (the Chosen People), will be dwelling in safety in the land of Israel, (their Promised Land), when Russia invades. The Chosen People and the Promised Land are integral components of the unconditional Abrahamic Covenant. Abraham was promised to father a great nation in Genesis 12:2. A great nation requires both a (promised) land for the people, and a (chosen) people for that land.

The parameters of the Promised Land are described in Genesis 15:18, Joshua 1:4 and Ezekiel 47:13-21. The promises to provide a Chosen People are located in Genesis 15:13, Exodus 32:13 and 2 Chronicles 20:7.

World War I prepared the Promised Land for the Chosen People, and World War II prepared the Chosen People for the Promised Land. With the collapse of the Ottoman Empire after World War I, the four hundred year reign of the Turks from 1517-1917 over the Middle East ended. This prepared the way for the Promised Land to be made available to the Jews scattered worldwide.

World War II was characterized by the genocidal attempt of the Jews by the Nazis. In fulfillment of another Ezekiel prophecy, the Jews found themselves residing in a desperate, helpless and hopeless holocaust condition. Ezekiel predicted that when this condition occurred, the regathering of the Jews back into Israel would follow.

"Then He said to me, "Son of man, these bones are the whole house of Israel. They indeed say, '*Our bones are dry, our hope is lost, and we ourselves are cut off!*' Therefore prophesy and say to them, 'Thus says the Lord GOD: "Behold, O My people, I will open your graves and cause you to come up from your graves, and bring you into the land of Israel." (Ezekiel 37:11-12; *emphasis added*)

The Turks attempted to steal the Promised Land, and the Nazis attempted to kill the Chosen People. Both attempts failed because the God of Abraham, Isaac and Jacob promised these patriarchs that they would possess this land and be the father of descendants forever. In addition, the Arabs of Psalm 83 will have attempted to destroy the Jews and confiscate the Promised Land prior to the fulfillment of Ezekiel 38. That too will fail.

This is why the third use of *My people Israel* in Ezekiel 39:7, already quoted, proves that the God of the Bible is a covenant keeping God. In the aftermath of Ezekiel 38 and 39, it will be undeniable that the Holy name of the Lord will have been upheld in the midst of the Chosen People, (Israelis), and their Promised Land of Israel.

Thus, the need for the Church to be on earth to witness the fulfillment of Ezekiel 38 and 39 is not necessary. The Christian Church may be here for the epic event, but there is a strong possibility that the true Christian believers could be caught up into the clouds in the Rapture event prior.

Ezekiel 39:9-10 clues us in to the types of weaponry the invaders possess. Israel will be able to convert the enemy weapons into fuel for at least seven years. The picture is of energy provision for the entire nation, rather than a few isolated households. Verse 9 says, "those who dwell in the cities," utilize this converted weapons-grade fuel. The widespread use and lengthy seven year span suggests that the weapons must be far more sophisticated than wooden bows and arrows, which would undoubtedly only last a short while. I mention this because some expositors today limit the weapons to wooden ones. I doubt nuclear non-proliferation will reduce Russian arsenals to wood between now and then.

There may actually be more than seven years' worth of fuel provided by these weapons, but the possibility looms large that the events occurring at the mid-point of the tribulation period interrupts the continued usage of the weapons. At this critical mid-trib point on the end-time's timeline, three-and-one-half years into the tribulation period, Israelis come under genocidal attack by the Antichrist. Thus, they are preoccupied with survival and probably not weapons conversion. As my editor and friend Gary Gaskin says; *"If I was under genocidal attack, I would be picking up a weapon to use it, rather than to burn it."* It is entirely possible that there could be eight-plus years of weapons fuel, but as a result of the maniacal campaign of the Antichrist, no Jews will be taking the time to harness the additional energy.

I don't believe that Gog of Magog and the Antichrist are the same individuals, nor do I believe their end times attempts to harm the Jews are motivated by the same reasons. Gog wants to possess Israel's great booty, but the Antichrist wants to destroy the Jews to prove that God's covenant making character is flawed. This is one of several reasons that the Antichrist seeks the genocide of the Jews. Another reason is to prevent Jesus Christ from returning to reign upon the earth.

According to Matthew chapter twenty three, Jesus will not return to Jerusalem until the leadership of Israel recognizes that He is their Jewish Messiah. If there are no Jews on earth, then there can be no formal recognition by Israelis of Jesus as the Messiah.

> ""O Jerusalem, Jerusalem, the one who kills the prophets and stones those who are sent to her! How often I wanted to gather your children together, as a hen gathers her chicks under *her* wings, but you were not willing! See! Your house (Second Jewish Temple) is left to you desolate; For I say to you, you shall see Me no more till you say, *'Blessed is He who comes in the name of the* LORD!*'""*
> (Matthew 23:37-39)

These missiles and rockets that are being converted to fuel in Ezekiel 39:9-10 probably include the ABCs of weaponry—atomic, biological, and chemical. We can presume this because these types of weapons already exist inside the arsenals of Russia and some of their cohorts. Additionally, the dead soldiers appear to require Hazmat (Hazardous Materials) teams to assist with their burial according to Ezekiel 39:14-16. The fascinating fact is that whatever the weapons configuration, Israel will possess the technological know-how to convert them into national energy. Today, whether it is cell phones or irrigation techniques, Israel is on the cutting-edge of technological advances.

In fact, Israel today is rapidly becoming a global economic powerhouse. It is an amazing phenomenon, a miracle in my estimation, that amidst the backdrop of a global economic catastrophe, Israel's economy is burgeoning almost exponentially. Below is a quote from my friend, the Israeli diplomat Yoram Ettinger.

> "*The London Financial Times reported: "in six hours of [Prime Minister Netanyahu's] talks with the Chinese leadership, they spent roughly ten seconds on the Palestinian issue, while revealing an unquenchable thirst for Israeli technology." Highlighting Israel's intensified and diversified global integration, the China-Israel 2013 trade balance exceeded $10BN, providing a tailwind to the currently negotiated free trade agreement, and enhanced by Chinese investments in some fifty Israeli high tech companies. The Japan Times reported the growing Japanese interest in Israeli business opportunities, tripling the number of reviews of Israeli companies.*
>
> *Moreover, foreign investments in Israel catapulted in 2013, achieving a seven- year high of $12BN, including $4BN in acquisition of Israeli companies by global giants such as Google, IBM, Cisco, AOL, Facebook, Apple and EMC. Furthermore, since January 2014, Israeli companies have raised over $500MN on Wall Street. Deloitte Touche – one of the top CPA firms in the world – crowned Israel as the fourth most attractive site for foreign investors, trailing only the USA, China and Brazil. According to the British Economist Intelligence Unit, "Israel's cluster of high tech companies, investors and incubators is enjoying a boom which has not been witnessed since the global tech bubble burst more than a decade ago." Neither Kazakhstan's billionaire Kenges Rakishev, nor Mexico's billionaire,*

Carlos Slim allowed the "Isolation Warning/Threat" to stop their flow of investments in Israel's high tech sector."

In fact, Israel, the Startup Nation, has become a critical Pipeline Nation that transfers to the American high tech industry a plethora of cutting edge technologies and applications, developed by Israel's brain power. This provides some 200 US high tech giants an edge over their global competitors, thereby contributing to US employment, research, development and exports. As stated by Microsoft's new CEO, Satya Nadella, "The two Microsoft research and development centers in Israel constitute a strategic factor, enhancing Microsoft's capabilities in many areas." This was echoed by Google's Chairman, Eric Schmidt, who also invests in Israel through his private venture capital fund, Innovation Endeavors: "Israel will have an oversized impact on the evolution of the next stage of technology. Israel has become a high tech hub. Israel is the most important high tech center in the world after the US." [93]

Ezekiel 39:11-16 describes the location of the mass burial grounds of the destroyed armies of Gog. A valley east of what is probably the Dead Sea is renamed the Valley of Hamon Gog, which means the "hordes or multitudes" of Gog, in Hebrew. Why I believe it refers to a valley in modern-day Jordan is explained in the chapter called, "Greater Israel," of my *Psalm 83, The Missing Prophecy Revealed* book.

We also find in Ezekiel 39:11-16 that the Israelis will be burying the dead in order to cleanse the land. This could imply two things. *One*, that the hordes of Gog's dead soldiers are contaminated, which would require a professional quarantined burial. This contamination could come from either the fallout from their atomic, biological and / or chemical weapons, or the deteriorating corpses strewn across the battlefield. *Two*, the Jews are adhering to their ancient Levitical Law according to Numbers 19:11-22 and Deuteronomy 21:1-9. These verses set forth specifications about the appropriate handling of dead bodies lying on the land of Israel.

Ezekiel 39:17-20 is an invitation "to every sort of bird and to every beast of the field" to partake of the sacrificial meal of the "flesh" and "blood" of the invaders. This passage is not for the faint of heart. I remember hearing prophecy expert Joel Rosenberg, teach this topic at a Calvary Chapel Chino Hills prophecy conference, and he brought tears streaming down from my eyes. Additionally foretold, the creatures are instructed, "to drink the blood" of the defeated "princes." This might imply that not only the Magog infantry, but their governments, are destroyed.

Ezekiel 39:21-29 concludes the chapter with a recap of some Jewish history and a promise to the faithful remnant of Israel that the Lord will pour out His spirit upon them in the end. The Holy Spirit will be bestowed to the faithful remnant when they recognize Christ as their Messiah. This is one of the rewards for believing in Jesus Christ. (John 14:16-17, 26, 15:26, 16:7).

Summary

Ezekiel 38 and 39 is one of the most important, well explained, and easy to understand prophecies in the Bible. This is because it foretells the coming of the marquis event, whereby the Lord upholds His holy name before the watchful eyes of humankind. The event is so epic that the Lord achieves the undivided attention of mankind. Israelis continuing to inhabit their homeland of Israel, after the prophetic wars of Psalm 83 and Ezekiel 38, will provide humanity with ample evidence to recognize that the God of the Bible is the one true God!

The timing of Ezekiel 38 is critical. It occurs in the end times when the Promised Land of Israel hosts the Chosen People (Israelis). The Rapture of the church could occur before, during or after the event. My personal view, which is further explained in the chapter called "Is the Ancient Prophecy of Elam a Pre-Tribulation Event?," is that the Ezekiel 38 is a post-Rapture, but Pre-Tribulation (Pre-Trib) event. I non-dogmatically believe that Ezekiel 38 finds fulfillment prior to the implementation of the Antichrist's "Mark of the Beast" campaign in Revelation 13:11-18.

Below are a few of my reasons for adopting the post-Rapture, but Pre-Trib. view for the timing of Ezekiel 38.

1. *My people Israel* – God calls the Israelis "My people Israel" three times in Ezekiel 38 and 39. (Ezekiel 38:14, 16 and 39:7). This suggests that the true believers within the Church need not be present. This is all about Israel and the Israelis. This is one reason I believe the Rapture could occur before Ezekiel 38 finds fulfillment.

2. *Israel alone is under attack* – The prophecy takes place in Israel and is an attack against Israelis. The Magog invaders *are not* attempting to destroy and plunder the Vatican, any nation, or any other religious entity or Christian denomination. If the Church was present on earth during the fulfillment of Ezekiel 38, it would possibly have been included in the attack with Israel, or mentioned among the protestors of Sheba, Dedan, or Tarshish, yet it is nowhere to be found. This is another reason I suspect that the Rapture might occur before Ezekiel 38 does.

3. *Upholding His Holy name* – The fact that the Lord chooses this end time's episode to uphold His holy name suggests that timing is important. Demonstrating His holiness by delivering Israel from the most massive Mideast invasion in all of history up to that point, gives humanity the opportunity to believe in God before being deceived by the Antichrist. The Antichrist becomes a central figure throughout the seven year Tribulation period. He rises to power through great deception according to 2 Thessalonians 2:8-12. A Pre-Trib fulfillment of Ezekiel 38 provides people with a clear choice between, believing in the holy promise keeping God of the Bible, or the unholy deceiver, the Antichrist.

4. *Israel burns weapons for seven years* – in addition to the reason above, I hold to the teaching that Ezekiel 39:9-10 presents another clue to the timing of Ezekiel 38 and 39.

"Then those who dwell in the cities of Israel will go out and set on fire and burn the weapons, both the shields and bucklers, the bows and arrows, the javelins and spears; and they will make fires with them for seven years. They will not take wood from the field nor cut down *any* from the forests, because they will make fires with the weapons; and they will plunder those who plundered them, and pillage those who pillaged them," says the Lord GOD." (Ezek. 39:9-10)

These Ezekiel verses suggest that Israel will possess the know-how to convert the advanced enemy weapons of mass destruction possessed by the Ezekiel 38 invaders into fuel, perhaps for heating, electricity, and other related energy needs. Israelis appear to utilize these weapons for energy consumption for a period of seven-years. This will be no problem during the peaceful first half of the tribulation, but not likely during the perilous second half, because Jews will be fleeing for their lives, rather than harnessing this energy.

Concerning the separation point between the first and second halves of the Trib-period, Christ warned the Israelis in Matthew 24:15-22 that they should flee for their lives when they witness the "abomination of desolation," because that signaled a period of "Great Tribulation" was coming. This abominable event occurs at the mid-point of the Tribulation period.

"Therefore when you see the *'abomination of desolation,'* spoken of by Daniel the prophet, standing in the holy place" (whoever reads, let him understand), "then let those who are in Judea flee to the mountains. Let him who is on the housetop not go down to take anything out of his house. And let him who is in the field not go back to get his clothes. But woe to those who are pregnant and to those who are nursing babies in those days! And pray that your flight may not be in winter or on the Sabbath. For then there will be great tribulation, such as has not been since the beginning of the world until this time, no, nor ever shall be. And unless those days were shortened, no flesh would be saved; but for the elect's sake those days will be shortened." (Matthew 24:15-22)

These Matthew 24 verses are part of the reason the second half of the Tribulation is commonly called the Great Tribulation. It stands to reason that if Christ instructs Israelis to flee immediately for their safety at the midpoint of the Tribulation period that the refugees won't be stopping along the way to convert anymore of these weapons in the process.

Therefore, many scholars suggest that Ezekiel 38 and 39 must conclude, not commence, no later than three and one-half years before the seven-years of tribulation even begins. This allows the Jews seven full years to burn the weapons before they begin fleeing for their lives. Realistically, it will probably take approximately a year to even collect, dismantle, and covert the weapons cache prior to that. It's even possible that there are more than seven years' worth of weapons available for fuel consumption, but the conversion process abruptly halts at the midpoint of the Tribulation when the abomination of desolation occurs.

Here's how this could break down incrementally in real time. Allow about one year for the Ezekiel 38 battle to occur and the weapons to be converted. Remember, assembling a coalition and mobilizing an invasion of the scope described in Ezekiel 38 is no twenty-four hour undertaking. Then consider an additional seven-year span to burn the weapons. And lastly, add in the final three and one-half years of Great Tribulation, for a total of eleven and one-half years.

If this hypothesis is correct, this means that at least (underscore at least because it's probably going to be longer) that from the time the Ezekiel 38 invasion begins until the second coming of Christ to set up His kingdom, there should exist at least eleven and one-half more years. I could be more technical on the timing, because Daniel 12:11-12 adds an additional seventy-five days to the equation. His infamous 'Seventieth Week' ends, and then the two and one-half month interval kicks in, at which time some Bible prophecy experts suggest that the sheep and goat judgment of Matthew 25:32-46 takes place."

In summary, some scholars teach that little or no time separates the Gog of Magog invasion from the Tribulation period, and others believe the invasion actually occurs during the Tribulation. I agree with those that teach the Ezekiel 38 invasion must conclude at least three and one-half years before the seven-years of tribulation commences. After the Ezekiel invasion Israel may have more than seven-years of weapons supply for energy consumption. They could have ten or more years for all we know. But one thing seems almost certain, that at the mid-point of the Tribulation period when the genocidal campaign of the Antichrist is in full swing, Israelis appear to be fleeing for their lives rather than converting enemy weapons into sources of fuel for energy.

Chapter 13

Are Jeremiah 49 and Ezekiel 38 the Same Prophetic Events?

"Turkey-Iran Alliance Looming?"

Israel National News 1/29/14

"Turkish PM visits Iran to establish council of cooperation, as interim agreement eases sanctions on Iran's nuclear program. Turkish Prime Minister Recep Tayyip Erdogan arrived in Iran on Tuesday, where he met Iranian President Hassan Rouhani to discuss establishing a high-level council of cooperation. The rapprochement follows eased sanctions on Iran's nuclear program."[94]

This chapter denotes the differences between Jeremiah 49:34-39 and Ezekiel 38 and 39. Several of these dissimilarities are substantial and serve to minimize the possibility that Jeremiah and Ezekiel are describing the same prophetic event.

It is common in the Bible for different prophets to describe additional details occurring within the same event. Whenever this occurs, the prophecies complement one another, and provide additional important information. Sometimes one prophet will designate the location, participants and some of the events that take place during the prophecy, while the other prophet gives the timing of the event.

The prophecies about the first coming of the Messiah are a perfect example. About three hundred predictions are dispersed throughout the writings of the Old Testament prophets. Isaiah 7:14 says the Messiah will be born of a virgin. Micah 5:2 designates the Messiah's birthplace of Bethlehem. Zechariah 9:9 foretells that the Messiah will present Himself while riding on a donkey. Isaiah chapter 53 explains that the Messiah would die for the sins of mankind. David writes in Psalm 22 about the crucifixion of the Messiah, describing the piercing of the Messiah's hands and feet (Psalm 22:16). Daniel 9:24-26 foretold the timing of Christ's first coming and subsequent death. All of these, and many more Messiah related prophecies were written before Jesus Christ came, and He fulfilled all of these predictions at the time of his first advent.

A few other examples of correlating details describing a prophetic event from the vantage point of different biblical prophets are;

- Portions of Jeremiah 49 that correlate with similar portions of Obadiah's sole chapter,
- The destruction of Damascus in Isaiah 17, and Jeremiah 49:23-27 and Amos 1:3-5,
- The Arab confederacy of Psalm 83:5-8 and that of Obadiah 1:7,
- Ezekiel 25:14, 37:10 and Obadiah 1:18 all refer to the Israeli Defense Forces in Bible prophecy,
- Ezekiel 38:2-3 concerning Meshech and Tubal (Turkey) and Ezekiel 32:26-28 also concerning Meshech and Tubal. (*Sometimes the same prophet adds more details to a prophetic event, but in a different portion of his writings*).

These are just a few amongst many more examples that could be cited. Each of these prophecies follows the pattern of providing details that greatly enhance our understanding of some specific prophetic event. They do not present differing or contradicting information, such as we find when comparing some of the details between Jeremiah 49 and Ezekiel 38. Clear contradictions mean that different prophecies exist. An example of this was provided in the chapter called "Psalm 83 or Ezekiel 38; what's Next?"

Different Battle Zones

It was pointed out in an earlier chapter that the events described in Jeremiah 49:34-39 take place inside of the borders of Iran. Elam is struck at the foremost of its might and this causes Iranian refugees to seek exile outside of their homeland.

Jer. 49:36 predicts that "*the four winds from the four quarters of heaven*" will be brought "*against Elam.*" Jer. 49:37 declares that the "*disaster*" comes "*upon*" the Iranians. Jer. 49:38 informs that the Lord will "*set*" His "*throne in Elam.*" These prophecies are geographically specific. They must occur within the borders of Elam, which is the Central Western region of modern day Iran.

Conversely, the Ezekiel 38 and 39 invasion, from start to finish, takes place in Israel according to Ezekiel 38:8, 16, 18, and 19 and Ezekiel 39:2, 4, 9, 11, and 17. At the time of the Ezekiel invasion, Israel may have enlarged their borders as a result of an IDF victory over the Psalm 83 countries, but there is no biblical basis to believe that any part of modern day Iran will be part of a future greater Israel.

There is one possible exception to the argument that Ezekiel 38 happens entirely within Israel, and it is found in Ezekiel 39:6 which says, "And I will send fire on Magog and on those who live in security in the coastlands." However, the "coastlands," already mentioned several times by Ezekiel (cf. Ezek. 26:15, 18; 27:3, 6-7, 15, 35), imply the farthest reaches of the known world."[95]

Ezekiel 38 Conspicuously Omits Elam and the Psalm 83 Populations

The fact that Ezekiel 38 omits Elam from the very specific list of populations that coalesce with Russia against Israel could be telling. Neither Elam nor any of the Psalm 83 countries are included in the Ezekiel 38 coalition. I think this is a conspicuous omission on Ezekiel's part.

Ezekiel 38 and 39 provides an enormous amount of meticulous details about the entirety of the Ezekiel invasion. It includes the participants, the spectators, the battle zone, the motive, the destruction involved, and the important details surrounding the aftermath events, i.e. *the mop-up of the war.* Why would Ezekiel overlook Elam and Israel's prime enemies today that are listed in Psalm 83? After all, the Ezekiel invaders have to travel over the lands of the Psalm 83 countries to even get into Israel.

Did Ezekiel Know About Psalm 83?

The first question to address is, was Ezekiel aware of Elam and the Psalm 83 populations of the Edomites, Ammonites, Moabites, and seven other populations? The answer for Psalm 83 is yes. Ezekiel listed the various Psalm 83 populations by one or more names about eighty-nine times in his forty-eight chapters.

Ezekiel mentions Edom, Edomite, or Edomites six times. Ammon, Ammonite, or Ammonites are written about six times also. Moab, Moabite, or Moabites are identified by Ezekiel three times. Egypt, Assyria, Tyre, Philistia and most telling even Gebal are included in Ezekiel's forty-eight chapters. In fact, Gebal, which is located in modern day Lebanon, is only listed in Ezekiel 27:9 and Psalm 83:7. Why does Ezekiel 27:9 include Gebal, but Ezekiel 38 omits Gebal from the list of invaders? It is safe to presume that if Gebal was a participant in Ezekiel 38, that Ezekiel would have included Gebal.

I believe the answer is quite obvious. The Psalm 83 populations are not involved in Ezekiel 38 and 39, because they are complicit in their own war prophecy. The Psalm 83 confederacy is probably soundly defeated prior by the IDF.

What About Elam; Did Ezekiel Know About Elam?

The second question is what about Elam? Did Ezekiel know about Elam? If Elam didn't exist at the time, or if the prophet was ignorant of its existence, then that could logically explain the omission of Elam from Ezekiel 38.

The truth is that Elam existed when Ezekiel 38 was penned, and the prophet was fully aware of its location at the time. Ezekiel actually issued a prophecy concerning Elam in chapter thirty-two.

Ezekiel authored his forty-eight chapters between 593-571 BC.[96] By the time Ezekiel 38 was written, Elam had already been identified in Genesis 10:22, 14:1, 14:9, Isaiah 11:11, 21:2 22:6, and Jeremiah 49:25:25 49:34-39. In fact, apart from Daniel 8:2 and Ezra 4:9, Ezekiel 32:24-25 represents the last biblical inscriptions of Elam in the Old Testament.

As you read the pertinent Ezekiel verses below, note that they were probably written around 585 BC.[97] This means that Ezekiel prophesied about Elam approximately eleven years after Jeremiah 49:34-39 was written.

> "There *is* Elam and all her multitude, All around her grave, All of them slain, fallen by the sword, Who have gone down uncircumcised to the lower parts of the earth, Who caused their terror in the land of the living; Now they bear their shame with those who go down to the Pit. They have set her bed in the midst of the slain, With all her multitude, With her graves all around it, All of them uncircumcised, slain by the sword; Though their terror was caused In the land of the living, Yet they bear their shame With those who go down to the Pit; It was put in the midst of the slain." (Ezekiel 32:24-25)

Since these verses were penned after Jeremiah prophesied about Elam, Ezekiel appears to be providing supplemental information regarding the events of Jeremiah 49:34-39. Ezekiel prophesies that many unsaved (uncircumcised) Elamites will be slain by the sword. The prophet mentions the sword two times in this passage. This seems to correlate with Jeremiah 49:37c, which says, *"And I will send the sword after them Until I have consumed them."*

Ezekiel connects more prophetic dots by acknowledging that Elam is guilty of causing "terror in the land of the living." The prophet also mentions this fact two times in these verses. This could be what fiercely angers the Lord and prompts Him to bring about Elam's severe disaster. Jeremiah 49:37b says, *"I will bring disaster upon them, My fierce anger,' says the LORD."*

Iran is notably the world's foremost sponsor of international terror. Below is a quote from the Council on Foreign Relations website.

"The U.S. State Department considers Iran the world's "most active state sponsor of terrorism." U.S. officials say Iran provides funding, weapons, training, and sanctuary to numerous terrorist groups--most notably in Iraq, Afghanistan, and Lebanon--posing a security concern to the international community."[98]

Other probable reasons that Iran is presently upsetting the Lord are;

- They are forcibly closing home churches, persecuting pastors, and imprisoning and killing Christians, especially since around 2012.[99]
- They are a Muslim nation that worships Allah rather than Jehovah, the God of the Bible,
- They are threatening to wipe Israel off of the map, and may soon have the nuclear wherewithal to accomplish this dastardly deed.

Jeremiah 49:34-39 and Ezekiel 32:24-25 are seemingly interrelated passages that describe the final destruction of Elam. Elam will experience a severe destruction that is subsequently followed by a period of restoration. Below is a chronological ordering of events that intertwine the two prophecies together.

- Elam will experience a disaster as a result of fiercely angering the Lord (Jer. 49:35, 37).
- Many Elamites will be killed; "slain by the sword" (Jer. 49:37) (Ezek. 32:24-25).
- Surviving Elamite refugees are subsequently scattered throughout the world (Jer. 49:36).
- The Lord topples the local, and perhaps, the national Iranian leadership and set up His throne in Elam (Jer. 49:38).
- The Lord will bring back the exiles that survived the disaster in Elam, and He will restore their fortunes (Jer. 49:39).
- The souls of the non-Christian Iranians (Elamites) that are destroyed during the disaster of Elam will be transported to the "Pit" of Hades, which is located in the "lower parts of the earth." This is the fate of these unbelievers for the "terror" they caused "in the land of the living." (Ezek. 32:24-25).

Elam's Disaster Will Be Massive

It is important to note that Ezekiel 32:25 mentions that there is a "multitude" of Elamite "graves" that will be filled with "slain" Iranians. This implies that the disaster of Jeremiah 49:37 is going to result in massive deaths and casualties. These deaths will certainly involve many unbelieving Iranians, which are referred to two times by Ezekiel as "uncircumcised."

Romans 2:28-29 points out that circumcision is more than an outward physical act, but consists of an indwelling of the Holy Spirit within the heart of a believer. John 14:15-17 clarifies that the indwelling of the Holy Spirit directly correlates with an individual's acceptance of Jesus Christ as their Savior. Identifying these Iranians as uncircumcised is synonymous with calling them unsaved or unbelievers.

The calamity in Elam may not be restricted to unbelievers though; it could also kill Iranian Christians. If so, the believers that are killed will be transported into heaven rather than the "Pit" of Hades. However, Ezekiel 32:24-25 does not apply to Iranian believers, but only addresses the fate of the uncircumcised unbelievers.

The Meshech and Tubal Clue

This next section continues to answer the question as to whether Ezekiel intentionally omitted Elam from Ezekiel 38 and 39. It has already been shown that Ezekiel was familiar with Elam, but there is more to consider concerning his omission of Elam. The conclusive clue for me is contained in Ezekiel's multiple references of Meshech and Tubal. Ezekiel writes about this dynamic duo in Ezekiel 32:26-28, 38:2-3, 39:1.

Ezekiel 32: Meshech, Tubal and Elam (no Persia)

Ezekiel 32:1-32 identifies seven significant populations among the slain. These peoples are listed in the order of Egypt, Assyria, Elam, *Meshech, Tubal*, Edom, and Sidon. Notice that Persia is not listed anywhere in Ezekiel 32. Iran was primarily identified by the western world as Persia until 1935. Modern day Iran is included in Ezekiel 32, but only under the banner of Elam!

Ezekiel 38: Meshech, Tubal and Persia (no Elam)

With the exceptions of Meshech and Tubal, Ezekiel 38 and 39 provides a lengthy list of entirely different populations than Ezekiel 32. These two peoples from Meshech and Tubal are alluded to in both Ezekiel 32 and Ezekiel 38.

Ezekiel 38 and 39 includes; Magog, Rosh, Meshech, Tubal, Persia, Ethiopia, Libya, Gomer and Togarmah. These nine comprise the Ezekiel invaders. The modern day identities of these invaders were provided in the earlier chapter called, "Introducing Ezekiel's Prophecy Concerning Persia." Also included in the prophecy are Israel, and the sideline spectators of Sheba (*Yemen*), Dedan (*Saudi Arabia*), Tarshish (*probably the UK*) and their Young Lions (*probably the USA*). Now notice that Elam is not listed anywhere in Ezekiel 38!

Exploring the prophecies of Meshech and Tubal

It is possible that Ezekiel 32 lists seven people groups in the chronological order of their respective judgments. Ezekiel 32:1-16 concerns Egypt's defeat by the Babylonians. This would be the first of the series of judgments relating to the peoples identified in Ezekiel 32.

Elam is listed third in the Ezekiel 32 lineup, just prior to the judgment of Meshech and Tubal. This may infer that Elam's judgment precedes theirs. The only other judgment concerning Meshech and Tubal within the Bible is in located in Ezekiel 38 and 39. According to Ezekiel 38:8, 16, this is an end time's prophecy. Many Bible prophecy experts believe that we are currently living in the last days, but they commonly teach that this prophecy still remains unfulfilled. Elam being listed before Meshech and Tubal in Ezekiel 32 might signify that Jeremiah 49:34-39 and Ezekiel 32:24-25 both happen before Ezekiel 32:26-28 and Ezekiel 38 and 39.

Ezekiel 32:26-28 May be Part of Ezekiel 38

Meshech and Tubal were the sons of Japeth, who was Noah's youngest son, according to Genesis 9:18. Both Meshech and Tubal settled in what is today modern day Turkey. In tandem, they show up together seven times in the Holy Scriptures, but only in Ezekiel 32 and 38 are they depicted in Bible prophecies.

> "Now the word of the LORD came to me, saying, "Son of man, set your face against Gog, of the land of Magog, the prince of Rosh, *Meshech, and Tubal,* and prophesy against him, and say, 'Thus says the Lord GOD: "Behold, I *am* against you, O Gog, the prince of Rosh, *Meshech, and Tubal.*" (Ezekiel 38:1-3; *emphasis added*)

> "And you, son of man, prophesy against Gog, and say, 'Thus says the Lord GOD: "Behold, I *am* against you, O Gog, the prince of Rosh, *Meshech, and Tubal*; and I will turn you around and lead you on, bringing you up from the far north, and bring you against the mountains of Israel. Then I will knock the bow out of your left hand, and cause the arrows to fall out of your right hand. You shall fall upon the mountains of Israel, you and all your troops and the peoples who *are* with you; I will give you to birds of prey of every sort and *to* the beasts of the field to be devoured. (Ezek. 39:1-4; *emphasis added*)

These above verses from Ezekiel 38 and 39 include three out of the four prophetic biblical references to Meshech and Tubal. They are clearly identified as members of the Gog of Magog invaders that come to take a spoil from Israel in the latter years. Meshech and Tubal, along with all the other Ezekiel 38 invaders, are destroyed, and subsequently "devoured" by the "birds of prey of every sort and *by* the beasts of the field."

Ezekiel 32 taken in correlation appears to add some concluding details surrounding the destruction of Meshech and Tubal.

> "There are Meshech and Tubal and all their multitudes, With all their graves around it, All of them uncircumcised, slain by the sword, Though they caused their terror in the land of the living. They do not lie with the mighty Who are fallen of the uncircumcised, Who have gone down to hell with their weapons of war; They have laid their

swords under their heads, But their iniquities will be on their bones, Because of the terror of the mighty in the land of the living. Yes, you shall be broken in the midst of the uncircumcised, And lie with *those* slain by the sword." (Ezekiel 32:26-28)

The unsaved Turks, (Meshech and Tubal), like the unsaved Iranians (Elam), will also wind up in the Pit of Hades at the time of their respective destructions. However, there is some dissimilarity between the final fates of the uncircumcised from Meshech and Tubal and their Elamite counterparts.

First, Meshech and Tubal don't take "their weapons of war" into Hades with them; rather their "swords" are laid "under their heads." *Second*, the iniquities of Meshech and Tubal become attached to their earthly bones. These two prophecies seem to correlate with some powerful aftermath events described in Ezekiel 39.

"Then those who dwell in the cities of Israel will go out and set on fire and burn the weapons, both the shields and bucklers, the bows and arrows, the javelins and spears; and they will make fires with them for seven years. They will not take wood from the field nor cut down *any* from the forests, because they will make fires with the weapons; and they will plunder those who plundered them, and pillage those who pillaged them," says the Lord GOD." (Ezekiel 39:9-10)

These above verses explain that the Israelis will use the weapons of war of the Ezekiel 38 invaders for apparent fuel or energy resources. This would be impossible if Meshech's and Tubal's weapons went with them into Hades. Maybe the weapons of Ezekiel 32:27 should be interpreted more figuratively than those of Ezekiel 39:9-10, which appear to be literal weapons. However, in both instances, these are clearly weapons that are associated with Meshech and Tubal in one way or another.

Moreover, Ezekiel 39:11-16 foretells of additional events that take place in the aftermath of the defeat of the Gog of Magog invaders. Ezekiel 39:11-12 informs that it will take Israel seven months to bury the multitude of dead Gog of Magog invaders, which includes those from Meshech and Tubal. The location of this mass graveyard will be named the Valley of Hamon Gog, which means the hordes of Gog. No such valley presently exists by that name, but that will change in the future.

> "It will come to pass in that day *that* I will give Gog a burial place there in Israel, the valley of those who pass by east of the sea; and it will obstruct travelers, because there they will bury Gog and all his multitude. Therefore they will call *it* the Valley of Hamon Gog. For seven months the house of Israel will be burying them, in order to cleanse the land. (Ezekiel 39:11-12)

Hamon Gog will someday be located in a valley east of some sea, and it will obstruct travelers. The obstruction of travelers may, or may not be, intentional. Perhaps the location is strategically located to increase the defensibility of Israel's borders.

Due to environmental and geographical reasons, the most logical and logistical valley for such a massive undertaking would be east of the Dead Sea somewhere in modern day Central Jordan. Presently, Jordan is not under Israeli sovereignty, which mitigates against this possibility. However, in the aftermath of an IDF victory over the Psalm 83 nations, Israel appears to take control over Jordan, which would then make this a viable option.[100] This possibility is explained in greater detail in my book called *Psalm 83: The Missing Prophecy Revealed, How Israel Becomes the Next Mideast Superpower*.

Ezekiel 39:13 declares that the burying of the dead is a national Israeli campaign that earns them notoriety from the observing nations. The verse reads, "Indeed all the people of the land will be burying, and they will gain renown for it on the day that I am glorified," says the Lord GOD."

After the seven month period expires, Israel sends out a team of professionals that work closely alongside a search party. The searchers seek out and mark all the exposed enemy bones, and then the professionals bury those bones in order to cleanse the land. The following verses suggest that this burial crew is comprised of either approved Jewish priests or skilled hazardous materials (HAZMAT) specialists.

> "They (the Israelis) will set apart men regularly employed, with the help of a search party, to pass through the land and bury those bodies remaining on the ground, in order to cleanse it. At the end of seven months they will make a search. The search party will pass through the land; and *when anyone* sees a man's bone, he shall set up a marker by it, till the buriers have buried it in the Valley of Hamon Gog." (Ezekiel 39:14-15)

In this section, we also find that the Israelis will be burying the dead in order to cleanse the land. This could imply two things. One, that the hordes of Gog's dead soldiers are contaminated, requiring a professional quarantined burial and two; that the Jews are adhering to their ancient Levitical Law. Concerning the latter, Dr. Ron Rhodes writes in his book *Northern Storm Rising*:

> *"From the perspective of the Jews, the dead must be buried because exposed corpses are a source of ritual contamination to the land (Numbers 19:11-22; Deuteronomy 21:1-9). The land must therefore be completely cleansed and purged of all defilement. Neither the enemies nor their belongings (their weapons) can be left to pollute the land!"*[101]

It is possible that the iniquity plagued bones of Meshech and Tubal, spoken of in Ezekiel 32:27, might have something to do with this cleansing of the land process. Perhaps these bones are toxic and the contamination is a manifestation of Meshech and Tubal's cursed effort to invade Israel. In other words, the weapons of the Ezekiel invaders may include WMD's of some sort that bleed into the bones of the invaders at the time of their destruction. Or, it may be as simple as the bones of Meshech and Tubal have become infected by pestilence during the seventh month period that it takes Israel to dispose of the dead.

Iran's Double Jeopardy: Persia is in Ezekiel 38, but Elam is in Ezekiel 32

At this point, it's important to discuss Iran's double jeopardy in the latter days. Iran is the subject of dual judgment prophecies, one in Jeremiah 49:34-39, and the other in Ezekiel 38 and 39. This means that the rogue nation will experience double trouble in the end times.

One of the strongest arguments for believing that Jeremiah's prophecy concerning Elam is not part of Ezekiel 38 is found in the observable omission of Elam in Ezekiel 38. Elam's exclusion from Ezekiel 38 appears to be intentional.

The prior section pointed out that Ezekiel was extremely familiar with Elam, and Meshech and Tubal because he predicted their final fates in Ezekiel 32. The prophet includes Elam in Ezekiel 32:24-25 and Meshech and Tubal in Ezekiel 32:26-28. These verses neatly blend into one another on the pages of the Bible. This congruency possibly suggests that Elam's judgment closely precedes that of Meshech and Tubal.

The astute Bible prophecy buff would be remiss not ask the following questions;

1. Why would Ezekiel lump Elam and Meshech and Tubal together in Ezekiel 32, but extract Elam from Ezekiel 38, which also incorporates Meshech and Tubal?
2. Why would Ezekiel substitute Persia in place of Elam in Ezekiel 38 alongside Meshech and Tubal?
3. Does this imply that Elam is the subject of its own prophecy, written by Ezekiel's contemporary Jeremiah, and is not involved in Ezekiel 38?

As Ezekiel is not physically with us today, I will go out on a limb and take advantage of author liberties by answering these questions as I believe he might. These answers will be presented in the language of our modern day vernacular. Treat the segment below as fiction that may not be too far-fetched.

1. The answer to question #1 is as follows:

"Elam is the subject of its own independent prophecy. Elam was not included in Ezekiel 38 because it is not part of this prophecy. Elam experiences the disaster revealed by Jeremiah 49:34-39 before Ezekiel 38 even occurs. Elam is listed in correlation with Meshech and Tubal in Ezekiel 32 because Jeremiah 49:34-39 is quickly followed by Ezekiel 38."

2. The answer to question #2 is as follows:

"Persia was identified in Ezekiel 38, because the Iranian Muslims that survive the disaster of Jeremiah 49:34-39, will coalesce with Russia for revenge against Israel. Iranian leaders will be dwelling in a weakened condition and extremely vulnerable after the fulfillment of Jeremiah's prophecy. Russian promises of restoration to religious, economic and military prominence will allure the Iranian leadership, hook, line, and sinker into the Magog Coalition. Iran will be allured by Russia's evil plan to capture Israel's inherent wealth of gas and other natural resources, along with the spoils of war captured by the IDF in the aftermath of Psalm 83. Iran will be among the first to enlist as an Ezekiel invader along with Turkey, (Meshech and Tubal)."

3. The answer to question #3 is as follows:

"The majority of surviving Elamites (Iranians) will be exiled globally and seek no part in the Gog of Magog invasion. Very few will return to fight alongside Russia, but many will come to a saving faith in the Messiah. They will have learned an invaluable lesson about the fatal flaws of the rogue Islamic regime and will flee to Christ for their peace and restitution. Many of the Iranians in their Diaspora will preach the gospel throughout the world."

Other Reasons Jeremiah 49:34-39
and Ezekiel 38 and 39 Differ

There are several other reasons why Jeremiah 49 and Ezekiel 38 may not be referring to the same prophecy. They are summarized below.

* *Good is in Elam's future, but not Persia's.*

Good is in store for Elam according to Jeremiah 49:38-39, but nothing good is in store for Persia. There is no mention anywhere within the Bible, of the Lord establishing His throne in Persia, or restoring the fortunes of the Persians in the latter days. This is why it is important for Iranians today to receive Christ now, and fortunately many are.

Some Iranians are extremely impoverished and cannot depart from Iran. Perhaps some of them will be among the exiles of Jeremiah 49:36. However, Jeremiah 49:36 is not necessarily the best and only exit strategy available to them. The ultimate exodus from harm's way for Iranians would be the Rapture prophesied in 1 Corinthians 15:50-52, 1 Thessalonians 4:15-18, Isaiah 26:20-21, John 14:1-3 and Revelation 4:1-5. However, no one knows whether Jeremiah 49:34-39 will find fulfillment before or after the Rapture. To read why both Jeremiah 49:34-39 and the Rapture are probably Pre-Tribulation events, read the chapter entitled "Is Ancient Prophecy of Elam is a Pre-Tribulation Event? "

Elam and Persia are
Different Geographical Locations

Not only do the battlefields differ in the prophecies involving Elam and Persia, but they both occupied different geographical locations. When Ezekiel and Jeremiah authored their prophecies, Elam was located in West Central, extending into Southwest Iran, and Persia covered most of the rest of modern day Iran. They were separated by the Zagros mountains. It wasn't until several decades after these prophets wrote, during the time of Cyrus the Great of Persia, that the territorial lines became somewhat blurred.

It is clumsy and potentially careless to lump Jeremiah 49:34-39 concerning Elam, with Ezekiel 38 and 39 that deals with Persia. Even though Iran today encompasses both ancient regions, this does not insulate the country from territorial judgments predicted millenniums ago in the Bible.

- *Elam Has Enemies, But Persia Has an Enemy.*

Jeremiah 49:37 points out that Elam has a plurality of enemies. On the contrary, Persia appears to have only one, and that is Israel. Although Ezekiel 38:13 identifies some sideline spectators, they do not appear to become involved in the defeat of the Ezekiel invaders. Ezekiel 38:18-39:6 informs us that the God of Israel defeats Russia and its coalition.

- *Elam is Defeated by the Sword, but Persia by Fire, Hail, and Brimstone*

Jeremiah 49:37 predicts Elam's destruction occurs via the sword, which probably alludes to a military victory. Whereas, Ezekiel 38:18-39:6 declares that an earthquake, flooding rain, great hailstones, fire, and brimstone are the weapons of warfare that the Lord uses to defeat the Ezekiel invaders.

Summary

Due to the various differences between Jeremiah 49:34-39 and Ezekiel 38 and 39, it is safe to conclude that these are two distinctly different prophetic events. Ezekiel appears to have intentionally omitted Elam and the Psalm 83 confederacy from the Magog alliance because they are not part of this alliance. Elam, Psalm 83 and Ezekiel 38 seem to be three different prophecies.

Iran experiences a double jeopardy in the end times. A disaster occurs in Iran as described in Jeremiah 49:34-39, but the Ezekiel 38 battle is fought in Israel, rather than on Iranian soil. In both prophecies Iran experiences massive destructions of epic biblical proportions.

Chapter 14

Is the Ancient Prophecy of Elam a Pre-Tribulation Event?

This chapter explores the probable Pre-Tribulation timing of Psalm 83 and Jeremiah 49:34-39. These topics will be explored in this order.

Some Bible prophecy teachers, such as Dr. David Reagan, Chuck Missler, me and many others, teach that some end time prophecies find fulfillment before the seven year Tribulation period (Trib-period) commences. There are several reasons this statement can be supported. Some of these reasons are listed below;

- Seven years of Trib-period are not enough time to fulfill all remaining unfulfilled prophecy,
- There appears to be a time-gap that exists between the Rapture and Trib-period that will probably experience the fulfillment of some Bible prophecies,
- Pre-trib prophecies have been fulfilled, setting precedent that more will follow,
- There are non-conforming prophecies, which predict details that don't seem to coincide with foreknown events that will be taking place during the Trib-period.

In the past it was commonly thought that the Pre-tribulation (Pre-trib) Rapture would occur, and the Trib-period would promptly follow. In essence, the thinking was that the Rapture was the trigger-point of the Trib-period. This is one reason that many end-times experts believed all remaining Bible prophecies had to find fulfillment during the Trib-period. In my book called *Revelation Road, Hope Beyond the Horizon*, I provide my reasons for believing that the Rapture of the Church probably precedes the Trib-period.

Consequently, this caused the relatively short Trib-period, spanning only seven years, to become the catch-all closet of all remaining unfulfilled Bible prophecy. Since some pending predictions could require a considerable amount of time to manifest, like the formation of the one world religion of the harlot in Revelation 17, this teaching becomes prohibitive. As it turns out, seven years of a Trib-period does not appear to be enough time to fulfill all the remaining unfulfilled Bible prophecies.

Complicating matters is the fact that some forthcoming predictions have definite time frames associated with them, whereas, many do not. For instance, the fifth trumpet locust plague of Revelation 9:1-12 lasts for five months. This trumpet judgment could certainly fit within the seven year Trib-period. However, the span of time it takes to implement a one-world religion, which Revelation 17:15 says presides over a multitude of peoples within many nations, could take many years if not decades. The Bible doesn't inform us how long it takes for this global religion to form, or how long until it gets desolated, which happens as per Revelation 17:16.

Additionally, the Bible predicts the formation of a global government that segues into ten separate kingdoms in Daniel 7:23-24. Since no specific time spans are specified within the Bible for this transformation to occur, we should suspect that this process could likewise consume quite a bit of time.

Therefore, eschatologists are wise to allot reasonable interludes of time between events. It seems illogical to restrict the rise and fall of such major international events to the confines of a seven-year time span. And, these are just a few prophetic events, leaving dozens more of equal or greater importance remaining.

Certainly, many events occur simultaneously, but others require the fulfillment of a prior event from which to build upon. For example, it appears that something must happen for Israel to become a peaceful people that dwell securely in the last days. These are prerequisite conditions that must be in place before Ezekiel 38 and 39 can occur. I believe Israel meets this requirement after the IDF defeats the Arab confederacy of Psalm 83.

Confounding timing issues further, is the probability that there exists a time-gap between the Rapture event and the Trib-period. There appears to be an unspecified period of time that follows the Rapture, but precedes the Trib-period. Lately, the realization has set in among many Bible teachers and students of prophecy that the Scriptures teach that the Trib-period begins by the confirmation of a false covenant confirmed by the Antichrist with the nation of Israel, rather than the Rapture. Dr. Tim LaHaye, the co-author of the bestselling "*Left Behind*" Christian book series, addressed this subject in a personal email to me.

> "*Pre-Trib. scholars are not agreed on whether the Rapture starts the Tribulation (Nothing in scripture says it does). Daniel 9:27 says the Antichrist will confirm a contract with Israel for one week (or seven years), which leads me to believe that starts the Tribulation. There is a high possibility that the Rapture could take place prior, but only God knows how long.*"[102]

Isaiah 28:15, 18 and Daniel 9:27 are the Scriptures providing details regarding this covenant. According to Isaiah's and Daniel's descriptions, this cunningly devised covenant is a seven-year peace-pact intended to lure Israel into a false sense of security. Those critical seven years result in a period of unprecedented worldwide woes. Armageddon, the mark of the Beast, and Mystery Babylon are just a few of the popularized biblical terms defining this period.

Somehow the content and confirmation of the Antichrist's false covenant becomes the straw that breaks the camel's back, provoking the Lord to finally judge unrighteous mankind. Some teach the treaty will be what brings about a temporary Mideast peace between the Arabs and/or Palestinians and the Jews. However, this teaching is primarily driven by geopolitical Middle East events, rather than sound biblical exegesis. Nowhere in Scripture does it declare that the false covenant alludes to a peace that is crafted between Arabs and / or Palestinians and the Jews.

According to Bible prophecy, Arab-Israeli peace appears to be achieved militarily, rather than diplomatically. The final resolution of the Arab-Israeli conflict appears to be what Psalm 83 is concerned with.

The Pre-Trib Prophecies of
Psalm 83 and Jeremiah 49:34-39

It appears that Psalm 83, Jeremiah 49:34-39 and Ezekiel 38 and 39 are events the commence before the Trib-period begins. Ezekiel 38 and 39 could overlap into the first half of the Trib-period, but it is doubtful that Psalm 83 or Jeremiah 49:34-39 will. These conclusions can be drawn through a process of deductive reasoning.

It is relatively easy to explain why Psalm 83 and Jeremiah 49:34-39 probably occur before Ezekiel 38. This next section will clarify why this is the most probable timing. If they occur prior, and it can be determined that Ezekiel 38 is a Pre-trib prophecy, then it is logical to conclude that Psalm 83 and Jeremiah 49:34-39 are also Pre-trib events.

Simply stated, the major premise is that if Ezekiel 38 finds a Pre-trib fulfillment, then the minor premise is, that any prophecies preceding Ezekiel 38, such as Psalm 83 and Jeremiah 49:34-39, are also Pre-trib prophecies. In the summary section of the chapter called "Overview of the Ezekiel 38-39 Prophecy," I provided my reasons for believing that Ezekiel 38 finds fulfillment before the Trib-period.

The Pre-Trib Timing of Psalm 83

It has already been argued in this book that Israel is not presently meeting all the prerequisite conditions for Ezekiel 38 to be considered an imminent prophecy. Atop the list is the fact that Israelis are not dwelling securely without walls, bars or gates. Israel will probably not be able to meet this requirement as long as the Psalm 83 prophecy remains unfulfilled.

Israel's enemies listed in Psalm 83 of Egypt, Lebanon, Syria, Iraq, Jordan, the Palestinians, Hamas, Hezbollah and more, prevent Israel from tearing down its security walls, fences and checkpoints. These Arab foes don't recognize Israel as the Jewish state and pose a constant threat to Israel. Until they change their disposition toward Israel, or are defeated in the Psalm 83 war, Israel will not be able to dwell securely. According to the Bible, Israel will achieve the national security it desperately seeks by winning the Psalm 83 war.

For this reason, I believe Psalm 83 precedes Ezekiel 38. However, there is another reason why Psalm 83 probably finds a Pre-trib fulfillment. A past dialogue between respected Bible prophecy expert Dr. Arnold Fruchtenbaum and me explains why.

The Fructhenbaum / Salus Dialogue

In December of 2009, while attending a Pre-Trib Rapture conference hosted by Dr. Tim LaHaye and Dr. Thomas Ice, I had the opportunity to interview the highly regarded prophecy expert, Dr. Arnold Fruchtenbaum, for Prophecy Update Radio. We talked about several prophetic topics, but of particular interest was our discussion centered upon the timing of Psalm 83.

Knowing that Dr. Fruchtenbaum has a healthy aversion to date setting and newspaper exegesis, I was respectfully careful in our interview not to corner him into pinpointing the exact timing of the fulfillment of the Psalm event. However, with that said, I'm very familiar with his general viewpoint regarding the final fulfillment of the prophecy. Arnold and I have bantered back and forth on the event timing on numerous occasions. I believe it is a Pre-Trib event, and Arnold had tended to place the final conclusion of the event into the "Great Tribulation", which would be the second half of the seven year tribulation period.[103]

Let me give you some background on this friendly, decade old timing debate between us. Regarding his placement of the Psalm in the Great Tribulation, I first discovered his viewpoint in his *Footsteps of the Messiah* book, where he clearly places the final fulfillment of the event in the Great Tribulation. Several years ago at a luncheon together, I seized the opportunity to ask him why he believed this. He opened up his Bible to the single book chapter of Obadiah and read:

> "For the day of Jehovah is near upon all the nations: as thou hast done, it shall be done unto thee; thy dealing shall return upon thine own head." (Obadiah 1:15, ASV)

He and I both concur this passage alludes to the timing of the fulfillment of Psalm 83; however, where we differ in opinion is that he believes the passage mandates that the event conclusion occurs in the day of Jehovah, and I read the passage as it occurs when the day of the LORD (Jehovah) draws near. The text says; "For the day of Jehovah is near", which implies that the day of the LORD will occur subsequent to the fulfillment of Obadiah 1:15. We both believe that the day of Jehovah encompasses at least the second three and one-half years of the Tribulation, and quite possibly the entire seven year period. Therefore, I suggest Psalm 83 occurs when the Tribulation period is relatively soon to happen, but not yet come.

A few friendly face to face meetings later, Arnold suggested that I write a book about the subject of Psalm 83, which is now published and is called *Isralestine, The Ancient Blueprints of the Future Middle East.* Although he believes we are in "*substantial agreement*" and *Isralestine* presents "*valid arguments*" on the details of the Psalm, he had remained fairly steadfast in his contrasting view of the timing of Psalm 83. Since the time of this interview, I have released an updated version of *Isralestine* entitled, *Psalm 83 – The Missing Prophecy Revealed, How Israel Becomes the Next Mideast Superpower.*

Subsequent to the publishing of *Isralestine*, our communications continued through radio interviews together, speaking at conferences with each other, and volleys of emails back and forth. His general feeling up to the time of the December, 2009, interview was that partial fulfillment of Psalm 83 occurred in the wars of 1948 and 1967, but the final fulfillment has not yet occurred.

Here is where things take an interesting twist. In our December, 2009, radio interview together, Dr. Fruchtenbaum answered several of my semi-pointed questions in a manner which suggested that he was open to other views of the final timing of Psalm 83. During the interview, I discovered that Dr. Fructhenbaum believes the majority of Psalm 83 finds fulfillment before the seven year Tribulation Period occurs, meaning more segments of Psalm 83 may yet occur as Pre-Trib events.

For instance, regarding the destruction of Damascus, he believes that Isaiah 17:1 may be part of Psalm 83 but he is not certain. However, if it is part of Psalm 83, he believes it will be a Pre-Trib event because there is no reference to the Day of the LORD throughout Isaiah 17.

Concerning God's manner of dealing with the Psalm 83 Arab confederacy, he "definitely" believes, as do I, that the Israeli Defense Forces (I.D.F.) will become divinely empowered to conquer these confederates as per Obadiah 1:18, Ezekiel 25:14, and elsewhere. We both believe that Asaph petitions God for this type of I.D.F. empowerment in Psalm 83:9-11.

About the midpoint of our radio interview, I asked Arnold a multi-layered question: first, if Israel is dwelling in a condition of peace guaranteed by the false covenant with the Antichrist in the first half of the tribulation, how could Psalm 83 occur, and second if Israelis are fleeing from the genocidal campaign of the Antichrist in the second half of the Tribulation, likewise, how could Psalm 83 occur? His comments can be summarized as follows:

> *"First, the purpose of the false covenant is to guarantee Israel's military security and, therefore, the I.D.F. will not likely be very active during the first three and one-half years of the Tribulation period. Thus when the "Abomination of Desolation" occurs at the midpoint of the Trib period, (Matthew 24:15) the I.D.F. won't be ready to "tackle it".*

> *"Second, the Jews will be fleeing from the Antichrist rampage during the second three and one-half years of the "Great Tribulation" and thus they won't likely be stopping in mid-flight to conquer the Psalm 83 confederates."*

Therefore, I pointedly asked him, then how can Psalm 83 find final fulfillment during the seven year Tribulation period? He said, "*That's why I believe the majority of Psalm 83 occurs Pre-Trib; before the actual tribulation*".

Wow! So what do you make of that? It sounds like he may be leaning toward a complete fulfillment, or at least a majority fulfillment, of Psalm 83 as a Pre-Trib event. What Dr. Fruchtenbaum and I are concluding in the nutshell version is the following:

The IDF won't be fighting the Arabs of Psalm 83 during the first half of the Trib-period, because Israel exists in the condition of a pseudo-peace. This false peace is broken during the middle of the Trib-period, which is when the Antichrist attempts to destroy the Jews. The IDF won't be fighting the Arabs of Psalm 83 in the second half of the Trib-period either, because they are fleeing from the genocidal campaign of the Antichrist.

A postscript to this radio interview occurred at a more recent Pre-Trib Rapture conference in December, 2013. I met up with Dr. Fructhenbaum there and asked him what he now believed was the timing of Psalm 83. Below is a direct quote from that conversation.

"*I now believe that Psalm 83:1-8 found fulfillment in the 1948 Arab-Israeli War of Independence, but the remainder of the Psalm (Psalm 83:9-18) remains unfulfilled.*"

Although, I disagree with this assessment about Psalm 83:1-8 being fulfilled in 1948, I do agree with him that Psalm 83 doesn't seem to fit in either the first of second half of the Trib-period for the reasons previously discussed.

There are two primary reasons that I don't believe Psalm 83:1-8 found fulfillment in 1948.

1. Psalm 83:1 beseeches the Lord to "*not keep silent*" about the Psalm. The verse reads, "*Do not keep silent, O God! Do not hold Your peace, And do not be still, O God!*" The fact of the matter is, that up until recently the Lord has kept silent about the Psalm. It has only been recently, over the past several years, that the Psalm has gained much notoriety about being a prophecy in modernity.

2. Psalm 83:6 identifies the Palestinian refugees as the "*tents of Edom.*" Listing a few members of the Psalm 83 confederacy, the verse reads, "*The tents of Edom and the Ishmaelites; Moab and the Hagrites.*" My research shows that the Palestinian refugees include Edomite descendants. In the Bible, the term the "*tents of*" can refer to refugee conditions. I believe the Psalmist was prophesying about the Palestinian refugees, and they didn't become a reality until after the 1948 Arab-Israeli War of Independence. The Palestinian refugees were a by-product of that war.

The Pre-Trib Timing of Jeremiah 49:34-39

This section explains why Jeremiah 49:34-38 probably happens before Ezekiel 38 and 39. Jeremiah 49:34-38 appears to find fulfillment before the Trib-period, but Jeremiah 49:39 seems to occur after the Trib-period, during the establishment of the Messianic Kingdom that follows. This can be deduced by recognizing that Jeremiah 49:39 promises the return of the Elamite exiles of Jeremiah 49:36. The regathering of exiles to restored fortunes is a recurring theme in the Messianic Kingdom. Examples of this are the Israelis (Ezek. 39:25-29), Egyptians (Ezek. 29:13-16), Assyrians (Isaiah 19:23-25), Jordanians (Jer. 48: 47 and 49:6) and others.

One of the reasons Jeremiah's prophecy concerning Elam probably precedes Ezekiel 38, is because of the Lord's promise in Jeremiah 49:39 to restore the fortunes of Elam. This verse precludes that the refugees of Jeremiah 49:36 survive the Ezekiel 38 prophecy by being exiled in other countries, and out of harm's way from Iran. If Jeremiah 49:34-38 did not occur before Ezekiel 38, then there might not be many exiles from Elam to regather in the millennium. This is because all Iranians of military service age, even those dwelling in the territory of ancient Elam, would be drafted to fight in Ezekiel 38. Presently, Iran has a mandatory military service law in place.

It is important to note that Ezekiel 38 and 39 make no promises to restore the fortunes of Persia. In fact, nowhere in the Bible are restored fortunes promised to Persia. This should be extremely troubling to Iranians because Persia is decisively defeated during the Ezekiel 38 invasion. If the Jeremiah 49:37 disaster in Elam does not occur before the Ezekiel 38 invasion, then many Iranians residing in the ancient territory of Elam will be forced to fight in Ezekiel 38.

Thus, in theory it makes more sense that Jeremiah's prophecy about Elam occurs before Iran invades Israel in the Ezekiel 38 prophecy. Ancient Elam could experience a relatively isolated disaster without preventing Persia from being involved in Ezekiel 38.

Ancient Elam represents approximately one-tenth of modern day Iran in size. Moreover, it is generally geographically isolated by the Zagros Mountains. Hypothetically, Iranian territory representing Elam could fall into the Persian Gulf or experience a nuclear disaster without forbidding the rest of Iran from going to war. This plausible nuclear disaster scenario is posited in the appendix titled, "Iran's Other Nuclear Time Bomb."

The fact that Elam is not part of the Ezekiel 38 invaders strongly suggests that the Jeremiah 49:37 disaster occurs before the Gog of Magog coalition forms. Otherwise, Ezekiel would have likely included Elam alongside Persia in his prophecy.

> "Persia, Ethiopia, and Libya are with them, all of them *with* shield and helmet." (Ezekiel 38:5)

Notice that Elam is omitted from the above verse. Perhaps Elam was not included because the prophet presumed that mentioning Persia would sufficiently represent modern day Iran in his prophecy. However, if this was the case, then why didn't Ezekiel take the same liberties when describing modern day Turkey? Ezekiel seems to identify all of Turkey in the Magog invasion by the ancient names of Meshech, Tubal , Togarmah and possibly Gomer. These four were all descendants of Noah's son Japheth, and they all seem to have settled in modern day Turkey.

> "The sons of Japheth *were* Gomer, Magog, Madai, Javan, Tubal, Meshech, and Tiras. The sons of Gomer *were* Ashkenaz, Riphath, and Togarmah." (Genesis 10:2-3)

The omission of Elam in Ezekiel 38, coupled with the fact that exiles from Elam must be protected from the devastation that occurs to Iran in Ezekiel 38, infers that Jeremiah 49:34-38 precedes Ezekiel 38. If Jeremiah's prophecy concerning Elam happens before Ezekiel 38, and Ezekiel 38 happens before the Trib-period, then it can be concluded that Jeremiah 49:34-38 is a Pre-trib event. The timing would be; the disaster of Jeremiah 49:34-38 finds a Pre-trib fulfillment, and the regathering of Jeremiah 49:39 carries over somewhat beyond the Trib-period into the millennium.

Summary

It is difficult to assess the actual timing of Jeremiah 49:34-39. The only solid clue we know is provided in Jeremiah 49:39, which references "*it shall come to pass in the latter days*." Through a process of deductive reasoning, it appears as though Psalm 83 and Jeremiah 49:34-39 find fulfillments before Ezekiel 38 and 39.

In my estimation, Jeremiah 49:34-38, Psalm 83, Ezekiel 38 and the Rapture all occur before the Trib-period. I non-dogmatically sequence the events as follows;

1. Jeremiah 49:34-39,
2. Psalm 83,
3. The Rapture,
4. Ezekiel 38 and 39,
5. The Trib-period.

The Rapture could occur before any of these events. This is why it is important to redeem the time, because believers could be caught up into the clouds to be with Christ before these other events take place.

Chapter 15

Supernatural Showdown- Supernatural Events Lead Many Iranians to Christ

"Supernatural Dreams and Visions Compel Muslims to Become Christian"

Yahoo News 5/8/09

> "Over the past few decades, increasing numbers of Muslims have begun to have supernatural dreams and visions of Isa, as Muslims call Jesus Christ. These dreams affect a cross section of Muslims. Young, old, men, women, and even (Islamic) fanatics have reported the dreams."[104]

"Iran's Christian Revolution Gains Momentum

CBN News 1/25/13

"Iran Clamps Down on Evangelical Christians"

Christian Post 10/26/11

As I author this final chapter, I find myself recounting the events that inspired me to write this book. It all began back in chapter one, on the TBN Praise the Lord TV set with

Reza Safa on August 30, 2013. Reza's enthusiasm about Jeremiah's prophecy concerning Elam left an indelible impression with me. I remember asking the Lord in a personal prayer shortly after our TV encounter, "What was that all about with Elam? Lord, are you trying to tell me something?"

Having written a couple of chapters about Elam in my *Revelation Road* and *Psalm 83* books, I was content to let the mainstream Bible prophecy experts run with it from there. Beyond that, the idea of treating Jeremiah 49:34-39 as another missing prophecy in desperate need of revealing had not occurred to me. The Psalm 83 prophecy, on the other hand, had cried out to me for a revealing like an elephant stomping and growling in my living room.

Psalm 83 presented eighteen timely prophetic verses, which has been simmering in the Middle East cauldron for several decades since the rebirth of Israel in 1948. To me, this was the prophecy to be on the lookout for. However, now I wonder if these mere six verses in Jeremiah 49:34-39 will precede Psalm 83. As I author this book, Mideast peace talks have reached a dead end, which makes Psalm 83 extremely relevant and timely, but at the same time, Iran's nuclear program dominates the mainstream news media, also making the predictions about Elam pertinent.

Both prophecies appear to be headed for a photo-finish. It's entirely possible that one could trigger the other. If Iran's nuclear program is struck, that might provoke its proxies of Hezbollah and Hamas into a missile launching campaign into Israel. Israel's retaliatory response could draw Syria, Egypt and Jordan into the fight if things escalate. Mideast events have been spiraling out of control, especially since the commencement of the Arab Spring of 2011.

Several other circumstantial signs followed the TBN TV show, which confirmed for me that it was time to amplify the light on the ancient prophecy of Elam. As I followed the Lord's lead, He led me to the works of important people who have their finger on the pulse of what's taking place inside Iran.

First, I encountered Allyn Huntzinger, who was a long time missionary in Iran until the Islamic takeover of the country in

1979. Allyn, who was referenced earlier in this book, somewhat tutored me through the growth of Christianity in Iran during this modern era. Equally as important, he familiarized me with Hormoz Shariat of Iran Alive Ministries, in addition to several other key individuals.

While I was reaching out to Hormoz Shariat for research, I read the book authored by Maryam Rostampour and Marziyeh Amirizadeh titled, *Captive in Iran*. This book inspired me further, as page by page these two incredible, Iranian Christian women described their testimony of imprisonment and torture turned into triumph.

These two wonderful witnesses, whom I like to call *"the Fiancées of Christ,"* were incarcerated in one of Iran's worst prisons for simply passing out free Bibles. The rogue, Islamic Iranian regime treats Bible peddlers worse than drug smugglers. The irony of this is that Iran ranks as one of the most drug afflicted countries in the world. Iranians are desperate for hope, and that's why the gospel message of Jesus Christ is resonating loud and clear in the spirits of many Iranians.

> "Blessed *are* those who are persecuted for righteousness' sake, For theirs is the kingdom of heaven. "Blessed are you when they revile and persecute you, and say all kinds of evil against you falsely for My (*Jesus Christ*) sake. Rejoice and be exceedingly glad, for great *is* your reward in heaven, for so they persecuted the prophets who were before you." (Matthew 5:10-12; *emphasis added*)

Iran has the fastest growing evangelical population in the world. Iran's Christian population is burgeoning at a 19.6% annual growth rate. Conversely, the evangelical population of the USA is slumping along at about a sluggish 0.8% pace.[105] American Christians can learn a valuable lesson from the evangelical harvest taking place in Iran.

Do Supernatural Events in Iran Fulfill Joel 2:29?

Supernatural events are transpiring in Iran in apparent fulfillment of a prophecy in Joel. The prophet issued a prophecy that apparently was intended to sequence into at least two parts. The first segment found fulfillment at the time of Pentecost. We are assured of this because the apostle Peter declares this in Acts chapter two. However, a second measure of the outpouring of the Holy Spirit appears to be taking place presently. The verses below inform that the Holy Spirit will be poured out two times.

> *Part one* - "And it shall come to pass afterward That *I will pour out My Spirit* on all flesh; Your sons and our daughters shall prophesy, Your old men shall dream dreams, Your young men shall see visions." (Joel 2:28; *emphasis added*)

> *Part two* - "And also on *My* menservants and on *My* maidservants *I will pour out My Spirit* in those days. And I will show wonders in the heavens and in the earth: Blood and fire and pillars of smoke. The sun shall be turned into darkness, And the moon into blood, Before the coming of the great and awesome day of the LORD. And it shall come to pass *That* whoever calls on the name of the LORD Shall be saved." (Joel 2:28-32; *emphasis added*)

The apostle Peter quotes all of these verses in Acts 2:17-21 to explain the supernatural events that took place on the day of Pentecost. As per the opening verses in Acts 2, it is safe to say that the Holy Spirit was poured out at the time of Pentecost. This event fulfilled at least part one foretold in Joel 2:28.

> "When the Day of Pentecost had fully come, they (*the apostles*) were all with one accord in one place. And suddenly there came a sound from heaven, as of a rushing mighty wind, and it filled the whole house where they were sitting. Then there appeared to them divided tongues, as of fire, and *one* sat upon each of them. And they were all filled with the Holy Spirit and began to speak with other tongues, as the Spirit gave them utterance. (Acts 2:1-4, *emphasis added*).

It is safe to say that Joel 2:28 has been accomplished. "*Your sons and our daughters shall prophesy, Your old men shall dream dreams,*

Your young men shall see visions." The Holy Spirit was poured out upon the apostles at Pentecost. Afterwards, the apostles issued prophecies (Revelation 1:3, 10:11) and had visions (Acts 10:10, 17 and Revelation 9:17).

However, not all of Joel's prophecy seems to have found historic fulfillment at Pentecost. It is doubtful that the accompanying events occurred at the time of Pentecost; *"wonders in the heavens and in the earth: Blood and fire and pillars of smoke, and that the sun shall be turned into darkness, And the moon into blood."* These events are reserved for a future fulfillment. Joel's time placement of these events is just *"before the coming of the great and awesome day of the LORD."*

This is where Joel 2:29 comes into the current picture, in Iran and elsewhere. This Scripture reads, *"And also on My menservants and on My maidservants I will pour out My Spirit in those days."* This is what's happening throughout various parts of the world presently. It is a burgeoning phenomenon in persecuted areas such as Iran. Both male and female believers are receiving an outpouring of the Holy Spirit. These Christian men and women are also experiencing dreams and visions. Further along in Acts chapter two, Peter declared that this would be the case.

> "For the promise (*the gift of the Holy Spirit*) is to you and to your children, and to all who are afar off, (*in distance and in time*) as many as the Lord our God will call." (Acts 2:39; emphasis added).

Does the Prophet Joel Predict the Super Blood Moon of 2015?

Some Bible teachers today believe that the blood moon tetrad, which consists of four full lunar eclipses that occur on the feasts of Passover and Tabernacles of 2014 and 2015, might be related to the blood moon of Joel 2:31. Case in point; I appeared on two different TBN Praise the Lord TV shows, where this correlation was explored.

On November 1, 2013, Pastor John Hagee mentioned this while introducing his bestselling book titled, *Four Blood Moons,*

Something is About to Change. Subsequently, on March 24, 2014, Pastor Mark Biltz posited a similar possibility while explaining parts of his bestselling book entitled, *Blood Moons, Decoding the Imminent Heavenly Signs.*

Hagee and Biltz believe that Genesis 1:14 informs that the heavens can serve as a means through which the Lord can communicate important information to mankind. They both point out that this Scripture seems to associate signs given during certain seasons with respect to the appointed feast days of the Lord.

"Then God said, "Let there be lights in the firmament of the heavens to divide the day from the night; and let them be for *signs and seasons,* and for days and years." (Genesis 1:14; *emphasis added*)

I interpret these *signs and seasons* as God's Amber Alert system, which serves to display heavenly banners at divinely appointed times. Since the tetrad of 2014 and 2015 happens on feast days of the Lord, Hagee and Biltz caution that something significant, especially concerning Israel, could be about to occur within this tetrad window period.

Mark Biltz points out that the lunar eclipse predicted by NASA to occur on September 28, 2015, is supposedly going to be a "Super Blood Moon." This means the moon will be at perigee, (its closest point), to the earth in its orbit. Furthermore, he says that this particular lunar eclipse will be visible to Israelis.

What is fascinating to consider, is that according to NASA's future forecasting, there will be no more blood moon tetrads falling on consecutive Jewish feast days for the rest of this century. This could possibly suggest that the "Super Blood Moon" on the feast of Tabernacles 2015 might fulfill the blood moon of Joel 2:31.

For an unbeliever, this possibility should be extremely troubling news, because Joel declares that this blood moon occurs, *"before the coming of the great and awesome day of the LORD."* The "day of the LORD" is commonly taught to represent the seven year Trib-period. This is when the Lord executes wrath upon a Christ rejecting humanity through the Seal, Trumpet and Bowl judgments described in the book of Revelation.

If you are an unbeliever reading this book, I would encourage you to become a believer right now. Every end time's Bible prophecy is converging, according to Dr. David Reagan's book entitled, *Living on Borrowed Time, The Imminent Return of Jesus.*

What are you waiting for; more signs that evidence that these are the biblically predicted last days? If you believe that Jesus Christ is the Savior of mankind and want to receive Him right now, then skip ahead to the appendix called "The Sinner's Salvation Prayer." This appendix will guide you through the process.

Elamites Are Familiar with Supernatural Events

According to Acts 2:9, the Elamites were among the first to hear the gospel message, and in Acts 2:37-39, they were among those that received Christ as their Savior. Additionally, the Elamites have a long history of experiencing the supernatural realm. Below are a few examples of Elamites encountering supernatural events.

1. Some of them are experiencing the supernatural outpouring of the Spirit today. This outpouring is causing many Iranians to convert to Christianity. (Joel 2:29)
2. Some Elamites were present to witness the supernatural experience that occurred at the time of Pentecost. (Acts 2)
3. Elamites that were alive when the Persian Empire conquered the Babylonian Empire, witnessed the fulfillment of prophecies written in Isaiah 44:27 – 45:3. Isaiah predicted the rise of King Cyrus the Great over a century before he rose to power. Predicting the future with 100% accuracy is a supernatural event.
4. Elamite ancestors were present when the Tower of Babel was being constructed in Genesis chapter 11.

An interesting antithesis might be made between the events of Babel (Genesis 11) and Pentecost (Acts 2). In both instances, languages were supernaturally affected. At Babel, foreign languages were used to disunite men that were not seeking God, but at Pentecost, foreign languages were used to unite men that were seeking God. At Babel, men were dispersed from one location into other parts of the world, but at Pentecost, men from other parts of the world were assembled into one location. In both instances, Elamites were present to experience these supernatural events.

Men from Elam were present at Pentecost. Acts 2:9 identifies them among the crowd, *"Parthians and Medes and Elamites, those dwelling in Mesopotamia, Judea and Cappadocia, Pontus and Asia."* These Elamites likely included Jews from Elam, and Elamite proselytes that converted to Judaism. Both groups could have been present to observe Pentecost (the Feast of Weeks).

In the historic Tower of Babel episode, we have a potential trail that traces Elamites to that tongue-twisting episode as well. Noah's son, Shem, fathered several sons, including Elam and Arphaxad. Elam fathered the Elamites.

> "The sons of Shem *were* Elam, Asshur, Arphaxad, Lud, and Aram." (Genesis 10:21)

These sons were among the descendant families of Noah, which through the generations formed into the nations that emerged within the world after the flood.

> "These (*including Elam and Arphaxad*) *were* the families of the sons of Noah, (*Japheth, Shem and Ham*) according to their generations, in their nations; and from these the nations were divided on the earth after the flood. (Gen. 10:32)

These verses are taken from Genesis ten, which is commonly called the "Table of Nations" chapter. It presents an extensive list of the descendants of Noah and provides a traditional ethnology of mankind's history in the postdiluvian world. Once upon a time some, if not all of the sons of Shem, spoke the same language.

> "Now the whole earth (*including Elam and Arphaxad*) had one language and one speech." (Gen. 11:1; *emphasis added*)
> "And the LORD said, "Indeed the people *are* one and they all have one language, and this is what they begin to do;

(*conspire against God*) now nothing that they propose to do will be withheld from them. Come, let Us (*including the Holy Spirit*) go down and there confuse their language, that they may not understand one another's speech.'" (Gen. 11:6-7; *emphasis added*)

After this infamous historic event we read that Elamites, like many of the other descendants of Noah, spoke differing languages and possessed different lands. At Babel, the Elamites became babblers like the rest of those present during the supernatural experience.

"These *were* the sons of Shem, (*including Elam and Arphaxad*) according to their families, *according to their languages*, in their lands, according to their nations. These *were* the families of the sons of Noah, according to their generations, in their nations; and from these the nations were divided on the earth after the flood." (Gen. 10:31-32; *emphasis added*)

"Therefore its name is called Babel, because there the LORD confused the language of all the earth; and from there the LORD scattered them abroad over the face of all the earth." (Gen. 11:9).

Iranians Respond to the Supernatural Realm

I'm not an expert on the Iranian culture, but there seems to be several reasons that the Holy Spirit has chosen to work through the supernatural realm to redeem throngs of Iranians to Christ. The supernatural sphere is certainly not alien territory to the Spirit. The Spirit of God is invincible in the invisible domain.

"*Bill, the Iranians are a very emotional people,*" Hormoz Shariat informed me while conducting a radio interview together for the purposes of promoting this book.

Hormoz Shariat, the man that Bible prophecy expert Joel Rosenberg calls, "The Billy Graham of Iran,"[106] imparted this important cultural information to me. This ethnic insight helps me to partially understand why so many Iranians respond favorably to the supernatural endeavors of the Holy Spirit.

Everybody dreams an occasional dream, but not everyone seems very adept at deciphering its potential spiritual significance. In December, 2012, I dreamt that I was being Raptured into the clouds above my house. Does that mean my generation will be Raptured? I hope so, but I am still taking daily walks in an attempt to live as long as possible. However, dreams are leading many Iranians to Christ. Converting to Christ through a dream is a big commitment, considering most Iranians have been brought up under the strong influence of Islam. Yet, testimonies like this are continually coming out of Iran.

Hormoz Shariat is a highly educated, American Iranian. He formerly lived in Iran until the Iranian revolution of 1979. Fortunately, he had left Iran just prior to the revolution to attend an American university. He became a Christian while living in America. As a child, he was raised in a Muslim household, and prior to coming to America, he was among the throngs of Iranian Muslims that would shout, *"Death to Israel, the little Satan, and Death to America, the great Satan."*

Conversely, now as a Christian that is on fire for Christ, he utilizes satellite TV as a means to spread the gospel into the Middle East. Hormoz is the founder of Iran Alive Ministries. He penetrates through the ethereal airways over the turban wrapped heads of the Islamic Mullahs, and preaches the gospel into the Farsi speaking countries of Iran, Afghanistan and Tajikistan. It is probably no coincidence that these three countries rank among the top ten of the fastest growing evangelical populations in the world. Iran is #1, Afghanistan #2, and Tajikistan #10.[107]

It is estimated that before the Islamic takeover of Iran in 1979, that there were about 500 Iranian Christians. However, now it is believed that over one million Iranians have become Christians. This estimate is probably very low. In actuality, there may be as many as three million Christian converts living inside of Iran. It is almost impossible to accurately assess the actual number.

Hormoz informed me that an Iranian Christian tends to feel compelled to preach the Gospel. They are not ashamed of their Christianity, but wear it proudly on their sleeves. He attributes this to the fact that before converting, they felt like helpless and hopeless hostages under the stranglehold of Islam and the ruling rogue

Islamic regime. Finding hope and peace in Jesus Christ, for them, is like a resurrection from the grip of death. This is why they are not easily dissuaded from preaching the gospel to their countrymen, even knowingly facing the fear of severe governmental persecution.

Along these lines, Hormoz informed me that he receives calls constantly from Iranians. These calls can be costly in two ways. One, it costs quite a bit of money in long distance charges to call from Iran to America. Two, the Iranian government often monitors outgoing calls.

Hormoz frequently reminds these callers to use caution whenever calling, but he says they don't always heed his advice. He says they generally exhibit an unparalleled boldness in their faith. Many of these callers want to give their testimony, or receive Christ, or express their gratitude for the work of Iran Alive Ministries. In most of these instances, the caller is prepared to face the severe persecution that could result as a consequence of their call.

Over the past couple of years, Christianity burgeoned in Iran to the point that the Islamic government proactively began closing down home churches and arresting pastors. The Iranian Christians are in desperate need of discipleship and Bibles. For many of them, the high point of their Christian daily walk is watching satellite TV shows like Shariat's on Iran Alive, and Reza Safa's on TBN's Nejat TV.

Hormoz told me that the Iranian government tries to scramble some satellite signals around Tehran, but it is presently almost impossible to stop the masses in Iran from tuning into these shows. He said millions of Iranians watch these programs. These ministries need our daily prayers and financial support to keep up the good work. Visit *http://www.iranaliveministries.org* to become a financial partner with Iran Alive Ministries.

Many Iranian Christians go to Turkey for discipleship. Turkey does not require a visa for up to a three month visit, and the Turkish government has not yet cracked down heavily on home churches. However, to legally depart from Turkey to another country requires time and money, which are commodities in short supply for many Iranian Christians. After their three month visitation, most of them return to Iran to disciple and evangelize.

Millions of Iranians Know Bible Prophecy

Millions of Farsi speaking Iranians, Afghanis and Tajikistanis were exposed to advanced Bible prophecy teachings about Elam in Jeremiah 49:34-39 and Persia in Ezekiel 38.

It was April 1, 2014, when I found myself sitting in the Iran Alive Ministries studio. With a wireless microphone on my sports coat lapel and an electronic translator device located in my left ear, it was time to teach Middle East related Bible prophecies to multitudes of Farsi speaking peoples. The experience was surreal to me. Seated next to me was Hormoz Shariat, and we were about to go live on satellite TV.

Let me preface the setting by saying that Hormoz Shariat regularly teaches about Jeremiah's prophecy concerning Elam, and Ezekiel's prophecy regarding Persia on his TV program. These prophecies are of great interest to Iranian Christians, because they address the future of Iran in Bible prophecy.

Hormoz believes, as do I, that Jeremiah 49:34-39 is a prophecy that remains unfulfilled. He reminds his viewers that Jeremiah 49:38-39 promises that the Lord will establish His throne in Elam and someday restore the fortunes of Elam. He excites his viewers by explaining that Elam is the only place, apart from Jerusalem, where the Lord promises to establish His throne upon the earth. He believes that day is coming soon, and that's why his ministry's mission statement reads *"Transforming Iran into a Christian Nation in This Generation."*

On this occasion, Iran Alive Ministries wanted to present a more in-depth teaching to its audience. Time was set aside to broadcast two, timely, half hour programs that would discuss the important prophecies described in Psalm 83, Jeremiah 49:34-39, Ezekiel 38 and the Rapture. Hormoz wanted to conclude with a discussion about the Rapture, because his audience was not that familiar with it, and the Bible refers to it as the blessed hope in Titus 2:13.

Roll…Camera…Action; It was time to unpack Bible prophecies in the Farsi language. Hormoz enthusiastically greeted his audience while I heard his translator's voice in my left ear. It was my first encounter with a translator while airing a live television show. I had been prepped moments beforehand to teach in small bite size pieces, to enable Hormoz to translate into Farsi. Usually, when doing a TV show the interview is semi-scripted, but not in this case. This was a total improvisational experience.

Fortunately, the two shows turned out excellent and millions of Iranians were the first to be exposed to the most important content of this book. It seems only fitting that the Lord invited the Iranians to a sneak preview of this prophetic revealing of this epic event that specifically involves their homeland.

Summary

Supernatural events are taking place throughout the world, and especially in Iran. Through the supernatural, the Lord is taking personal responsibility to redeem as many of the lost as possible. Miracles, healings, dreams, visions and personal encounters with Christ are at the forefront of the Christian harvest that is taking place in Iran, Afghanistan, Tajikistan and other parts of the world.

Christian satellite TV reaches millions, and readies them to receive Bibles that people like Maryam Rostampour and Marziyeh Amirizadeh smuggle in at the risk of severe persecution. Many Iranian Christian converts have been incarcerated, persecuted and in some instances, killed, for attempting to freely worship Christ and spread the Gospel.

Amidst the backdrop of the ruthless reign of the repressive, Iranian Islamic rogue regime, multitudes of Iranians are converting to Christianity. According to Jeremiah 49:38-39, Iran will someday become a Christian nation. However, before that time comes, it appears that a nuclear showdown in Iran will occur.

A disaster happens in ancient Elam that causes many Iranian exiles to flee into other world nations. Who knows if you, as a reader of this book, might be called to receive one of these refugees into your own household? If the Lord tarries and asks you to become a part of an Elamite exile's exit strategy, are you willing? I believe that they would gladly receive you if the circumstances were reversed.

Pray, prepare and think about it........!

Appendices

Appendix 1

The Text of Psalm 83 and Ezekiel 38:1-39:20

The Text of Psalm 83:1-18
(New King James Version)

1. Do not keep silent, O God! Do not hold Your peace, And do not be still, O God!

2. For behold, Your enemies make a tumult; And those who hate You have lifted up their head.

3. They have taken crafty counsel against Your people, And consulted together against Your sheltered ones.

4. They have said, "Come, and let us cut them off from being a nation, That the name of Israel may be remembered no more."

5. For they have consulted together with one consent; They form a confederacy against You:

6. The tents of Edom [Palestinians refugees including West Bank Palestinians] and the Ishmaelites [Saudis]; Moab [central Jordanians] and the Hagrites [or Hagarenes— Egyptians];

7. Gebal [Lebanese], Ammon [northern Jordanians], and Amalek [Arabs of the Sinai area];Philistia [Palestinians of the Gaza, including Hamas] with the inhabitants of Tyre [Lebanese, including Hezbollah];

8. Assyria [Syrians and northern Iraqis] also has joined with them; They have helped the children of Lot. Selah

9. Deal with them as with Midian, as with Sisera, as with Jabin at the Brook Kishon,

10. Who perished at En Dor, who became as refuse on the earth.

11. Make their nobles like Oreb and like Zeeb, Yes, all their princes like Zebah and Zalmunna,

12. Who said, "Let us take for ourselves The pastures of God [Promised Land] for a possession."

13. O my God, make them like the whirling dust, like the chaff before the wind!

14. As the fire burns the woods, and as the flame sets the mountains on fire,

15. So pursue them with Your tempest, and frighten them with Your storm.

16. Fill their faces with shame, that they may seek Your name, O LORD.

17. Let them be confounded and dismayed forever; Yes, let them be put to shame and perish,

18. That they may know that You, whose name alone is the LORD, are the Most High over all the earth.

The Text of Ezekiel 38:1-23
(New King James Version)

1. Now the word of the LORD came to me, saying,

2. Son of man, set your face against Gog, of the land of Magog, the prince of Rosh, Meshech, and Tubal, and prophesy against him,

3. and say, 'Thus says the Lord GOD: "Behold, I *am* against you, O Gog, the prince of Rosh, Meshech, and Tubal.

4. I will turn you around, put hooks into your jaws, and lead you out, with all your army, horses, and horsemen, all splendidly clothed, a great company *with* bucklers and shields, all of them handling swords.

5. Persia, Ethiopia, and Libya are with them, all of them *with* shield and helmet;

6. Gomer and all its troops; the house of Togarmah *from* the far north and all its troops—many people *are* with you.

7. "Prepare yourself and be ready, you and all your companies that are gathered about you; and be a guard for them.

8. After many days you will be visited. In the latter years you will come into the land of those brought back from the sword *and* gathered from many people on the mountains of Israel, which had long been desolate; they were brought out of the nations, and now all of them dwell safely.

9. You will ascend, coming like a storm, covering the land like a cloud, you and all your troops and many peoples with you."

10. 'Thus says the Lord GOD: "On that day it shall come to pass *that* thoughts will arise in your mind, and you will make an evil plan:

11. You will say, 'I will go up against a land of unwalled villages; I will go to a peaceful people, who dwell safely, all of them dwelling without walls, and having neither bars nor gates'—

12. to take plunder and to take booty, to stretch out your hand against the waste places *that are again* inhabited, and against a people gathered from the nations, who have acquired livestock and goods, who dwell in the midst of the land.

13. Sheba, Dedan, the merchants of Tarshish, and all their young lions will say to you, 'Have you come to take plunder? Have you gathered your army to take booty, to carry away silver and gold, to take away livestock and goods, to take great plunder?'"

14. "Therefore, son of man, prophesy and say to Gog, 'Thus says the Lord GOD: "On that day when My people Israel dwell safely, will you not know *it*?

15. Then you will come from your place out of the far north, you and many peoples with you, all of them riding on horses, a great company and a mighty army.

16. You will come up against My people Israel like a cloud, to cover the land. It will be in the latter days that I will bring you against My land, so that the nations may know Me, when I am hallowed in you, O Gog, before their eyes."

17. Thus says the Lord GOD: "Are *you* he of whom I have spoken in former days by My servants the prophets of Israel, who prophesied for years in those days that I would bring you against them?

18. "And it will come to pass at the same time, when Gog comes against the land of Israel," says the Lord GOD, "*that* My fury will show in My face.

19. For in My jealousy *and* in the fire of My wrath I have spoken: 'Surely in that day there shall be a great earthquake in the land of Israel,

20. so that the fish of the sea, the birds of the heavens, the beasts of the field, all creeping things that creep on the earth, and all men who *are* on the face of the earth shall shake at My presence. The mountains shall be thrown down, the steep places shall fall, and every wall shall fall to the ground.'

21. I will call for a sword against Gog throughout all My mountains," says the Lord GOD. "Every man's sword will be against his brother.

22. And I will bring him to judgment with pestilence and bloodshed; I will rain down on him, on his troops, and on the many peoples who *are* with him, flooding rain, great hailstones, fire, and brimstone.

23. Thus I will magnify Myself and sanctify Myself, and I will be known in the eyes of many nations. Then they shall know that I *am* the LORD.'"

The Text of Ezekiel 39:1-20
(New King James Version)

1. And you, son of man, prophesy against Gog, and say, 'Thus says the Lord GOD: "Behold, I *am* against you, O Gog, the prince of Rosh, Meshech, and Tubal;

2. and I will turn you around and lead you on, bringing you up from the far north, and bring you against the mountains of Israel.

3.   Then I will knock the bow out of your left hand, and cause the arrows to fall out of your right hand.

4.   You shall fall upon the mountains of Israel, you and all your troops and the peoples who *are* with you; I will give you to birds of prey of every sort and *to* the beasts of the field to be devoured.

5.   You shall fall on the open field; for I have spoken," says the Lord GOD.

6.   And I will send fire on Magog and on those who live in security in the coastlands. Then they shall know that I *am* the LORD.

7.   So I will make My holy name known in the midst of My people Israel, and I will not *let them* profane My holy name anymore. Then the nations shall know that *I am* the LORD, the Holy One in Israel.

8.   Surely it is coming, and it shall be done," says the Lord GOD. "This *is* the day of which I have spoken.

9.   "Then those who dwell in the cities of Israel will go out and set on fire and burn the weapons, both the shields and bucklers, the bows and arrows, the javelins and spears; and they will make fires with them for seven years.

10. They will not take wood from the field nor cut down *any* from the forests, because they will make fires with the weapons; and they will plunder those who plundered them, and pillage those who pillaged them," says the Lord GOD.

11. "It will come to pass in that day *that* I will give Gog a burial place there in Israel, the valley of those who pass by east of the sea; and it will obstruct travelers, because there they will bury Gog and all his multitude. Therefore they will call *it* the Valley of Hamon Gog.

12. For seven months the house of Israel will be burying them, in order to cleanse the land.

13. Indeed all the people of the land will be burying, and they will gain renown for it on the day that I am glorified," says the Lord GOD.

14. "They will set apart men regularly employed, with the help of a search party, to pass through the land and bury those bodies remaining on the ground, in order to cleanse it. At the end of seven months they will make a search.

15. The search party will pass through the land; and *when anyone* sees a man's bone, he shall set up a marker by it, till the buriers have buried it in the Valley of Hamon Gog.

16. *The* name of *the* city *will* also *be* Hamonah. Thus they shall cleanse the land."'

17. "And as for you, son of man, thus says the Lord GOD, 'Speak to every sort of bird and to every beast of the field: "Assemble yourselves and come; Gather together from all sides to My sacrificial meal Which I am sacrificing for you, A great sacrificial meal on the mountains of Israel, That you may eat flesh and drink blood.

18. You shall eat the flesh of the mighty, Drink the blood of the princes of the earth, Of rams and lambs, Of goats and bulls, All of them fatlings of Bashan.

19. You shall eat fat till you are full, And drink blood till you are drunk, At My sacrificial meal Which I am sacrificing for you.

20. You shall be filled at My table With horses and riders, With mighty men And with all the men of war," says the Lord GOD.

Appendix 2

Iran's Other Nuclear Nightmare

Olivier Guitta: Iran's other nuclear timebomb

National Post 3/31/14

This appendix was going to include the above National Post article.[108] The op-ed piece was to be inserted because it alluded to the potential structural damage and environmental dangers that a significant earthquake might cause to the Bushehr nuclear facility and the surrounding areas. Unfortunately, the policies of the National Post (publisher) prohibited me from including this short, but extremely pertinent treatise.

For those of you that would like to read the essay, it can be accessed at this website link: *http://fullcomment.nationalpost. com/2014/03/31/olivier-guitta-irans-other-nuclear-timebomb/*

In lieu of posting this article in this appendix, I will paraphrase what the expose pointed out. To preface the potential relevancy of the information in this appendix, remember that Jeremiah 49:34-39 issues a prophecy that informs us that someday a disaster takes place in the territory of ancient Elam. The Bushehr facility exists within the boundaries of Elam. Jeremiah does not specifically predict that an earthquake is the cause of the calamity in Elam, but we cannot rule out this possibility.

"For I will cause Elam to be dismayed before their enemies
And before those who seek their life. I will bring disaster
upon them, My fierce anger,' says the LORD; 'And I will

send the sword (military invasion) after them Until I have consumed them." (Jer. 49:37; *emphasis added*)

The Hebrew prophet declares that the disaster results from the Lord's fierce anger, and it is accompanied by a military invasion, but this invasion may not be the sole reason for the catastrophe. Perhaps an earthquake may come into play as part of this Bible prophecy. The Bushehr nuclear facility is located in one of the most active seismic regions in the world.

As I author this appendix, important world leaders are working frantically to strike a deal with Iran concerning its nuclear program. They want Iran's estimated 19,000 centrifuges to stop, or at least slowdown, from spinning. It is estimated that 2,500 to 3,000 centrifuges spinning constantly could produce a nuclear bomb in about a year's time. Conversely, 19,000 centrifuges, spinning at the same rate can generate an atomic bomb in about 6 to 7 weeks. [109]

However, turning centrifuges could take a back seat to another larger looming issue. Across the gulf, the Arab states of the GCC (Gulf Cooperation Council) are preparing for the possible implications of a significant earthquake in Bushehr. These concerned neighbors are planning the construction of one of the world's largest pipelines. This canal system could be up to 2,000 kilometers (1242 miles) in length, and extend from Oman in the south, to Kuwait in the north.

The goal of the GCC is to provide potable and drinkable water to their member countries of Oman, UAE, Qatar, Bahrain, Saudi Arabia, and Kuwait. The project could be ready by 2020, at a cost of $7 to $10.5 billion.

"Gulf states try to tackle water woes"

Al Jazeera 1/22/14

"Threats to the GCC countries' water supply, say some analysts, are magnified by the fact that they rely heavily on desalinating water from a single source: the (Persian) Gulf." [110]

These oil rich Arab states recognize that all their liquid black gold can't insulate them from a nuclear disaster at Bushehr. Not only are they concerned about a potential military strike on the facility, but also about a devastating earthquake in close proximity to that location. Bushehr was constructed with German, Iranian and Russian parts at the intersection of three tectonic plates.

In America, the three most important words in Real Estate are often considered to be, "location, location and location." However, the German, Iranian and Russian contractors who built the Bushehr nuclear reactor apparently translated these English words as "tectonic, tectonic and tectonic!" As such, the world's least monitored nuclear site stands to be the GCC's worst nightmare.

Below are a few categorized quotes from the Olivier Guitta National Post article. These quotations are interwoven amidst my comments. The Guitta assessments adequately address the legitimate GCC trepidations about the Bushehr nuclear facility.

Facility Concerns

- "A 40-year-old design."
- "A 30 year old coolant system that runs on two different technologies."
- An untrained staff that is ill-equipped" to face any kind of accident."

A case in point is, "In February, 2011, a broken water pump caused small metallic pieces to infiltrate the reactor cooling system, forcing the unloading of the fuel rods…" "Indeed, in May, 2011, Iranian scientists themselves concluded this, in a report that was subsequently leaked."

Location Concerns

- "It (Bushehr) is situated in a zone that has experienced several deadly and very intense earthquakes — including as recently as April of last year. A 6.3 magnitude earthquake hit Bushehr."
- "Much closer" to the GCC countries "than it is to other large Iranian cities." It is a 412 mile drive from Bushehr to Kuwait City, but it is a 665 mile trip from Bushehr to Tehran.

- Wind patterns put the GCC nations at higher risk than Iran. Northwesterly winds "would actually push the potential radioactive leak right towards the aforementioned (GCC) neighboring countries and the Strait of Hormuz."
- Geography puts the GCC nations at a higher risk than Iran. "Iran's major population centers could be partially sheltered by the Zagros Mountains, a large mountain range about 550 miles long and 150 miles wide, which could act as a shield."

Olivier Guiita closes the article with the following comments.

"The Gulf countries are even more concerned than Iran itself about a potential nuclear accident…" "The number of direct victims could be in the thousands, with hundreds of thousands more facing long-term cancer risks."

"The impacts on international relations and global trade in this economically vital area of the world cannot be predicted, but would clearly be devastating."

Appendix 3
The Sinner's Salvation Prayer

"In an acceptable time I have heard you, And in the day of salvation I have helped you." Behold, now *is* the accepted time; behold, now *is* the day of salvation. (2 Corinthians 6:2).

The most important life decision one can make is to receive Christ as his personal Lord and Savior. It is the sinner's passport to a forgiven and changed life, so that they can enter paradise. However, sin is not allowed in heaven; therefore, Christ came to remedy the sin problem confronting mankind. He was sent because God so loved the world that He wished none would perish, but all would inhabit eternity.

"For God so loved the world that He gave His only begotten Son, [Jesus Christ] that whoever believes in Him should not perish but have everlasting life." (John 3:16).

"And this is eternal life, that they may know You, the only true God, and Jesus Christ [Begotten Son of God] whom You have sent." (John 17:1-3).

These passages point out that people are perishing, to the great displeasure of God, Who loves them immeasurably. He wishes that none would perish, but that everyone would inhabit eternity with Him and His only begotten Son, Jesus Christ. Of the utmost importance to eternal life is the knowledge of these two.

Sin Separates Us from the Love of God

The apostle John reminds us in 1 John 4:8, 16 that God is love; but, man lives in a condition of sin, which separates him from God's love. Romans 8:5-8 explains how sin manifests into carnal behavior, which creates enmity between God and man. So then, those who are in the flesh cannot please God. (Romans 8:8).

The book of Romans also instructs us that sin entered into the world through Adam, and spread throughout all mankind thereafter. Additionally, Romans informs us that sin is the root cause of all death, but through Jesus Christ eternal life can be obtained.

> "Therefore, just as through one man [Adam] sin entered the world, and death through sin, and thus death spread to all men, because all [men] sinned." (Romans 5:12).

> "All we like sheep have gone astray; We [mankind] have turned, every one, to his own way; And the LORD has laid on Him [Jesus Christ] the iniquity of us all." (Isaiah 53:6).

> "For the wages of sin *is* death, but the gift of God *is* eternal life in Christ Jesus our Lord. (Romans 6:23).

> If this makes sense to you, and you:

- Will humble yourself and recognize you are a sinner, separated from your Creator and living under the curse of sin,

- Believe that Jesus Christ took your punishment for sin so that you could be pardoned, as the only way to be saved,

- Want to repent and start letting God make changes in your life, to be in right relationship with Him,

- And, want to do it right now,

Then you have come to a right place spiritually. It is the place where millions before you, and many of your contemporaries alongside you, have arrived. By the grace of God, you have only one final step to take to complete your eternal journey. This is because salvation is a gift of God. Christ paid the full price for all sin, past, present, and future, when He sacrificed His life in Jerusalem about 2,000 years ago. Your pardon for sin is available to you through faith in the finished work of Jesus Christ completed upon His bloodstained cross. His blood was shed for us. He paid sins wages of death on our account.

You must now take the final leap of faith to obtain your eternal salvation. It is your faith in Christ that is important to God.

> "But without faith *it is* impossible to please *Him*, [God] for he who comes to God must believe that He is, and *that* He is a rewarder of those who diligently seek Him." (Hebrews 11:6; *emphasis added*).

> "In this you [believer] greatly rejoice, though now for a little while, if need be, you have been grieved by various trials, that *the genuineness of your faith, being much more precious than gold that perishes*, though it is tested by fire, may be found to praise, honor, and glory at the revelation of Jesus Christ, whom having not seen you love. Though now you do not see *Him*, yet believing, you rejoice with joy inexpressible and full of glory, receiving the end of your faith—the salvation of *your* souls." (1 Peter 1:6-9; *emphasis added*).

Before the necessary step to salvation gets introduced, it is important to realize and appreciate that salvation is a gift provided to us through God's grace. We didn't earn it, but we must receive it. If you are one who has worked hard to earn everything you have achieved in life, then you are to be commended. However, there is nothing you as a sinner could have done to meet the righteous requirement to cohabit eternity with God. In the final analysis, when we see our heavenly Father in His full glory, we will all be overwhelmingly grateful that Christ's sacrificial death bridged the chasm between our unrighteousness, and God's uncompromising holiness.

> "But God, who is rich in mercy, because of His great love with which He loved us, even when we were dead in trespasses, [sin] made us alive together with Christ (*by grace you have been saved*), and raised *us* up together, and made *us* sit together in the heavenly *places* in Christ Jesus, that in the ages to come He might show the exceeding riches of His grace in *His* kindness toward us in Christ Jesus. *For by grace you have been saved* through faith, and that not of yourselves; *it is the gift of God,* not of works, lest anyone should boast." (Ephesians 2:4-9; *emphasis added*).

The Good News Gospel Truth

The term gospel is derived from the Old English "god-spell," which was understood to mean "good news" or "glad tidings." In a nutshell, the gospel is the good news message of Jesus Christ. Jesus came because God so loved the world that He sent His Son to pay the penalty for our sins. That's part of the good news, but equally important is the "Resurrection."

This is the entire good news gospel:

> "For I delivered to you first of all that which I also received: that Christ died for our sins according to the Scriptures, and that He was buried, and that He rose again the third day according to the Scriptures" (1 Corinthians 15:3-4).

Christ resurrected, which means He's alive and able to perform all of His abundant promises to believers. The Bible tells us that He is presently in heaven, seated at the right hand side of God the Father, waiting until His enemies become His footstool.

> "But this Man, [Jesus Christ became a Man, to die a Man's death] after He had offered one sacrifice for sins forever, sat down at the right hand of God, from that time waiting till

His enemies are made His footstool. For by one offering He has perfected forever those who are being sanctified." (Hebrews 10:12-14).

The resurrection of Christ overwhelmingly serves as His certificate of authenticity to all His teachings. He traveled through the door of death, and resurrected to validate His promises, prophecies, and professions. This can't be said of the claims of Buddha (Buddhism), Mohammed (Islam), Krishna (Hinduism), or any of the other host of deceased, human, non-resurrected, false teachers. All the erroneous teachings they deposited on the living side of death's door were invalidated when they died and lacked the power to conquer death itself, as Jesus had done. One of Christ's most important claims is:

> "Jesus said to him, "I am the way, the truth, and the life. No one comes to the [heavenly] Father except through Me."" (John 14:6)

This is a critical claim, considering eternal life can only be obtained by knowing the heavenly Father, and Christ, whom He (the Father) sent, according to John 17, listed at the top of this appendix. Most importantly, the resurrection proves that death has an Achilles heel. It means that its grip can be loosed from us, but only by Christ who holds the power over death.

> ""O Death, where is your sting? O Hades, where is your victory?" The sting of death *is* sin, and the strength of sin *is* the law. But thanks *be* to God, who gives us the victory [over Death and Hades] through our Lord Jesus Christ." (1 Corinthian 15:55-57)

How to be Saved —You Must Be Born Again

"Jesus answered and said to him, [Nicodemus] "Most assuredly, I say to you, unless one is born again, he cannot see the kingdom of God."" (John 3:3)

Jesus told Nicodemus, a religious leader of his day, that entrance into the kingdom of God required being born again. This is a physical impossibility, but a spiritual necessity, and why faith plays a critical role in your salvation. You can't physically witness your new birth; it is a spiritual accomplishment beyond your control, which happens upon receiving Christ as your Lord and Savior. God takes full responsibility for your metamorphosis into a new creation at that point.

> "Therefore, if anyone *is* in Christ, *he is* a new creation; old things have passed away; behold, all things have become new." (2 Corinthians 5:17)

You must trust God to perform on His promise to escort you through the doors of death into eternity, and to process you into the likeness of Christ meanwhile. This is the ultimate meaning of being born again; and alongside Christ, it is a responsibility undertaken by the third member of the Trinity, the Holy Spirit. Christ holds the power over Death and Hades, but the Holy Spirit is your "Helper" that participates in your spiritual processing.

> "I *am* He [Jesus Christ] who lives, and was dead, and behold, I am alive forevermore. [Resurrected] Amen. And I have the keys of Hades and of Death." (Revelation 1:18)

> "If you love Me [Christ], keep My commandments. And I will pray the Father, and He will give you another Helper [Holy Spirit], that He may abide with you forever— the Spirit of truth, whom the world cannot receive, because it neither sees Him nor knows Him; but you know Him, for He dwells with you and will be in you." (John 14:15-17)

> "These things I have spoken to you while being present with you. But the Helper, the Holy Spirit, whom the Father will send in My name, He will teach you all things, and bring to your remembrance all things that I said to you." (John 14:25-26)

In order for you to successfully cross over from death to eternal life, at the appointed time, God has to work His unique miracle. Christ's resurrection demonstrated He possesses the power to make your eternity happen. Death wasn't eliminated in the resurrection, it was conquered. Death still serves its purpose on Earth by providing the sinner his due wage. Isaiah 65:20 informs that death continues to serve its purpose even in the Messianic Kingdom, where Christ reigns over a restored Earth for 1,000 years.[111]

> "No more shall an infant from there *live but a few* days, Nor an old man who has not fulfilled his days; For (*in the Messianic Kingdom*) the child shall *die* one hundred years old, But the sinner *being* one hundred years old shall be accursed." (Isaiah 65:20; emphasis added)

This is why the full gospel involves both God's love and power. His love for us would be of little benefit if it ended with our deaths. His love and power are equally important for our eternal assurance. Therefore, we see in Romans 10, the following:

> "But what does it say? *"The word is near you, in your mouth and in your heart"* (that is, the word of faith which we preach): that if you confess with your mouth the Lord Jesus and believe in your heart that God has raised Him from the dead, you will be saved. For with the heart one believes unto righteousness, and with the mouth confession is made unto salvation. For the Scripture says, *"Whoever believes on Him will not be put to shame."* For there is no distinction between Jew and Greek, for the same Lord over all is rich to all who call upon Him. For *"whoever calls on the name of the Lord shall be saved.""* (Romans 10:8-13)

These Romans verses sum it up for all who seek to be saved through Christ. We must confess that Jesus Christ is Lord, and believe in our hearts that God raised Him from the dead.

The Sinner's Prayer for Salvation

Knowing that confession of Christ as Lord, coupled with a sincere faith that God raised Him from the dead, are salvation requirements, the next step is customarily to recite a sinner's prayer in order to officiate one's salvation.

Definition of the Sinner's Prayer

A sinner's prayer is an evangelical term referring to any prayer of humble repentance spoken or read by individuals who feel convicted of the presence of sin in their life and desire to form or renew a personal relationship with God through His son Jesus Christ. It is not intended as liturgical like a creed or a Confiteor. It is intended to be an act of initial conversion to Christianity, and also may be prayed as an act of recommitment for those who are already believers in the faith. The prayer can take on different forms. There is no formula of specific words considered essential, although it usually contains an admission of sin and a petition asking that the Divine (Jesus) enter into the person's life.[112]

Example of the Sinner's Prayer

Below is a sample Sinner's Prayer taken from the Salvation Prayer website. If you are ready to repent from your sins, and to receive Jesus Christ as your personal Lord and Savior, read this prayer will all sincerity of heart to God.

Dear God in heaven, I come to you in the name of Jesus. I acknowledge to You that I am a sinner, and I am sorry for my sins and the life that I have lived; I need your forgiveness.

I believe that your only begotten Son Jesus Christ shed His precious blood on the cross at Calvary and died for my sins, and I am now willing to turn from my sin.

You said in Your Holy Word, Romans 10:9 that if we confess the Lord as our God and believe in our hearts that God raised Jesus from the dead, we shall be saved.

Right now I confess Jesus as the Lord of my soul. With my heart, I believe that God raised Jesus from the dead. This very moment I receive Jesus Christ as my own personal Savior and according to His Word, right now I am saved.

Thank you Jesus, for your unlimited grace which has saved me from my sins. I thank you Jesus that your grace never leads to license for sin, but rather it always leads to repentance. Therefore Lord Jesus transform my life so that I may bring glory and honor to you alone and not to myself.

Thank you Jesus, for dying for me and giving me eternal life. Amen.[113]

Congratulations and welcome into the household of God!

Below are the congratulatory words and recommendations also taken from the Salvation Prayer website. If you just prayed the Sinner's Prayer, please be sure to read this section for further guidance.

"If you just said this prayer and you meant it with all your heart, we believe that you just got saved and are born again. You may ask, "Now that I am saved, what's next?" First of all you need to get into a Bible-based church, and study God's Word. Once you have found a church home, you will want to become water-baptized. By accepting Christ you are baptized in the spirit, but it is through water-baptism that you show your obedience to the Lord. Water baptism is a symbol of your salvation from the dead. You were dead but now you live, for the Lord Jesus Christ has redeemed you for a price! The price was His death on the cross. May God Bless You!"[114]

Remember, being born again is a spiritual phenomenon. You may have felt an emotional response to your commitment to Christ, but don't be concerned if fireworks didn't spark, bands didn't march, sirens didn't sound, or trumpets didn't blast in the background at the time. There will be plenty of ticker-tape for us in heaven, which is where our rewards will be revealed. If you meant what you said, you can be assured God, Who sent His Son to be crucified on our behalf, overheard your every word. Even the angels in heaven are rejoicing.

"Likewise, I say to you, there is joy in the presence of the angels of God over one sinner who repents." (Luke 15:10).

Welcome to the family…!

Appendix 4

Is the Church identified in Psalm 83?

Appendix is based upon an article from the author written on 8/13/2010

Linked here -
http://prophecydepot.blogspot.com/2010/08/is-church-hiding-in-psalm-83.html

Recently I received an email asking a very interesting Church related question regarding the *"hidden ones"* of Psalm 83:3.

> *They* [Arab confederates] *have taken crafty counsel against Your people* [national Israel], *And consulted together against Your sheltered* [hidden] *ones. (Psalm 83:3; NKJV) Some translations use the word "hidden" instead of sheltered.*

> Question: *I have a question concerning Psalm 83:3 and its link with Isaiah 26:20. The last section of the Psalm verse reads." and consulted against thy hidden ones ", and Isaiah explains who these are that are hiding. I understand these passages refer to the Saints/Church.*

> *That being the case would not the inference in the psalm be that the Church has already been taken before the fulfillment of that prophecy? Kindest Regards - Garry M.*

Bill's Answer: Brother Gary, I don't believe the Church is identified anywhere in Psalm 83. Furthermore, since the Rapture is an imminent event, Psalm 83 is about to occur, and the Church is still present, it is very possible that Christians may witness the final fulfillment of Psalm 83.

In Psalm 83:3, the Hebrew word for "hidden" in "hidden ones" is Tsaphan. This word does not appear in Isaiah 26:20 or anywhere else in the book of Isaiah. The first usage of Tsaphan is in Exodus 2:2-3 alluding to the baby Moses being hidden by his mother from Pharaoh's edict of death in Egypt. At the time all Hebrew males were being killed at birth in order to keep the Hebrew ethnicity weak and enslaved. However, a remnant led by Moses ultimately survived and departed for the Promised Land.

Typologically, from an end time's perspective, the mother of Moses likely represents national Israel and Moses, the faithful end time's remnant that eventually emerges from within it. Similarly, the next usage of Tsaphan is found in Joshua 2:4 whereby Rahab was hiding the two spies. These two also typologically signify a select sub-group or remnant of Israel.

I believe that Psalm 83:3 alludes to both national Israel (Your people), which exists today in a condition of unbelief, and the faithful remnant (hidden ones) that comes out from national Israel in the end times in a condition of belief. Although the faithful remnant hasn't emerged yet from within Israel, one will in the Tribulation period. Today, they are "Tsaphan", within national Israel. Presently, they remain unidentified but probably exist on the world scene somewhere unknowingly. However, omniscient God knows who and where they are.

Psalm 83 represents a genocidal attempt of the Jews and the final destruction of the Jewish State, that the name Israel be remembered no more. (Ps. 83:4). Geo-politically the Arab confederates want to destroy Israel and confiscate the Promised Land. We see this stage setting in the Middle East today. Geo-prophetically, Satan wants to destroy all Jews worldwide, especially the infamous coming faithful remnant, to prove God is not a covenant keeper.

In Genesis 13:15, 22:17, and elsewhere, God unconditionally promised Abraham, Isaac, and Jacob, descendants forever. In Genesis 15:18 these patriarchs were presented with the Promised Land, which exists from the Nile River in Egypt to the Euphrates in Iraq and Syria. The Psalm 83 Arabs dwell upon a majority of this "Holy Land" today. They want to destroy the Jews and possess the land (Psalm 83:12).

Psalm 83 represents the first of three end time's genocidal attempts against the Jews. Ezekiel 38 & 39 appears to follow soon and sequentially on the heels of Psalm 83. In Ezekiel's prophecy Russia, Iran, Turkey, and several other nations will confederate to kill the Jews and confiscate the plunder and booty that Israel will possess after they defeat the Psalm 83 confederacy.

Lastly, the Antichrist will muster up his Armageddon forces in the Tribulation Period in a final Jewish genocidal attempt. This is when the Tsaphan, faithful remnant, of Israel will emerge. They become the saved remnant of Romans 9:27 and 11:26. They are also the "sons of the living God" in Hosea 1:10 and Romans 9:26. I believe the Psalmist Asaph was informing us that Israel's Arab enemies will attempt to kill all Jews, even the hidden faithful end time's remnant, so that God's promises to Abraham, Isaac, and Jacob would be broken.

Although the Church may be here to witness Psalm 83, it does not appear to be identified anywhere in the Psalm. Psalm 83 is Satan's attempt to inspire the Islamic Arabs who hate and surround Israel, to destroy the Jews and the Jewish State in order to prove God is a promise breaker. In fact, the Church needs to come out of hiding on Psalm 83 and preach the possibility that it's about to find final fulfillment.

Appendix 5
The Treasured Ones of Psalm 83

Appendix is based upon an article from the author written on 2/9/2011

Linked here:
prophecynewsstand.blogspot.com/2011/02/treasured-ones-of-psalm-83.html

Comment - Dear Mr. Salus - I regularly receive emails from Bible Prophecy and as a matter of fact, I pray Psalm 83 every night for the total defeat of Israel's satanic enemies. Regarding your article "*Is the Church Identified in Psalm 83?*" I would like to bring the following to your attention. In my Bible Ps.83.3 reads as follows:

"They are making secret plans against your people; they are plotting against those you protect."

I feel that this translation of vs.3 is far more descriptive, especially in light of current events that are leading up to Psalm 83, which I believe will be the next "happening" in the prophetic Mid-east calendar. It never ceases to amaze me how much different Bible translations differ. Yours in Christ – J.M. - South Africa

Bill's Response – Dear J.M. thanks for your comment. In 2010, Chuck Missler and I discussed this topic at a Southern California prophecy conference we were speaking at. Chuck is studying the possibility that the "hidden" or "treasured" ones in Psalm 83:3 could represent true born again Christians. He presented a couple arguments in support of this view. However, for the reasons expressed in, (*refer to the Appendix called Is the Church Identified in Psalm 83*)and those listed below, I believe the "hidden ones" probably represent the faithful remnant inside national Israel.

1. To make the "hidden ones" the Church implies the confederacy of Psalm 83:6-8 wages a multi-front war against Israel and true Christian believers. It seems that geography alone would defeat this plan. The Psalm 83 confederacy is centered in the Mideast, but true believers are scattered throughout the world. The confederates surround Israel, making it an easy target. However targeting Christians would require a worldwide campaign headquartered in the Middle East which is unlikely.

2. The mandate of Psalm 83:4 is to destroy the Jewish State, "that the name Israel be remembered no more." This mission is very specific regarding Israel.

3. The motive of Psalm 83:12 is the capture of the Promised Land of Israel. Thus, the mandate and motive of the Psalm 83 confederacy are entirely regarded with the Jewish people and the land of Israel.

4. The Hebrew word for "hidden" is Tsaphan and is first used in Exodus 2:2-3 identifying Moses being hidden in the basket from Pharaoh's persecution.

5. The second usage is in Joshua 2:4 describing Rahab hiding the two spies.

In these initial usages the Hebrew word Tsaphan best represent the faithful inside national Israel. Therefore, I suggest the "hidden ones" of Psalm 83:3 represent the faithful remnant that will surface out of today's national Israel and survive both Psalm 83 and ultimately the Tribulation. The caveat is that if there is a significant generational gap between Psalm 83 and the Tribulation, which I doubt, then the hidden ones in Psalm 83 probably represent the Messianic Jewish community dwelling inside Israel when Psalm 83 occurs.

Endnotes

1 The article about Jeremiah prophecy on Elam is called *Mighty Muscles Flex in the Mideast*. It was written on 6/24/10 and was still located at this weblink as of 1/15/14 *http://prophecynewsstand.blogspot.com/2010/06/mighty-muscles-flex-in-mideast.html*. The two books were *Revelation Road, Hope Beyond the Horizon*. (2012) and the *Psalm 83: The Missing Prophecy Revealed, How Israel Becomes the next Mideast Superpower*. (2013)

2 (Matthew 28:19, Mark 16:15) These verses encourage believers to preach the gospel of Christ throughout the world.

3 *Epicenter* was published by Tyndale House Publishers. Tyndale's website is *http://www.tyndale.com*

4 The map was created by Koinonia House Ministries and the modern-day equivalents are only a consensus.

5 US State Department website was accessed on January 16, 2014 at this website: *http://www.state.gov/j/ct/list/c14151.htm*

6 The Elamites may have been among the nations that came against Babylon in Jer. 50:9.

7 Netanyahu quote taken on 2/25/14 from this website: *http://www.ynetnews.com/articles/0,7340,L-4491413,00.html*

8 Jerusalem Post article was on the Internet as of 2/26/12 at this link: *http://www.jpost.com/LandedPages/PrintArticle.aspx?id=343555*

9 Image of Iran's military sites was taken from the Internet on 1/28/14 at this website. *http://commons.wikimedia.org/wiki/File:Military_installations_of_Iran_-_2002.jpg*

10 *CAVEAT*: These above statements by the author may not apply to the entire country of Iran, but to the affected area characterized by Elam, which would be west central Iran today. Since Iran's enemies are primarily located to its west, many of Iran's military installations are located in or around the ancient territory of Elam.

11 Sean Osborne's quote was taken from his Internet blogsite on 1/22/14 at this link *http://www.eschatologytoday.blogspot.com/2014/01/global-sitrep-b5-13-lords-fierce-anger.html*

12 Reshith translations taken from Strong's Hebrew and Greek Dictionaries H7225.

13 Construction of Bushehr information was taken from this website on 1/20/14 *http://en.wikipedia.org/wiki/Bushehr_Nuclear_Power_Plant*

14 Related article to GCC concerns about Bushehr was found on the Internet on 1/20/14 at this site: *http://english.alarabiya.net/en/views/news/middle-east/2013/07/24/Iranian-radiation-a-threat-to-GCC-water-security-.html*

15 Religions of Iran taken from the Internet on 1/28/14 at this website: *http://en.wikipedia.org/wiki/Religion_in_Iran*

16 The quote from CBS News was taken from the Internet on 1/28/14 at this Internet site: *http://www.cbsnews.com/news/iran-pre-emptive-strike-against-enemies-possible/*

17 The quote from the Diplomat was taken on 1/28/14 from this Internet site: *http://thediplomat.com/2013/05/a-grand-coalition-against-iran/*

18 This quote was taken from the Internet on 1/28/14 at this Internet site: *http://english.alarabiya.net/en/views/news/middle-east/2013/07/24/Iranian-radiation-a-threat-to-GCC-water-security-.html*

19   This quote is taken from the Internet as of 1/28/14 at this site: *http://www. futuredirections.org.au/publications/food-and-water-crises/28-global-food-and-water-crises-swa/1230-gcc-co-operates-on-critical-water-security-measure-in-response-to-fears-of-iranian-nuclear-radiation.html*

20   Jerusalem Post headline taken from Internet on 5/5/14 at this website link: *http://www. jpost.com/Iranian-Threat/News/Iran-terror-network-prolific-US-report-says-350981*

21   Chathath translation taken from "The New American Hebrew and Greek Dictionaries" and "Strong's Hebrew and Greek Dictionaries. H2865

22   Jeremiah's usages of the phases are located in (Jer. 19:7, 9, 21:7, 34:20-21, 46:26, 49:37)

23   The quote from Breitbart was taken on 1/31/14 from this Internet site: *http://www.breitbart. com/Big-Peace/2014/01/29/Israel-Defense-Official-We-are-Entering-an-Era-of-Fire*

24   Population estimates between Sunnis and Shia's in Bahrain were taken from the Internet on 1/29/14 at this website: *http://www.globalpost.com/dispatch/news/ regions/middle-east/121211/bahrain-uprising-protests-islam-sunni-shiite*

25   Hebrew word translations for "raah" taken from the New American Standard Hebrew and Greek Dictionaries.

26   The definition of the word Hebrew was taken from the Easton Bible Dictionary.

27   Quote taken from the Internet on 7/18/2011 at this link: *http://en.wikipedia.org/ wiki/List_of_earthquakes_in_Iran*: all the earthquake information was gathered at this web link.

28   The definition of throne was taken from the Internet on 2/3/14 at this website: *http://www.merriam-webster.com/dictionary/throne*

29   *New American Standard Hebrew and Greek Dictionaries*

30   Global Firepower website with specific 2013 rankings was taken on 3/16/14 at this link: *http://www.globalfirepower.com/countries-listing.asp*

31   Definition of the Hebrew word "sar" was taken from Strong's Hebrew and Greek Dictionaries

32   Jack Kelley's article on the subject of Elam is located on the Internet as of 2/7/14 at this site: *http://gracethrufaith.com/end-times-prophecy/prophecy-elam/*

33   Psalm 83: *The Missing Prophecy* Revealed by Bill Salus chapter 14, pages 153-155

34   Study the distinctions between Syrians and Assyrians at the Assyrian International News Agency (AINA) at this Internet site: *http://www.aina.org/articles/assyrians.htm*

35   Location of Pathros was taken from the Parsons Bible Atlas from QuickVerse 6.0 Bible software.

36   Quote taken from the Internet on 3/4/13 from this website: *http://online.wsj.com/ news/articles/SB10001424052702303560204579246142096554348*

37   The interpretation by James B. Jordan was written in 1996 and is posted on the Internet. It was accessed for the purposes of this book on 3/6/14 at this Internet link: *http://www.biblicalhorizons.com/biblical-chronology/8_03/*

38   This quote was taken from the Internet on 3/4/14 from this website link *http:// www.farsinet.com/persiansinbible/pib10/chapter9.pdf*
      It is part of a PDF document entitled "CHAPTER 9 WHY IS ELAM SO SIGNIFICANT? (CITADEL OF SUSA - CAPITAL OF ELAM). The related website link appears to be *http://www.farsinet.com/persiansinbible/*. The main website appears to be *http://www.farsinet.com*.

39   Allyn Huntzinger's information was taken from Internet on 3/9/14 at this website: *http://www.farsinet.com/persiansinbible/pib10/chapter9.pdf*.   This website provides a four-page reading entitled: CHAPTER 9 WHY IS ELAM SO SIGNIFICANT? (CITADEL OF SUSA - CAPITAL OF ELAM)

40   Esther 1:2

41   Information taken from the Internet on 3/4/14 at this website: *http://www.iranchamber.com/history/cyrus/cyrus_charter.php*

42   This point is made about the 10 minute mark into the documentary video called "Iran the Forgotten Glory." *http://farsmovie.com/eng/index.htm*

43   Pasargadae was one of the oldest residences of the Achaemenid kings. This inscription information was taken from the Internet on 3/4/14 at this website: *http://archaeology.about.com/od/athroughadterms/qt/achaemenid.htm*.

44   The Achaemenid Empire was the name of the first Persian Empire.

45   Cyrus was spoken about in Bible prophecy by Isaiah 44:28-45:1 before he was even born.

46   These city population stats were taken on 3/4/14 from a Google search using the words, what is the population of, and then by the city.

47   This was the population of Ahvaz, Iran as of 2006 as per this website that was accessed on 3/4/14 *http://en.wikipedia.org/wiki/Ahvaz*

48   Quote taken from James B. Jordan. It was accessed from the Internet on 3/10/14 at this website: *http://www.biblicalhorizons.com/biblical-chronology/8_03/*

49   The time period of the Persian Empire was taken from the Internet on 3/10/14 from this website: *http://www.flowofhistory.com/units/pre/2/FC15*

50   Esther 2:7 points out the Esther and Mordecai were cousins.

51   Jack Kelly's quote was taken from the Internet on January 13, 2014 at this website: *http://gracethrufaith.com/end-times-prophecy/prophecy-elam/*

52   The timeline of the Babylonian conquest of Elam was taken from the Internet on 3/12/14 at this website: *http://www.scaruffi.com/politics/persians.html*. Technically speaking, the Medes participated with the Babylonians during the conquest over the Assyrian Empire at the time. As such, the Medes rather than the Babylonians exerted more sovereign control over the territory of Elam.

53   Information about the Persian conquest of Elam was taken from the Internet on 3/12/14 at this website: *http://www.scaruffi.com/politics/persians.html*

54   Jack Kelly's quote was taken from the Internet on January 13, 2014 at this website: *http://gracethrufaith.com/end-times-prophecy/prophecy-elam/*

55   King Artaxerxes ruled for forty years from 465-425 according to Easton's Bible Dictionary.

56   Jack Kelly's quote was taken from the Internet on January 13, 2014 at this website: *http://gracethrufaith.com/end-times-prophecy/prophecy-elam/*

57   Time Period of Cyrus was taken from the Internet on 3/12/14 from this website: *http://www.ancient.eu.com/Cyrus_II/*

58   Quote taken from The Bible Knowledge Commentary: Old Testament in the commentary section of Ezra 1:1.

59   The time period of King Ahasuerus was taken from Holman Bible Dictionary, under the title of Xerxes, which was another name for King Ahasuerus.

60   The war between the Jews and the Canaanites (Judges 4-5). The war between the Jews and the Midianites (Judges 6-8).

61   Jack Kelly's quote was taken from the Internet on January 13, 2014 at this website: *http://gracethrufaith.com/end-times-prophecy/prophecy-elam/*

62   The Greek name for Elam was taken from Easton's Bible Dictionary, under the title of "Elam."

63   Headline taken from worldtribune.com and was accessed over the Internet on 4/5/14 at this website: *http://www.worldtribune.com/worldtribune/WTARC/2010/me_iran0785_08_16.asp*

64   Quote about Elam is from *The Footsteps of the Messiah* book, chapter 20, section C-6 pages 510-511. By Dr. Arnold Fruchtenbaum

65   Joel Rosenberg's presentation was uploaded on YouTube on November 1, 2011, and can be watched on YouTube at this website: *https://www.youtube.com/watch?v=9WvQIcSCgiI*

66   Quote taken from the section of commentary covering Jeremiah 49:34-38 by John Walvoord and Roy Zuck.

67   McTernan quote taken from the Internet on 4/7/14 at this website link: *http://www.defendproclaimthefaith.org/elam_letter_days.html*

68   Quote about Egypt is from *The Footsteps of the Messiah* book, chapter 20, section C-6 pages 509. By Dr. Arnold Fruchtenbaum

69   Populations of Egypt and Algeria taken from the Internet on 4/7/14 from this website: *http://en.wikipedia.org/wiki/List_of_Arab_countries_by_population*

70   Military rankings of Egypt and Saudi Arabia taken from the Internet on 4/7/14 from this website: *http://www.globalfirepower.com/countries-listing.asp*

71   This headline comes from the National Post article linked at this site as of 4/7/14 *http://fullcomment.nationalpost.com/2014/03/31/olivier-guitta-irans-other-nuclear-timebomb/*

72   Iranian Diaspora population statistics were taken from Allyn Huntzingers book called Persian in the Bible chapter 18 on page 85.

73   Headline taken from the Internet on 4/29/14 at this website: *http://www.wnd.com/2012/02/ayatollah-kill-all-jews-annihilate-israel/*

74   Dates of Medo-Persian empire taken from this Internet site on 1/4/14 *http://www.princeton.edu/~achaney/tmve/wiki100k/docs/Persian_Empire.html*

75   Lifespan of Cyrus the Great taken from the Internet on 1/9/14 at this website: *http://www.cyrusthegreat.net/*

76   Dates of the Greek Empire were taken from this Internet site on 1/9/14: *http://www.scaruffi.com/politics/greeks.html*

77   Quote was made on 2/1/12 and taken from the Washington Post over the Internet on 1/9/14 at this link: *http://www.washingtonpost.com/world/middle_east/iran-says-it-launched-satellite/2012/02/03/gIQARNuDmQ_story.html*

78   Quote was made on 2/1/12 and taken from the Washington Post over the Internet on 1/9/14 at this link: *http://www.washingtonpost.com/world/middle_east/iran-says-it-launched-satellite/2012/02/03/gIQARNuDmQ_story.html*

79   Quote was made on 8/14/13 and taken from the Jerusalem Post over the Internet on 1/9/14 at this link: *http://www.jpost.com/Iranian-Threat/News/Khamenei-Zionist-regime-will-disappear-from-map*

80   Quote was made on 11/20/13 and taken from the Haaretz over the Internet on 1/9/14 at this link: *http://www.haaretz.com/news/middle-east/1.559135*

81   Khamenei quote taken from Al Jazeera website on 4/30/12 at this link: *http://www.aljazeera.com/news/middleeast/2011/10/201110222010936488.html*

82   This assessment was emailed to me on 5/1/14 from Sean Osborne. Osborne's blogsite is located at this link: *http://eschatologytoday.blogspot.com/*

83   Examples of typological usages in the Bible of mountain or mountains are Daniel 2:45, Ezek. 37:22, Ezek 19:9

84   Mark Twain quote gathered from the Internet on 11/3/12 at this site: *http://zionismandisrael.wordpress.com/2008/08/28/mark-twain-in-the-holy-land/*

85   New American Standard Hebrew and Greek dictionaries. *Yashab*: to dwell. *Betach*: securely.

86   Other biblical use examples of Yashab Betach in tandem are Deut. 12:10, Ezek. 28:26.

87   Holman Bible Dictionary says that Solomon became the third king of Israel and reigned forty years about 1000 BC.

88   Curse-for-curse-in-kind is a phrase I first heard from Dr. Arnold Fruchtenbaum of Ariel Ministries. The phrase aptly describes the curse component of Gen. 12:3

89   List of nations and their relationship to Israel can be found on the Internet as of 5/7/14 at this website: *http://en.wikipedia.org/wiki/International_recognition_of_Israel*

90   Information about Josephus connecting Magog with the Scythians was collected from "The Old Testament Volume" of the *New Commentary on the Whole Bible*—Based on the classic commentary of Jamieson, Fausset, and Brown. It can be located in the commentary regarded with Ezekiel 38.

91   Information accessed from the Internet on 7/8/11 at this link: *http://en.wikipedia.org/wiki/Scythians*

92   Author recommended books and/or articles, and/or videos presentations covering Ezekiel 38 are *Northern Storm Rising* by Dr. Ron Rhodes; *Epicenter* by Joel Rosenberg; *The Magog Invasion and the The Alternative View to the Magog Invasion* by Dr. Chuck Missler; and *The Footsteps of the Messiah* by Dr. Arnold Fruchtenbaum.

93   Yoram Ettinger's quote was taken from his website on 5/5/14 at this website link: *http://www.theettingerreport.com/OpEd/OpEd---Israel-Hayom/Is-Israel-Isolated--(1).aspx*

94   Headline taken on 4/29/14from this Internet website on 4/29/14: *http://www.israelnationalnews.com/News/News.aspx/176855#.U2BFCNJOVjo*

95   Quote taken from The Bible Knowledge Commentary in the section of Ezekiel 38:1-8.

96   The dating of the Book of Ezekiel was taken from the Internet on 4/21/14 from this website link: *http://www.internationalstandardbible.com/E/ezekiel-1.html*

97   The 585 BC date for the writing of Ezekiel 32 was taken from the Bible Knowledge Commentary: Old Testament in the commentary section of Ezekiel 32. *"Ezekiel 32:17-21. Ezekiel's last of seven prophecies against Egypt came in the 12th year, on the 15th day of the month. The month was not named, but many interpreters assume it was the same month as the previous prophecy (v. 1). If so, the date of this message was March 17, 585 B.C."*

98   Quote about Iran as a sponsor of terrorism was taken from the Internet on 4/23/14 at this website: *http://www.cfr.org/iran/state-sponsors-iran/p9362*

99   Hormoz Shariat of Iran Alive Ministries informed me that Iran has been cracking down hard on Christian pastors and home churches in Iran over the past couple of years.

100   The supporting Scriptures for the Israeli takeover of Jordan are in Jeremiah 49:1-6, Zephaniah 2:8-9, and Isaiah 11:14.

101   Northern Storm Rising – Russia, Iran, And the Emerging End-Times Military Coalition Against Israel - Page 159 under "The Burial of Enemy Bodies for Seven Months (Ezekiel 39:11-12,14-16) Published by Harvest House - Copyright 2008. Authored by Dr. Ron Rhodes.

102   Tim LaHaye quote taken from my book entitled *Revelation Road, Hope Beyond the Horizon* on page 138.

103   Footsteps of Messiah Chapter 20, section C, pages 498-499

104   Headline was taken from the Internet on 5/13/14 from this website: *http://voices.yahoo.com/supernatural-dreams-visions-compel-muslims-to-3285772.html*

105 Jason Mandryk, *Operation World: The Definitive Prayer Guide to Every Nation* (Colorado Springs, CO: Biblica Publishing, 2010), 916.

106 Joel Rosenberg's reference to Hormoz Shariat as the Billy Graham of Iran can be found on the Internet as of 6/16/14 at this web site link: *https://twitter.com/JoelCRosenberg/status/457269128056045568*

107 Jason Mandryk, *Operation World: The Definitive Prayer Guide to Every Nation* (Colorado Springs, CO: Biblica Publishing, 2010), 916.

108 This headline comes from the National Post article linked at this site as of 4/7/14 *http://fullcomment.nationalpost.com/2014/03/31/olivier-guitta-irans-other-nuclear-timebomb/*

109 Centrifuge numbers were collected from the Internet on 5/21/14 from this website: http://www.israelnationalnews.com/News/News.aspx/180837#.U31SF9JOVjo

110 GCC water pipeline information collected from the Internet on 5/21/14 from this website: http://www.aljazeera.com/indepth/features/2014/01/gulf-states-tackle-water-woes-20141226487523277.html

111 The Messianic Kingdom was the high-point of Old Testament prophecy. Revelation 20:4 informs that is lasts for 1,000 years.

112 Sinner's Prayer quote taken from Wikipedia over the Internet on 8/13/11 at this link: *http://en.wikipedia.org/wiki/Sinner's_prayer*

113 Sinner's prayer example was copied from the Internet on 8/13/11 at this website link: *http://www.salvationprayer.info/prayer.html* (slight emphasis was added in this appendix).

114 Quote welcoming those who prayed the sinner's prayer into the family of God copied over the Internet on 8/13/11 at this link: *http://www.salvationprayer.info/prayer.html*.

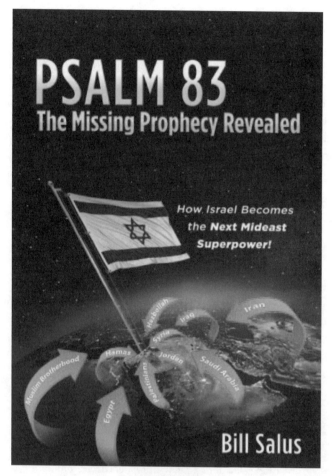

Psalm 83
The Missing Prophecy Revealed

An ancient prophecy written over 3000 years ago reveals that the Arab states and terrorist populations, which presently share common borders with Israel, will soon confederate in order to wipe Israel off of the map. These enemies of Israel are depicted on the red arrows upon the book cover image, and their mandate is clear:

> They have said, "Come, and let us cut them off from being a nation, That the name of Israel may be remembered no more." (Psalm 83:4).

Psalm 83 predicts a climactic, concluding Arab-Israeli war that has eluded the discernment of today's top Bible scholars, and yet, the Middle East stage appears to be set for the fulfillment of this prophecy. While many of today's top Bible experts are predicting that Russia, Iran, Turkey, Libya, and several other countries are going to invade Israel according a prophecy in Ezekiel 38, this timely book explains how Psalm 83 occurs prior. Discover how Israel defeats their ancient Arab enemies, and why Americans need to stand beside Israel in this coming war! Here are a few endorsements from the experts:

"Invaluable New Insights"

– Dr. David Reagan, the founder of Lamb and Lion
Ministries and host of Christ in Prophecy Television

"I wish I would have written it"

– Dr. David Hocking, the founder
of Hope for Today Ministries

"Groundbreaking"

– Dr. Thomas Horn, bestselling author
and founder of Raiders News Network.

Buy your copy of Psalm 83, the Missing Prophecy
Revealed at *http://www.prophecydepot.com*

Revelation Road
Hope Beyond the Horizon

You are invited on a one-of-a-kind reading experience. Enjoy a novel and biblical commentary at the same time. This unique book is designed with appeal for both fiction and non-fiction audiences. George Thompson believes his grandson Tyler lives in the final generation. Lovingly, he prepares the lad for the treacherous road ahead. All young Tyler wanted was a chance to join his sister at Eastside Middle School in the fall, but the Arab Spring led to an apocalyptic summer disrupting his plans. Middle East wars and nuclear terror in America quickly turned his world upside down. Join the Thompson's on their journey through the Bible prophecies of the end times, and discover how their gripping story uncovers the silver lining of hope against the backdrop of global gloom and doom. The commentary section explains how their story could soon become your reality!

America and the Coming
Mideast Wars DVD

According to ancient Bible prophecies a series of Mideast wars are coming and America plays a vital part in these apocalyptic battles. Will the USA support Israel and be divinely blessed, or will America put the Jewish state into harm's way and come under divine judgment? America and the Coming Mideast Wars is a DVD that cuts to the biblical chase of what currently matters most in America and the Middle East.

"The Future for Israel, Iran, and the Arab States," is the first lesson, and it points out that Israel is the victor of a climactic concluding Arab-Israeli war predicted over 3000 years ago in Psalm 83. It also identifies the prophecies concerning the desolations of Egypt, Syria, Iran, and many other countries currently dominating the Mideast news.

"America's Role in the Coming Prophetic Wars," is the second teaching that explains America's crucial role in the Psalm 83 war, the Ezekiel 38 Magog invasion, and the Armageddon campaign of the Antichrist.

"The TV Interviews" are included as a bonus feature that provides the viewer with additional new insights about the future of America and the countries and terrorist populations of the Middle East.

Visit *http://www.prophecydepot.com*
to purchase these and other products.